# A Good Dusting

# A Good Dusting

## A Centenary Review of the Sudan campaigns 1883–1899

## HENRY KEOWN-BOYD

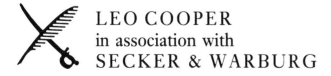

LEO COOPER
in association with
SECKER & WARBURG

*To The Memory of the Brave Men*
*On Both Sides*
*Who Fought in These Campaigns*

First published in Great Britain 1986 by Leo Cooper
in association with Martin Secker & Warburg Limited
54 Poland Street, London W1V 3DF

Copyright © 1986 Henry Keown-Boyd
Maps – Copyright © 1986 Chester Read

ISBN 0-436-23288-X

Printed and bound in Great Britain by
Butler & Tanner Limited, Frome and London

# Contents

CONTENTS

# Illustrations

## Maps

# Acknowledgements

So many people and institutions have been so helpful that I do not know where to start or finish. I hope any unmentioned helpers will overlook my bad manners and worse memory with a philosophical shrug.

In no particular order I thank most especially Miss Lesley Forbes of the Oriental Section of Durham University Library, the staffs of the National Army Museum Reading Room, the Ministry of Defence Library and the Library of the Institute for Commonwealth Studies, Mrs Gill and Mr Redman of the West Sussex Record Office, Mrs Harding of the Kent Archives Office, numerous regimental secretaries and regimental museum curators, the Marquess of Salisbury and Mr R. H. Harcourt-Williams, Brigadier G. Fitzgerald, Mr William Hale, Brigadier Jed Palmer, Brigadier Maurice Lush, Colonel and Mrs H. S. P. Hopkinson, Lieutenant-Colonel David Trafford-Roberts, Mrs Hall and her father the late Mr Hal Kitchener, Mr Richard Hill, Canon Graham Morgan, Miss Maira Roberts, Colonel E. Windsor-Clive, Colonel P. Adair, Mrs Maxse, Miss MacLean of Ardgour, Mr A. Hunter Service, Mr M. W. Daly, Mr Howard Dodsworth, Mr David Harvey, Messrs George and Edward O'Farrell, my brother David who read the manuscript and Mrs Kathleen Clinton who typed it.

An early inspiration was my late half-brother, Bill, whose grandfather, Captain Dalison of the Scots Guards, was one of the casualties of these campaigns.

I am also greatly indebted to Captain Chester Read, CBE, RN (Rtd) who drew the maps and battle plans and to Tom Hartman, whose guidance as editor was invaluable.

# Author's Note

There are numerous English versions of Arabic words, names and place names. The present author's choices of spelling are unashamedly haphazard and no particular rule has been followed. Furthermore, it should be borne in mind that many of the place names used by the British commentators of the time, such as Churchill or Alford and Sword, were quite unrecognisable to the local inhabitants then, and are the more so today.

The old-fashioned spelling "Soudanese" is used throughout this book only in reference to the Black battalions of the Egyptian Army.

# Introduction

No writer of fiction could have invented the story of the Sudan over the last twenty years of the nineteenth century and expect to be taken seriously. No element of drama, except perhaps romantic love, is missing and every leading character is an exaggeration of his kind. All the human stereotypes without whom no series of Boys' Own adventure stories was complete are there. So too are the geographical clichés; burning deserts; choking dust storms; a mighty river; a ruined palace; a deserted capital.

The fanatical Mahdi urges his wild adherents against their cruel oppressors; the lonely Christian hero is beset by his Muslim foes, whom he admires, and is betrayed, at least in his own mind, by his friends whom he despises. There is capture, torture, massacre, escape; there are chains, dungeons, whipping posts and gallows. A desperate rescue attempt fails by a few hours. The unbreakable British square is broken, not once but twice, by the most ferocious warriors since the Vikings.

Then the fire dies down and for a decade and more only occasional sparks fly up. But the world's greatest power must avenge itself and punishment must be inflicted. A mighty army sets forth on its inexorable march. A railway is constructed through harsh terrain under impossible conditions. Finally a great battle is staged and, after feats of incredible but futile heroism, a medieval host is slaughtered by the invincible combination of nineteenth century discipline and the first glimmers of twentieth century technology.

The fire goes out.

Will it be rekindled?

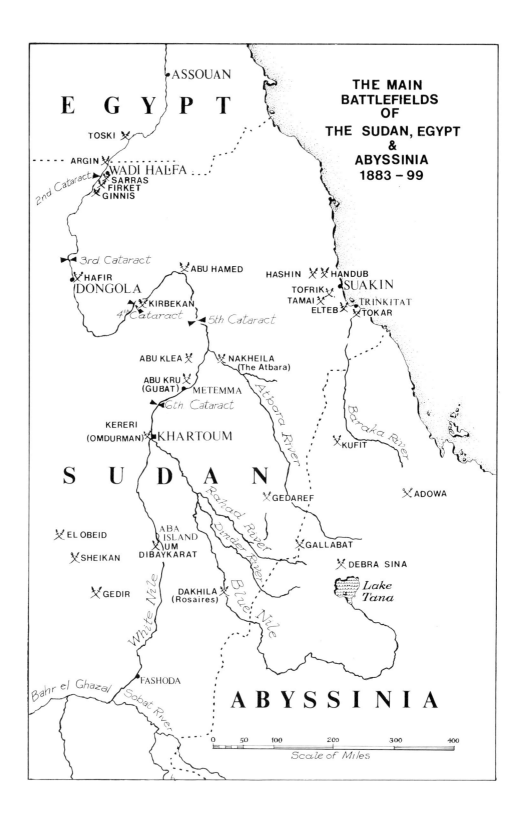

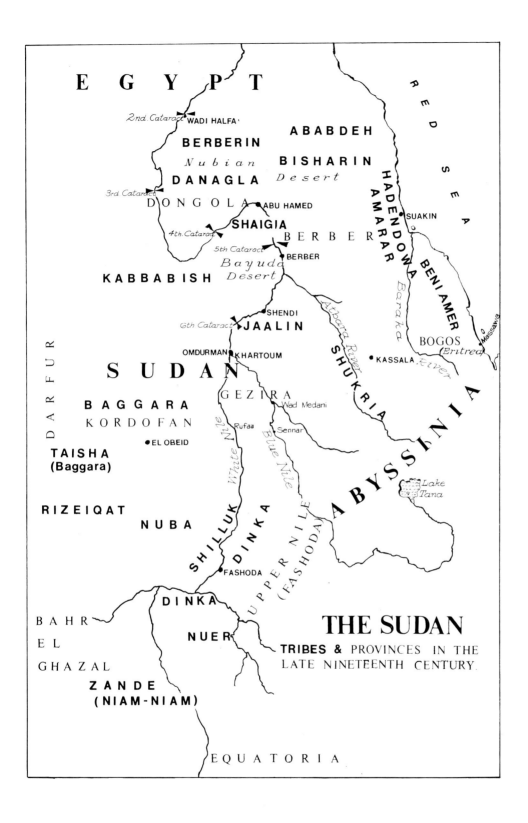

EGYPT

2nd Cataract — WADI HALFA

BERBERIN

ABABDEH

BISHARIN

*Nubian*

DANAGLA

*Desert*

HADENDOWA

3rd Cataract

AMARAR

DONGOLA — ABU HAMED

SHAIGIA

RED SEA

4th Cataract

BERBER

SUAKIN

5th Cataract — BERBER

BENI AMER

*Bayuda*

KABBABISH

*Desert*

*Baraka*

BOGOS
(Eritrea)

Massawa

SHENDI

*Atbara River*

6th Cataract — JAALIN

OMDURMAN — KHARTOUM

SHUKRIA

KASSALA

*Atbara River*

DARFUR

SUDAN

BAGGARA

GEZIRA

KORDOFAN

Wad Medani

ABYSSINIA

TAISHA
(Baggara)

Rufaa

Sennar

*White Nile*

*Blue Nile*

*Lake
Tana*

RIZEIQAT

NUBA

SHILLUK

DINKA

UPPER NILE

(FASHODA)

FASHODA

DINKA

THE SUDAN

BAHR
EL
GHAZAL

NUER

TRIBES & PROVINCES IN THE
LATE NINETEENTH CENTURY.

ZANDE
(NIAM-NIAM)

EQUATORIA

# PART ONE

# Expulsion

# 1 The Haboub

During the latter half of the nineteenth century the slave trade aroused in the hearts and minds of liberal Europeans the same emotions as apartheid does today. By the 1870's it had been suppressed in many parts of the world, but in the Sudan it flourished.

It was primarily an export business but also a fundamental element in the social and economic structure of the Sudan itself. The slavers, mostly Sudanese Arabs of the Baggara, Jaalin and Danagla tribes, with their private armies hunted and captured their prey, the negro and Nilotic tribes of the South, conveying them by river and on foot northwards to Egypt and to Suakin for shipment to what is now Saudi Arabia, the Persian Gulf, Turkey and beyond. Many of the more warlike young men were inducted into the slavers' own armed bands or into the Egyptian Army. These troops, or bazingers[1] as they were known, served their masters, the Egyptians and later both the Mahdiya and the British with loyalty and courage.

Under a series of treaties and firmans, the Khedives of Egypt, descended from the great Mohamed Ali, ruled their own country, the Sudan, and some pockets of territory in what is now Eritrea, Ethiopia and Somalia, under Ottoman suzerainity. This book is not intended to deal with Egypt's financial circumstances at that time. Suffice it to say that Khedivial extravagance and ministerial corruption had forced Egypt into vast borrowing from the European Powers, primarily Great Britain and France. This indebtedness led, in the nature of things, to greatly increased western influence in Egypt, both political and moral. Furthermore, from September, 1882, onwards, after the suppression by British troops of Arabi's[2]

[1] Believed to be named after the tribe from which such soldiers were originally recruited, and perhaps the original breeders of the African hunting-dog known as the Basenji.
[2] An Egyptian nationalist army officer, a forerunner of Nasser.

rebellion against the Khedive, the country came under what was in effect if not in name, British rule.

Thus European liberals, through their governments, were able to put great pressure on the Khedives to take measures to suppress the slave trade, although it was implied that existing slaves could remain in situ for the time being. This was sensible as the trade in slaves was far more repulsive than the condition of slavery itself. Indeed, it would be no exaggeration to suggest that the lot of a slave in an Arab or Turkish household was generally less disagreeable than that of a Victorian domestic drudge in England.

The Khedive Ismail realized that in order to achieve any success in this ambitious endeavour and ingratiate himself with western public opinion he would have to dismiss many of the senior officials of the Sudan Government, Turko-Egyptians who were themselves heavily involved in the slave trade, and replace them with Europeans. This he proceeded to do and by one means or another he recruited a remarkable group including one of the leading figures of our story, the dynamic and deeply religious British officer, Charles Gordon, whom he appointed Governor-General of the Sudan in 1877 after previous service against the slavers in Equatoria. Among the others were the Italian soldier of fortune and explorer, Romolo Gessi, Gordon's most trusted lieutenant and most successful scourge of the slave-barons; Edward Schnitzer, known to history as Emin Pasha, an eccentric German scientist; Frank Lupton, a young English ship's officer and the Austrian Christianized Jew, Rudolf Slatin, destined to become the servant and confidant of the Mahdi's successor, a pasha, a baron, a general in the British Army and the holder of two knighthoods.

The selection of these men and others was haphazard but what is important is that they were at least partially successful and their very success contributed in no small measure to the political, religious and military "haboub"[3] which was to engulf the Sudan.

For the purposes of comparison with our own times let us try to imagine that the unpopular government of an overtaxed industrialized nation should seek to outlaw the motor industry on the grounds of the anti-social effect of motor cars. Shareholders, managers and workers are faced with ruin and unemployment and their customers with having to walk. An ambitious firebrand of a shop-steward with the gift of rhetoric and already popular for his widely shared political beliefs, travels the country calling upon one and all to unite in overthrowing an oppressive, grasping and incompetent régime. If, at the same time in this rather unlikely scenario, that régime lacked effective security forces and had great difficulty in transporting those which it had from one place to another, a revolution might not only be attempted but might well succeed.

---

[3] Sudanese colloquial Arabic for a severe dust storm.

Haboub over Khartoum.

Thus the suppression, or partial suppression, of the slave trade was a major cause of discontent in the Sudan at this time. There is no stricture against slavery in the Koran and its attempted abolition was not only economically damaging to the Sudanese but morally and philosophically incomprehensible. Equally intolerable was the corrupt and oppressive nature of the Turkiya (Egyptian Government). In particular the riverain tribes, the majority of whom scratched a basic existence by cultivating narrow irrigated strips along the banks of the Nile, were the milch cows of the government and its officials, who, since Mohamed Ali's conquest of the Sudan in the early part of the century, had imposed upon them a confiscatory system of taxation, extorted by bashi-bazooks[4] with the khourbash (hippopotamus-hide whip). Sometimes the same tax would be levied twice or even three times, once for the government, once for the Mamour (Governor) and once more for the bashi-bazooks themselves. A peasant would be taxed for using his own sakieh (water-wheel) or fined for not using it and so on.

A catalyst for this discontent was needed and sooner or later was bound to appear. Virtually the only unifying factor among the Sudanese Arab tribal groupings was Islam and therefore it was inevitable that this catalyst should take religious form. The appearance of a Mahdi el Muntazer or Expected One in Muslim countries was not before, and has not been since, an unusual

[4] Armed militia, mostly from the Shaigia tribe of the Korti area of the Sudan or half-castes of Turkish and Albanian descent.

Tribesmen of the Upper Nile from whom many of the soldiers of both the Mahdiya and the Egyptian Army were recruited.

phenomenon. Most pass unnoticed and others are suppressed by co-operation between the religious and secular authorities. What was different about Mohamed Ahmed Ibn el Sayyid Abdullah was his timing. He appeared at the very moment when everyone was looking for him.

It must be admitted that the Mahdi, Mohamed Ahmed, bore little resemblance to our militant shop-steward in the analogy suggested above. The son of a boat-builder who claimed descent from the prophet, he was born near Dongola in the 1840s. Moving south Mohamed Ahmed studied Islam under various sheikhs at Berber, Khartoum and elsewhere, eventually establishing himself as a hermit on Aba Island on the White Nile some 150 miles south of Khartoum. Here he followed a harsh and ascetic way of life and soon built up a reputation for extreme holiness. His fame began to spread and in due course he was joined by one Abdullahi Ibn el Sayyid Mohamed whilst he and his disciples were building the tomb of a holy man at Messalamia. Abdullahi was himself the son of a holy man or fiki of the Taisha clan of the great Baggara cattle-owning and slaving tribe of Kordofan and Darfur.

Of the character of the Mahdi really we know little. Only a handful of articulate Europeans ever met him and their impressions were not altogether unfavourable.

On the Sudanese side the effusions of propaganda at the time, and to some extent since, have done no more than to produce a cloudy and insubstantial figure. There is no doubt that the hard core of his following sincerely believed in him and his holiness. Many others jumped on his bandwagon and a diminishing few opposed him. At his military and administrative abilities we can only guess. So feeble and inadequate was the Egyptian opposition to him and so fanatically brave and ferocious were his own warriors (ansar)[5] that once having won their allegiance he could hardly lose. His real triumph and skill lay in his ability to win that allegiance. Nevertheless, he was probably a better general than any of his leading followers and, as we shall see, the destruction of Hicks Pasha's expedition, supervised by the Mahdi himself, was a skilful exercise in harassment and attrition, the coup de grâce coming only after the enemy had been prostrated by heat, thirst and fear.

As he died within six months of the fall of Khartoum it is difficult to say much about his administration for he had little opportunity to govern. There is evidence from Slatin and others that by the time of his death, still only in his forties, soft living and the harem had taken their toll. This strange and slightly unreal figure will forever remain an enigma but perhaps we should let his extraordinary record speak for itself.

In under four years he had acquired a tenuous mastery over all but the extremities of the Sudan, an area of nearly one million square miles. He had killed or captured some forty thousand Egyptian troops. He had defied successfully the greatest power on earth, Great Britain, killed one of her national heroes and forced her soldiers, perhaps the finest in the world, to withdraw. Aided only by harsh climatic conditions, an inhospitable terrain and the natural fighting instincts of his followers, he had accomplished all this without military training, with few modern weapons and no outside allies. Furthermore, and perhaps even more astonishing, the precarious and ramshackle edifice which he had erected survived under a less charismatic successor for another thirteen years.

Even in terms of the great sweep of history, it was a truly astounding achievement.

The first rumours that an unusually popular and revered fiki was preaching an anti-government line reached Khartoum in early 1881 when a sheikh with whom Mohamed Ahmed had quarrelled denounced him to the Governor-General, Raouf Pasha. At first Raouf shrugged off the warning but later received confirmation of the potential danger from other sources. He sent a crony, one Abu Suud, to interview the Mahdi on Aba Island and instruct him to come to Khartoum and explain himself. This the Mahdi had no intention of doing, knowing full well that he would be arrested and killed or allowed to die in prison. But he made no attempt at prevarication and in the course of the interview so

---

[5] Literally 'helpers'. Tribal warriors armed with swords and spears.

alarmed Abu Suud with his fierce denunciations of the Turkiya and all its evil and blasphemous works that the man feared for his life and fled back to Khartoum.

On receiving his subordinate's report Raouf decided that this upstart Dongolawi should be dealt with, but the hot summer months had arrived and it was not until August that two companies of Egyptian regulars were sent by steamer to Aba to arrest the turbulent priest and his followers. Delay had not served to improve the military skills of the officers of this small but historic punitive expedition and although the overall commander, again Abu Suud,[6] was cautious enough to remain on his steamer in midstream, the two company commanders decided to disembark their troops and advance upon the Mahdi's village from opposite directions in the middle of the night. Inevitably the Mahdi was forewarned, left the village with his followers and set up an ambush for the unwary Egyptians. Upon reaching the deserted village, the rival companies opened fire simultaneously inflicting serious casualties on each other. The Mahdists sprang the ambush, killed most of the Egyptians and captured their weapons. The few who escaped back to the steamer returned to Khartoum with the sinister news of the Mahdi's first military success, word of which spread like wildfire through the Sudan.

At first the Egyptian Government was inclined to blame Raouf Pasha for failure to crush what it believed to be no more than a minor rebellion and, in May, 1882, replaced him with an able and resolute Syrian, Abdel Qadir Pasha Hilmi, who was already Minister for Sudanese Affairs. Abdel Qadir did not confine himself to military means of defeating Mohamed Ahmed but made use of political and religious propaganda methods and even resorted to such hoary old tricks as gifts of poison food and the hiring of assassins. On one occasion he asked the authorities in Cairo to prepare letter bombs, proving that not all his methods were old-fashioned. The turmoil at home in Egypt, in the throes of the Arabi rebellion and the British invasion, did not help Abdel Qadir whose requests for additional troops (and, indeed, letter bombs) were ignored. However, he had been encouraged by a major, if temporary, set-back to the Mahdi when the ansar were repulsed with heavy losses at El Obeid in September, 1882. This check followed soon after the total destruction of an Egyptian force under Yusef Pasha el Shellali at Gedir but El Obeid's reprieve was short-lived and starvation forced the garrison into submission in January, 1883. Although Mahdist losses had been heavy, most of the Egyptian Army's black troops took service in the jehadiya[7] after capture and were to serve the Mahdi and his successor loyally and well for the next fifteen years.

---

[6] Abu Suud died shortly afterwards, reputedly poisoned by the relatives of the Egyptian soldiers killed in the Aba expedition.

[7] 'Warriors of the Holy War'. Riflemen who were the Mahdist army's equivalent to bazingers.

In the Gezira Abdel Qadir took the field himself, inflicting several reverses on Mahdist supporters but was abruptly dismissed in April, 1883. It was becoming clear to the Egyptian Government that its officer corps, demoralized by events both in Egypt and the Sudan, was unwilling and unable to cope with the emergency. The Khedive turned to the British, now effectively rulers of Egypt, for help in the Sudan but their response was far from positive. Certainly no British troops were to be made available and serving British officers were not to be employed there, but if the Khedive wished to employ foreign officers, or even retired or "half-pay" British, that was his affair.

The man the Egyptians needed to pull their fat out of the Sudanese fire had to be one, irrespective of nationality, of almost super-human military and administrative ability. The man they found was a very ordinary mortal.

# 2 Sheep to the Slaughter

"Whatever measure the Government will take will be in the direction of making effective arrangements with regard to bringing all the difficulties to an end".

W. E. GLADSTONE

Apart from the bare outlines of his rather undistinguished career in the Indian Army (Bombay Staff Corps), little is recorded of the first fifty-two years of the life of El Farik (Lieutenant-General) William Hicks Pasha, perhaps because there is little to record. He had been caught up in the Indian Mutiny and had taken part in Napier's Abyssinian expedition. Otherwise his life had been one of ordinary peacetime soldiering in India.

Redundant and without private means, he was one of many middle-aged, middle ranking British officers seeking employment around the world. One source[1] describes how his name was picked out of a hat in a room at Shepheard's Hotel by Valentine Baker Pasha, Chief of the Egyptian Gendarmerie. The mystery is how his name came to be in the hat in the first place, as the successful candidate would be required to lead a third-rate army into wild and inhospitable country against hordes of fierce tribesmen flushed with the success of a series of victories over government forces.

From his letters to his wife Sophie the impression is gained of a decent, conscientious family man concerned about his future career and financial prospects but not overambitious. Success against the Mahdi, he felt, might lead to a reasonable job in Cairo, perhaps second-in-command of the Gendarmerie, where Sophie and the children could join him. Not for him the Governor-Generalship of the Sudan rather casually suggested by Lord Dufferin.[2] "Some men are born great, some achieve greatness and others have greatness thrust upon them," he quoted to Sophie, "I am to be of this last!"

[1] General Stuart-Wortley's unpublished Reminiscences of Egypt.
[2] British Ambassador to Istanbul, at the time temporarily in charge of Egyptian affairs.

The Evans Memorial at Rhuddlan
Church, North Wales.
The inscription reads:

*Major Edward Baldwin Evans son of*
*John and Jane Evans born at Rhuddlan*
*Oct. 8th 1843 and killed while serving as*
*Interpreter and Chief of Intelligence with*
*Hicks Pasha's army at El Obeid in the*
*Soudan, November 1883*
*This monument is erected by his sisters in*
*loving remembrance.*

He had little say in the selection of most of his European staff,[3] of whom, in general, he had a low opinion. De Coetlogon, his headquarters staff officer, he considered "useless, rude and insubordinate". Colborne, nicknamed "Dishonest John", although the son of a Field-Marshal, was a disreputable drunk who scratched a living from freelance journalism. The young militia officers, Massey and Forestier-Walker, were "helpless as babies", according to Hicks, and had failed their examinations for regular commissions. Massey could not even read a compass and nearly died of thirst after losing himself on patrol. Forestier-Walker, in command of the Nordenfeldt machine-gun battery, failed to teach his men how to work the guns (probably he did not know himself) and was condemned by Hicks to three days' non-stop training in the desert from which he collapsed with heat exhaustion and was invalided back to Cairo. Colborne and an ill-tempered giant called Martin, who beat up the Officers' Mess servants, were also invalided in due course with unspecified complaints, although in Colborne's case it is not difficult to guess at the nature of the ailment. As for Warner, "there was nothing to be got out of him".

[3] See Appendix A for details of the staff.

Evans,[4] a civilian interpreter and self-styled intelligence officer, does seem to have been recruited by Hicks himself when, down on his luck in Egypt, he had leapt at the chance of any employment. But he was no greater success and for unspecified reasons put in his resignation, which Hicks refused and was later withdrawn. With Farquhar, his Chief of Staff, the German von Seckendorf and the Austrian Herlth, Hicks recorded his satisfaction, even going so far as to describe Herlth, a cavalry officer with eleven years' service in the Imperial and Royal Army, as "excellent". At one point he applied for an officer of his own choice, a certain Captain Charles Campbell of the Royal Welsh Fusiliers, who, if he arrived at all, had the good fortune to arrive too late as he did not take part in the Kordofan expedition.

A tower of strength at a lower level was Brady, an ex-sergeant major of the Royal Horse Artillery, privately employed by Hicks as a sort of general factotum. He may have spent a good deal of his time coping with two drunken reporters attached to Hicks's army, O'Donovan of the *Daily News* and Vizetelly, a freelance war artist. A third, Frank Power[5] of *The Times*, was driven temporarily mad by the sun and shot his own camel. Hicks had trouble with O'Donovan even before leaving Khartoum when the Irishman caused a fracas in the *suk* (bazaar).

The Egyptian officers were even less promising than the British. Often totally ignorant of their profession, the Sudan was to them, as to their men, a place of punishment, fear and death. Language too was a problem. Neither Hicks nor the other Europeans (except Evans) knew any Arabic and few of the Turko-Egyptians, including the new Governor-General, Ala el Din Pasha, spoke any European language. The Egyptian Government had quibbled over the interpreters' salaries and the quality of those eventually recruited was low, no doubt causing a great deal of misunderstanding and exacerbating an already impossible situation. With the German and Austrian officers Hicks had to converse in a mixture of German and French.

As for the troops, the Egyptian "regular" infantry consisted mainly of time-expired conscripts and former members of Arabi's mutinous army, many of whom had been transported to the Sudan in chains, some with self-inflicted wounds by which they had hoped to escape forcible re-enlistment. Nevertheless, Hicks was not unimpressed by the physique and endurance of these men and Colborne, for what it is worth, does not write too disparagingly of them in his book *With Hicks in the Sudan*, a slightly misleading title as Colborne had been invalided to Cairo before the Kordofan expedition started.

Also included in the army were bands of Bashi-bazooks, Albanian, Turkish and

---

[4] Edward Evans, a civilian who had been Arabi's interpreter at his trial, is the only member of the expedition to whom a monument was erected. This stands in the churchyard at Rhuddlan in North Wales and was placed there by his sisters.

[5] Also British Consul in Khartoum.

Sudanese cut-throats quite without discipline and concerned only with loot and pillage, although Hicks felt that the Albanians at least had some fighting potential.

To Hicks' already insuperable problems was added a decrepit Circassian official, Suleiman Pasha el Niazi, as titular head of the "Sudan Army". This polite old gentleman took his duties seriously and saw to it that Hicks was obstructed and hindered in every conceivable way with the time-honoured thoroughness of the Middle Eastern bureaucrat through the centuries to this day.

If this was not enough, the Kordofan expedition was to be accompanied by the Governor-General himself, who was unlikely not to have something to say about the conduct of operations.

We do not know what all these people, British, German, Austrian, Turkish, Egyptian, Sudanese and the rest, thought of Hicks. Presumably the more intelligent among them realized that he was completely out of his depth.[6] He complained to Sophie that he could not make friends with any of his officers. Perhaps he had the smell of doom about him. The attitude of his senior Turko-Egyptian colleagues was ambivalent. Jealous of the trust placed in him by Cairo and anxious to assert their own authority (and probably to get their hands on the army's funds), at the same time they were glad to make him the scapegoat for failure and disarray. We were not there and we do not know but it seems likely that Hicks for his part tended to rub people up the wrong way, did not have the subtlety to get what he wanted and lacked the drive and self-confidence required for successful military organization and command.

Having arrived in Khartoum in early March, 1883, and after a month of intensive training, Hicks felt his army was as ready for active operations as it was ever likely to be. However, for once wisdom prevailed and as summer was coming on it was decided to test the troops in a short preliminary campaign on the White Nile south of Khartoum. After a few skirmishes, and the burning of the Mahdi's now deserted village on Aba Island, a sharp engagement with a Mahdist force under Omar el Makashfi took place at Marabia between Kawa and Jebelein. This resulted in a surprising victory for Hicks and he returned to Khartoum with new confidence. Unfortunately this was soon dissipated by the constant quarrelling between him and the Egyptians. In July he sent in his resignation to Cairo, which, unluckily for him, was refused but resulted in the removal of his principal tormentor, the elderly Suleiman el Niazi, who was promoted to the Governorship of the Eastern Sudan. Shortly after this Hicks was officially confirmed as C-in-C Sudan, promoted to the rank of Farik and his salary increased from £1,200 to £2,000 per annum.

Despite almost universal disbelief in the possibility of success, the main

---

[6] The memoirs of Giegler Pasha, a German official of the Sudan Government, recently translated into English by Mr R. Hill, tend to confirm this.

expedition against the Mahdi in El Obeid left Khartoum on 7 September, 1883. Until the recent discovery of Hicks's letters to his wife, the precise size of his force had never been accurately established and estimates had been complicated by the separate departures from Khartoum of Hicks and the Governor-General, who linked up at El Dueim on the White Nile. It is now know that his army consisted of 8,300 regular infantry, 1,100 bashi-bazooks, 100 cuirassiers (horsemen in chain mail), 800 tribal irregulars, sixteen guns and six Nordenfeldt machine-guns. No less than 5,000 camels provided transport but the army was encumbered by some 2,000 camp-followers.

Perhaps the most extraordinary aspect of the tragedy which was about to unfold is that everyone realized what was likely to happen yet nobody attempted to stop it happening. It was as though the expedition had acquired a will of its own which drove it inexorably towards its predestined fate. Doubtless Hicks himself felt it would be dishonourable not to attempt to fulfil his contract without direct instructions from London or Cairo. Also he needed the job. The British Government confined itself to complaining that Hicks should not correspond with Sir Edward Malet, the British Agent in Cairo, but with the Khedivial Government direct. No doubt the Prime Minister, Gladstone, would have jumped on the bandwagon of success but, having already described the Mahdist rising as a struggle for freedom, by distancing himself and his government from Hicks, he hoped to avoid the consequences of failure.

Twelve days later Hicks reached El Dueim without incident and was joined by Ala el Din Pasha, the Governor-General. Faced with the choice of two routes to El Obeid, the longest was chosen in the belief that it was the better watered. Now they must march west away from the river and fifteen guides, several of them Mahdist agents, were employed. At this point, Hicks himself describes the situation on 3 October in his last despatch following the deliberations of a Council of War.

"On leaving Duem . . . to march by the Khor el Nil to Melbeis and Obeid, I decided that my line of communication should be secured by posts of 200 men each left in strongly fortified positions at the following places (here he lists twelve posts between twelve and thirty-two miles apart). At all these places I was informed that water would be found. Large quantities of biscuits were to arrive at Duem; and as we were unable to leave a single camel at the base, 1000 were ordered to be purchased and forwarded to Duem . . . The biscuits would then, with ammunition and other stores be pushed on to the front from post to post, and in case of a reverse, a line of retreat secured, the troops falling back upon these depots where we should be certain of finding supplies of food, ammunition and water.

"But . . . I was informed by the Governor-General that it was useless for me to expect any supplies to be pushed up from Duem; that the soldiers left at the posts

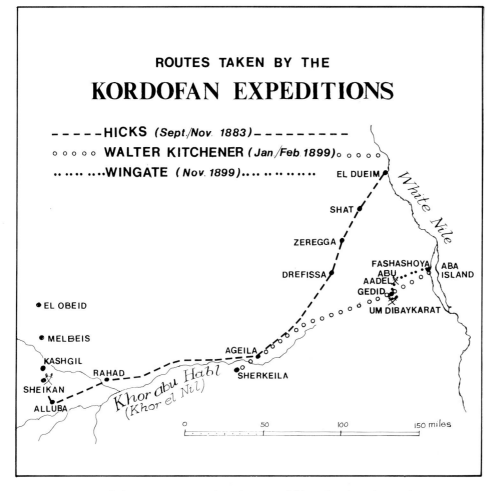

ROUTES TAKEN BY THE

# KORDOFAN EXPEDITIONS

- - - - - HICKS (Sept./Nov. 1883) - - - - - - - -

○ ○ ○ ○ ○ WALTER KITCHENER (Jan./Feb. 1899)○ ○ ○ ○ ○

· · · · · · · · · · WINGATE (Nov. 1899)· · · · · · · · · · · ·

would not guard the convoys – in fact they would be afraid to do so; that to ensure supplies being forwarded an army would be required with each convoy. . . .

"The Governor-General requested me to abandon the idea of having this line of posts, to give up my line of communication and line of retreat and to advance with the army *en l'air* with 50 days supply of food only, the Arabs (Mahdists) closing in on our rear.

"I am naturally very averse to this but if, as H.E. assures me it is a fact that the posts will not be supplied from the base at Duem and supplies would not be forwarded through them, I should in garrisoning these posts only be weakening my fighting force without gaining any advantage. I have therefore called a council, have had the matter explained and requested the members to record their opinion."

Of the five senior officers at the council, apart from Hicks himself, four, including Colonel Farquhar, apparently agreed with the Governor-General and one sought a compromise by which the first four posts would be manned and further troops sent for from Cairo. Hicks accepted the majority opinion.

The folly is breathtaking. No supplies to be brought forward. No certainty of sufficient water en route. No secure line of retreat. For another ghastly month they staggered on, constantly harassed by the enemy who had denuded the countryside of what little sustenance it offered, the officers bickering, the men fatalistically despairing. From the diary of Abbas Bey, secretary to the Governor-General, it is clear that well before the end officers and men alike had lost confidence in Hicks and Farquhar. This diary, which was found on the battlefield of Omdurman nearly 15 years later, is one of only two semi-reliable sources of information about the last few weeks of the expedition's existence. The other is the verbal evidence of Hicks' cook, Mohamed Nur el Barudi,[7] who escaped death by pretending to be a doctor.

Any morale which remained was further damaged by a propaganda barrage of letters from the Mahdi demanding surrender or death.

The end came on 5 November, 1883, on a wooded plain called Sheikan, a few miles south of El Obeid. According to Barudi the force was advancing in three squares through thick bush when the dervishes launched their main and final assault led by the emirs Wad Nejumi, Abu Girgeh and Abdel Halim. In the wild confusion the squares fired on each other, were soon broken and the massacres began. Barudi's account, later corroborated by Mahdists as well, tells how Hicks and his European staff sold their lives dearly at the end.[8] For all their shortcoming they died in the best traditions of their caste. Nor did the Turkish warrior instincts of Ala el Din desert him and he was cut down fighting his way to Hicks's side.

One European had escaped, temporarily, with his life by deserting to the Mahdi a few days before the final slaughter. This was Gustav Klootz, an officer's servant and former Prussian Uhlan. Later there were rumours that he had been given some military command in the Mahdi's army but in reality he was treated with the same mixture of indifference and cruelty as the other European prisoners of the

---

[7] Barudi had a remarkable career. He had served Gordon in the Southern Sudan, Uganda and Abyssinia and afterwards various Governor-Generals in Khartoum before being employed by Hicks. After Sheikan, where he was severely wounded, he acted for the next six years as medical officer to Wad Nejumi, deserting to the Anglo-Egyptian army a few days before the battle of Toski in 1889. As may be imagined he was of considerable value to the Intelligence Department and later continued his culinary activities on the domestic staff of the Director of Intelligence, Wingate.

[8] Not everyone agreed with this version. Gordon believed there had been no battle and that the entire army had died of thirst. Marquet, a French merchant in Khartoum, told Colonel Stewart that Hicks had been shot by the Governor-General's men! The Qadi Ismail Abdel Qadir who, several years later, at the Khalifa's command, wrote a highly fanciful book about the rise of the Mahdi, claimed that "el Hiksi" was killed fleeing from the battle. It should be noted that none of these people was an eye-witness, but only Gordon's theory can be entirely ruled out.

Fires burning over the Sud, a vast area of swamp feared by generations of explorers and administrators.

Mahdiya (except Slatin). Eventually he tried to escape to Abysinnia and died en route. Only a few hundred of the rank and file out of a total of about 11,000 survived the slaughter at Sheikan.

It is a tale of unrelieved carelessness, stupidity and weak, divided command. One is reminded, although the circumstances are quite different, of the Argentine invasion of the Falklands ninety-nine years later, with its lack of appreciation of the power of the enemy and the elements, untrained and unwilling conscripts, inexperienced and quarrelsome commanders and a background of political misjudgement.

Before turning our attention to the consequences of the Hicks and other débâcles suffered by the Egyptians, let us go back two and a half years to 30 April, 1881. On this day Romolo Gessi, the former Governor of Bahr-el-Ghazal Province, died.

Of all the foot-loose adventurers who found their way into the Khedivial service in the Sudan in the 1870s, Gessi was the most remarkable and, as the hammer of the slave traders, the most successful. His place of birth is uncertain but he is thought to have been born in Istanbul of an Italian father and an Armenian mother in about 1830. His association with Gordon started while he was serving as an interpreter with the British Army in the Crimea but he learnt his trade as an irregular soldier under Garibaldi in the wars for Italian independence. Unhindered by the rigidity of a formal 19th century military education, Gessi was not only a highly skilled and daring guerrilla campaigner but an engineer, an explorer and an accomplished tribal diplomat with the genetic ability of the Levantine to learn any language very quickly.

He was an honest-to-goodness mercenary who did the job he had been hired to do to the best of his considerable ability. It is unlikely that high-flown religious and moral thoughts such as those which plagued his chief Gordon entered much into his philosophy.

In January, 1881, rumours of the burgeoning influence of the Mahdi were beginning to reach Khartoum when Gessi arrived there after a nightmarish journey through the Sud[9] from the south. He had been dismissed as Governor of Bahr el Ghazal though the intrigues of Christian Giegler Pasha, an allegedly corrupt German official of the governorate in Khartoum.[10] He was seriously ill and arrangements were made to get him to Egypt via Berber and Suakin but the ordeal of the journey by boat and camel in tremendous heat was too much for him and he expired shortly after his arrival at the French hospital at Suez.

All this is history but we may indulge a little in the realms of speculation. Had Gessi lived he might well have been recalled and employed against the Mahdi. His unique ability to weld together two second-class elements, Egyptian regulars and tribal irregulars, into a viable fighting force might well have been more than enough to deal with the Mahdist uprising in its early stages. No one even approaching Gessi's calibre was ever pitted against Mohamed Ahmed. At the height of the seige of Khartoum Gordon cried out for his dead friend and comrade and Housman wrote a eulogy for all the Gessis of this world:

> "What God abandoned these defended
> And saved the sum of things for pay"

---

[9] A vast area of swamp in the Southern Sudan through which the White Nile meanders.
[10] According to Colonel Stewart, Giegler, originally a telegraph engineer, amassed a fortune of some £40,000 in the course of his career as an official of the Sudan Government, an accusation understandably denied by Giegler himself.

# 3 The Christian Hero

Gordon, despite his successes against the slave traders, despairing of his ability to cleanse the Augean stables of the Sudan adminstration and upset by the deposing of the Khedive Ismail under Anglo-French pressure, had resigned as Governor-General of the Sudan in 1879.

The destruction of Hicks alarmed not only the Egyptians but the British as well. Gladstone and his Liberal Government wished to steer well clear of the Sudan and, as we have seen, had washed their hands of Hicks. But who was this Mahdi and what was he up to? Might he threaten Egypt, the Canal, the route to India? Even, and such a thing could barely be contemplated without a shudder, India herself? The finest jewel in the Imperial crown might be endangered by the disaffection of her millions of Muslims and the spectre of a second Mutiny flickered before the eyes of ministers. And what if those tiresome French tried to exploit the Sudan situation to the disadvantage of Great Britain? And did not Her Majesty's Government have some responsibility for the remaining Egyptian garrisons in the Sudan? After all, the Egyptian Army in Egypt itself was now undergoing British reorganization. Yes, and what about the European civilians there, mostly Greeks and a few Italians? Britain was friendly with these two nations and had supported them against Turks and Austrians respectively.

Why not send someone to report? Harmless word, report. But who? What about that unusually intelligent cavalry officer, Colonel Stewart?[1] He knew all about the Sudan and had recently produced a fine report on the place – let him do another one. No, he's not really senior enough and we must have someone well known, a

[1] Lieutenant-Colonel J. D. H. Stewart of the 11th Hussars, assisted by Messadaglia Bey, an able Italian official of the Sudan administration, had produced a comprehensive report on the Sudan which had been submitted to Parliament in February, 1883.

celebrity. Sir Samuel Baker[2] was a bit past it but there was Gordon – yes, why not Gordon? Very unruly fellow and Baring[3] doesn't want him but he is held in high esteem at home, in Egypt and, above all in the Sudan. Let Stewart go with him to steady him down; very steady fellow Stewart. There's the solution – Gordon with Stewart – to report.

The decision taken, there is a sudden frenzy of activity. Between 15 and 18 January, 1884, there is barely time for Gordon to dash back to London from the Continent,[4] rush down to Devon to consult Baker, back to London for government briefings, then to Charing Cross, Calais and Brindisi. Much is overlooked in the rush, including clear instructions. What is the purpose of his mission, is he simply to report, is he to attempt to defeat or negotiate with the Mahdi or to try to evacuate the Egyptian garrisons and European civilians? HMG is happy just to be seen to be doing something. Baring is worried by the whole idea and Gordon himself, from almost the first telegraph office in France, starts an endless stream of telegrams which is to abate only when the means of sending them is denied him. Within hours of leaving Brindisi he orders his ship to by-pass Port Said and sail straight through the Canal to Suakin, thus to avoid any discussion with Baring and the Egyptians, and, above all, to avoid meeting the Khedive Tewfik who, by stepping onto his deposed father's throne, had incurred Gordon's enmity. However, under telegraphic pressure from the Foreign Secretary, Lord Granville, eventually he agrees to go to Cairo. Here a further hectic round of activity ensues, in the course of which a chance encounter with the powerful slave baron, Zubeir Pasha Rahma, now under open arrest in Cairo, persuades Gordon that his old adversary is the man to save the Sudan from Mahdism and never mind the price in terms of a reversion to tacit acceptance of the slave trade.[5]

Here, briefly, we have an unusual glimpse of Gordon the realist. He knew better than anyone that the revolt in the Sudan, under a veneer of religious purity, was a rebellion against Egyptian oppression and the destruction of the slave trade. Not only was Zubeir a slaver but a leading member of one of the most powerful slaving tribes, the Jaalin. On the other hand his connections and ties with Egypt

[2] Sir Samuel Baker, a famous hunter and explorer, had preceded Gordon as the spearhead of the Khedive's campaign against the slave trade.
[3] Sir Evelyn Baring (later The Earl of Cromer), Sir Edward Malet's successor as British Agent and Consul General in Egypt. He was the de facto ruler of Egypt from 1883 to 1907.
[4] There is some confusion about Gordon's movements during these four days. He had been in Belgium to discuss a possible appointment in the Congo with King Leopold and may have returned there to inform the King of the new situation.
[5] It is particularly remarkable that Gordon should have come to this conclusion in view of the death of Zubeir's son Suleiman at the hands of Gessi, a deed for which Zubeir held Gordon, as Gessi's superior, responsible. However, Gordon told Baring he had "a mystic feeling" about Zubeir.

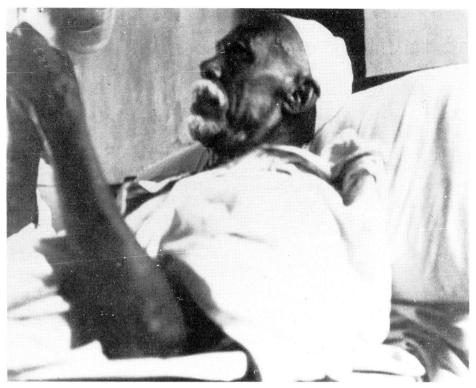

Zubeir Pasha in old age. This photograph was probably taken by Sir Reginald Wingate in about 1912.

were strong. He claimed descent from the Abassides.[6] Gordon was telling the British and Egyptians that they had a choice; either accept the loss of the Sudan to the Mahdi with whom they could not deal or hand it over to Zubeir with whom they could. Even Baring, the most practical of men, was stunned by the suggestion but did not hide from himself or from his masters at home the merits of the argument.

The discussion lingered on long after Gordon had left Cairo and it was not until March that Granville informed Baring that the plan was unacceptable to the Government, Parliament and the British people. In fact even Gladstone had come to realize the strength of the case for allowing Zubeir to go back to the Sudan but could not carry a Cabinet majority with him. The anti-slavery lobby was powerful and vocal and the move would have been seen by it as an unforgiveable betrayal of a cause which the Liberals had so enthusiastically supported. Better, the Government decided, to risk anarchy and chaos in the Sudan than to offend

[6] Formerly the ruling dynasty in Egypt, of Syrian origin.

against the liberal conscience – a political philosophy not unfamiliar to us in our own generation. In any case Zubeir might have failed and the Government would have brought down a storm of protest upon itself for nothing. But anyone who doubts Zubeir's qualifications for the job should read his extraordinary life and adventures as recounted "in his own words" to the Intelligence Officer and writer, Na'um Bey Shuqair, and later published as a book, *Black and White Ivory* by H. C. Jackson, shortly before Zubeir's death in 1913.

On the night of 26 January, 1884, Gordon, Stewart and their entourage, which included a Darfur princeling, the Emir Abdel Shakoor, and his 23 wives, steamed out of Cairo railway station. The first irrevocable step towards total British involvement in the Sudan for the next seventy years had been taken and Gordon had exactly one year to live.

While in Cairo, Gordon had been re-appointed Governor-General of the Sudan by the Khedive, a far cry from his original reporting role. This appointment, emanating from Gordon himself, had not been contemplated by the British but Baring was aware of it and it must have had at least the tacit assent of HMG. He was also equipped with a variety of firmans and proclamations, one of which announced the intention of the Egyptian Government to withdraw its garrisons and hand over the Sudan to the descendants of its orginal rulers, hence the Darfur princeling[7] described by Stewart as "a common-looking, unintelligent, badly dressed native". Apparently against Stewart's advice, Gordon revealed this policy to the elders of Berber on his arrival there, a major blunder and an extraordinary one for a man with Gordon's experience of the Arab mind. Presumably he sought to offer the carrot of local power to his audience but the effect was further to weaken confidence in the Egyptian will to resist the tide of Mahdism.

Gordon's character was so complex as to defy analysis and several commentators have doubted his sanity. All his decisions were taken on impulse, usually altered and sometimes regretted. Religious to the point of mania his attitude to earthly authority was once succinctly expressed by the harassed Baring in a letter to Granville. "It is as well that Gordon should be under my orders," he wrote, "but a man who habitually consults the Prophet Isaiah when he is in a difficulty is not apt to obey the orders of anyone."

He possessed the fearlessness of a man who, on balance, preferred to die than to live. He was contemptuous of anyone who disagreed with him or did not come up to his standards and as he changed his mind hourly it was difficult to agree with him for very long. He did not believe in making life easy for himself or others. For example, when the hopelessness of the situation in Khartoum became obvious

---

[7] He took to heavy drinking, perhaps in anticipation of the trials awaiting him on his return to his homeland, declined to go beyond Dongola and eventually returned to Cairo.

even to him, he refused to order Stewart either to leave or to stay. It is difficult to escape the conclusion that he wished to place his unfortunate subordinate in an invidious position, which, had Stewart survived, he would undoubtedly have succeeded in doing.

Strangely enough, Gordon's journal written during the siege of Khartoum is not a moving document although it does contain flashes of humour. He does not seek to excite sympathy for himself and he has little praise for superiors, equals or subordinates but a good deal of condemnation for all. He does not seem to have been close to Stewart, a much shrewder man, and it is difficult to know what they thought of each other. Doubtless Stewart was exasperated by Gordon who, in turn, probably resented him. Stewart, for as long as he could, reported direct to Baring who set more store by his opinions than he did Gordon's.

The more one studies Gordon and his mission to Khartoum, the more one is convinced that Baring's early resistance to both was right and should have been maintained, as Baring himself admits in his book, *Modern Egypt*; but, in the end, he bowed to the consensus. It should have been obvious that the mission itself, whatever it was supposed to achieve, was hopeless. By the time Gordon reached Khartoum no one man, except, conceivably, Zubeir, could have saved the Sudan from Mahdism or rescued the Egyptian garrisons.[8] The British Government concealed from itself the unwelcome fact that only the use of large numbers of first-class regular troops, British or Indian, could have saved the situation and even then at great risk.

Gordon and Stewart arrived at Khartoum on 19 February, 1884, and immediately set to work re-establishing morale. Debts were cancelled, prisoners freed from dungeons, chains removed, troops paid, extra food distributed to the poor. The first months were relatively uneventful compared to the turmoil in other parts of the Sudan. We will examine the position in the East later, but in the West, Rudolf Slatin, the Austrian Governor of Darfur, having already become a Muslim in the hope of maintaining the loyalty of his men, had surrendered in the previous December. He was no Gessi but nor was he a coward. He had resisted the onslaught of Mahdism to the limits of his meagre resources and claimed to have fought twenty-seven battles, but from then on he cannot be blamed for devoting himself to his own survival and a great survivor he proved to be.

By the beginning of 1884 the Mahdi's tentacles were reaching into the remotest areas of the South and in April Frank Lupton, who had replaced Gessi as Governor of Bahr el Ghazal Province, was forced to surrender by his native officers, despite having himself embraced Islam.

Elsewhere small Egyptian garrisons held out here and there. In the swamps of

---

[8] Except those which could be evacuated through Abyssinia by arrangement with King Yohannes as was subsequently negotiated.

Equatoria Emin Pasha remained more or less unmolested but totally isolated, eventually to be "rescued", much against his will, by the famous explorer Stanley, who had set out from the mouth of the Congo specifically to find Emin and bring him to safety, which he succeeded in doing after a two-and-a-half-year journey of incredible hardship. Emin, on arrival in Zanzibar, rewarded him by falling (or jumping) out of a window and quite seriously injuring himself.

Meanwhile in Khartoum the Christian Hero remained, in his own imaginative Arabic,[9]

> "*Wa ana mawjood hona zey el hadeed*
> *wa ashoof el Inglez el jadeed*"

> I am here like iron and (will)
> see the new (newly-arrived) English.

[9] This couplet appears in his Journal. He knew very little Arabic and probably composed it with the aid of a dictionary.

# 4 "So 'ere's to you, Fuzzy-Wuzzy"

In the Eastern Sudan the Egyptians were faring no better. The Beja[1] tribesmen in the Suakin area under Osman Digna, a slave merchant of mixed Turkish and Hadendowa descent, had inflicted a series of reverses on Egyptian troops in the last quarter of 1883. At one such action the British Consul at Jeddah and Suakin, Commander Moncrieff, was killed. Only one Egyptian official displayed any courage or determination in the face of the Mahdist onslaught. This was Tewfik Bey, a Cretan, whose efforts at resistance were eventually undermined by the same disastrous Suleiman el Niazi who had so trammelled Hicks in his attempts to prepare for the Kordofan expedition.

By this time the Egyptian Government had a serious manpower problem on its hands. The remnants of the old Egyptian army had been despatched to Khartoum with Hicks in the spring of 1883. There remained in Egypt only the raw recruits for the new British-officered army and a motley mixture of policemen and gaolbirds known as the Gendarmerie under Valentine Baker Pasha, a force of even lower martial quality than Hicks's army had been. However, the government was determined to despatch several thousand of these highly reluctant heroes to defend Suakin despite the opposition of some of their Turkish officers, doubtless fully aware of the shortcomings of their men.

In due course most of the objectors, perhaps persuaded by Baker's infectious confidence and the presence of a dozen or so other European officers, agreed to go and the Gendarmes arrived at Suakin in December, 1883, with instructions

[1] The Beja are an important tribal grouping in the Eastern Sudan of Hamitic origin with their own language. They include the Hadendowa, Amarar, Bisharin and several other tribes on the Red Sea littoral up to the Egyptian frontier. From their great shocks of buttered hair they were nick-named Fuzzy-Wuzzys by the British troops.

to maintain a largely defensive posture. However, anxious to re-establish a reputation tarnished by scandal,[2] Baker soon put his force on the offensive, trans-shipped to Trinkitat and marched on 4 February, 1884, to relieve the besieged garrison at Tokar. At a place called El Teb what followed was the now familiar pattern of swift and ferocious dervish attack, Egyptian confusion, panic and massacre. Out of an original strength of 3,700 about half were killed or captured and eleven of the European officers killed.[3] The victors reaped a rich harvest in weapons, including a number of cannon, machine guns and three thousand rifles. Baker survived and, despite having ignored his instructions, seems to have been acclaimed rather than reprimanded for leading this rabble to its destruction.

Stung by these reverses to its Egyptian protégé and concerned by the threat to its toe-hold on the Red Sea Coast, in the same month the British Government lashed out in exasperation. Two brigades of British infantry, a cavalry regiment (19th Hussars), several companies of Mounted Infantry, some artillery, Marines and a Naval Machine Gun detachment under the command of Major-General Sir Gerald Graham VC, a personal friend of Gordon and a fellow sapper, were despatched from Egypt to Suakin. At the same time another cavalry regiment, the 10th Hussars, was diverted there en route from India to England.

On 29 February Graham, having trans-shipped the bulk of his force from Suakin to Trinkitat, advanced to confront Osman Digna's dervishes, all the infantry in one large square. Osman's warriors, flushed with their recent slaughter of Baker's Gendarmes and equipped with their captured weapons, naturally assumed that by meeting this new army of "Turks" on the same battlefield, El Teb, the same tactics would have the same result. One concession to their new-found wealth in military hardware was made when they opened fire with the Krupp guns served by captured Egyptian gunners, but this was soon silenced by Graham's own artillery. Tired of wasting time, the dervishes then rose from their prepared positions and, for the first time, flung themselves upon the British square.

These "Turks", however, were different. Far from throwing down their rifles and vainly begging for their lives in gibbering terror as was expected of them, they proceeded calmly to mow down the charging tribesmen with steady volleys from their Martini-Henry .450s. Forewarned of the sheer velocity of a charging dervish, many of the British troops had nicked their bullets to make dum-dums, thus adding to the stopping power of their heavy single-shot rifles. Even so many

---

[2] Colonel Valentine Baker, brother of the famous explorer Sir Samuel Baker, was a distinguished cavalry officer and Colonel of the 10th Hussars, when, at the height of his career, he was charged with molesting a young woman on a train. There was little evidence against him but he was convicted on a wave of public indignation led by the Queen herself, imprisoned and cashiered from the Army. He took service first with the Turks then the Egyptians and died in Cairo in 1887.

[3] Among them the Captain Forestier-Walker who had been invalided from Hicks' army.

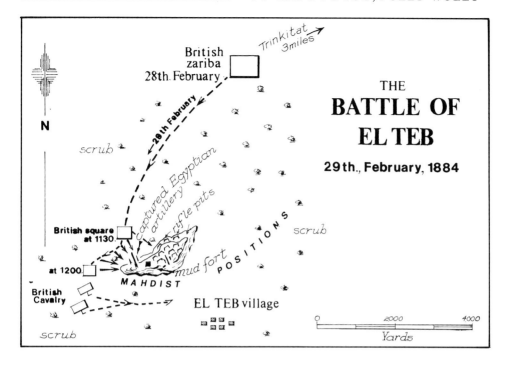

dervishes reached the square and had to be engaged with the bayonet,[4] a weapon with which the British infantryman of the day was nearly as proficient as the dervish with his sword or spear. One warrior sprang clean over the front rank (which knelt) of the square and impaled himself on a bayonet in the rear rank. "Howzat, sir?" appealed the amazed Tommy to his officer. "Well caught!" was the reply.

The initial assault beaten off, the square advanced majestically towards the dervish defences, every yard of the way disputed, but by 2 o'clock in the afternoon these positions had been taken, including a small mud fort where some Egyptian prisoners were found chained to their guns. Dervish losses were estimated at over 2,000 and British casualties amounted to 35 killed and 155 wounded.

Although a cavalryman, Quartermaster-Sergeant William Marshall,[5] was awarded the Victoria Cross for rescuing a wounded officer, the cavalry as a whole does not seem to have distinguished itself. Victorian cavalry officers tended to charge at every opportunity even when the circumstances were unsuitable, as was

[4] These were made of low-quality steel and as they frequently bent and buckled were the subject of some controversy.
[5] See Appendix B for citations.

Captain Arthur Wilson RN
won the Victoria Cross at
the Battle of El Teb.

usually the case in the Sudan. At El Teb, instead of waiting for the waves of
assaulting dervishes to break themselves on the infantry square and then pursuing
them as they withdrew, Brigadier-General Herbert Stewart, commanding the
cavalry, allowed both his regiments to charge groups of the enemy which had not
yet engaged the infantry. In so doing they galloped past or over many others
concealed on the scrub-covered ground and were surprised when attempting to
return. The result was that not only did they suffer relatively heavy casualties,
twenty killed and forty-eight wounded out of the total mentioned above, but when
eventually they were required to chase the retreating Fuzzy-Wuzzys, their horses
were quite out of puff and unable to fulfil the one role in which they could have
been of real value.

Despite the overall success of the action General Graham was dissatisfied with
the performance of at least one of his battalions, chiding the Black Watch for
moving too slowly into the attack and wasting ammunition. As the morale and

Quartermaster-Sergeant
William Marshall, 19th
Hussars, won the
Victoria Cross at the
Battle of El Teb.

performance of the soldiery was based largely on a spirit of inter-regimental competitiveness,[6] the scornful and mocking jeers from the men of other regiments were to have unfortunate consequences less than a fortnight later.

On reaching Tokar, Graham found that an unusual compromise had been reached between the Egyptian defenders and their Beja besiegers under which the fort was occupied by both sides! It is not very clear what happened on Graham's arrival there but it would seem that the news of their defeat at El Teb had caused the dervishes to withdraw from the fort and eventually 600 Egyptian men, women and children were evacuated to Egypt. Tokar having been

---

[6] Sometimes with near lethal results. For example, Private Frank Ferguson of the 20th Hussars wrote home from Egypt describing a pitched battle between his own regiment and the Shropshire Light Infantry in the canteen at Abbassyieh Barracks near Cairo on Christmas Day, 1886, which put eighteen men in hospital and one in the lunatic asylum!

A Beja tribesman ready for battle. This one happens to be a "Friendly".

abandoned by both sides, Graham withdrew his force to Trinkitat and thence by ship to Suakin.

By 12 March news reached Graham of a large concentration of dervishes at Tamai, a few miles inland from Suakin, and on the 13th an engagement took place which has passed into history as the first of two occasions on which Sudanese tribesmen "broke the British square" and inspired Kipling's famous poem:

> "So 'ere's to you, Fuzzy-Wuzzy, at your 'ome in the Soudan;
> You're a pore benighted 'eathen but a first-class fightin' man;
> . . .
> An' 'ere's to you, Fuzzy-Wuzzy, with your 'ayrick 'ead of 'air –
> You big black boundin' beggar – for you broke the British square!"

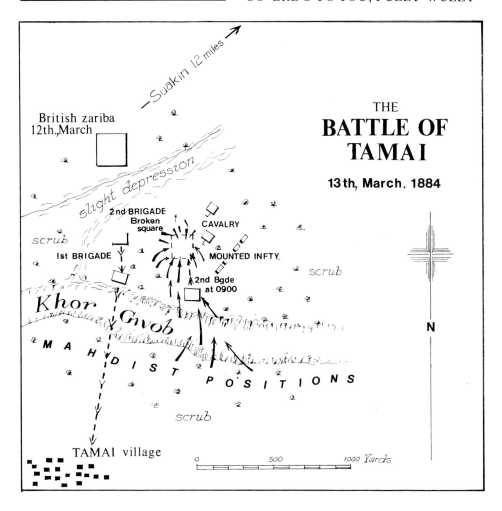

The British infantry brigades marched on Tamai in separate squares. 1st Brigade, under Major-General Sir Redvers Buller VC, consisted of the 1st Bn Gordon Highlanders, 2nd Bn Royal Irish Fusiliers and 3rd Bn 60th Rifles (KRRC). 2nd Brigade, under Major-General Davis, was made up of the 1st Bns Black Watch, York & Lancasters and Royal Marine Light Infantry with a Royal Naval Gardner Machine Gun detachment. The two brigades were advancing in echelon with 2nd Brigade on the left when large numbers of the enemy were sighted in and around a ravine known as Khor Gwob. What happened then is shrouded in the mists of battle and time.

The square formation, already obsolete in the 1880s, had been developed largely as a defence against cavalry. Based on the theory that staunch, well-disciplined troops kneeling (front rank) and standing (rear rank) rigidly shoulder to shoulder presented an almost impenetrable barrier to even the most determined attacker, the square had proved itself as a defensive formation in the years before the development of the bolt-action magazine rifle made it hopelessly vulnerable. However, it was difficult to manage in attack, movement inevitably creating gaps which could be exploited by a swift and agile enemy.

At Tamai it seems that General Graham, riding with the 2nd Brigade, upon sighting the dervishes on the edge of the Khor, ordered the Black Watch on the left front of the square to charge. We do not know why he did this or even if, in reality, any such order was given. Whatever orders were or were not given or by whom, the Black Watch, smarting from the intolerable insults of a fortnight before (which doubtless had continued since) were not backward in rushing forward, leaving the left flank and rear of the York and Lancasters, who either had not received or not heard any order to charge, exposed to the dervish *pièce de résistance*, the mass attack pressed home with unbelievable speed and ferocity. Thus the square was penetrated and the York and Lancasters hurled back into the sailors and marines in rear of the square which was soon broken up into small groups of desperately fighting men, once again sword and spear against bayonet, the dervishes slashing first at the hands to disarm and then at the head and body to kill and maim.

Fortunately 1st Brigade on their right and the cavalry and Mounted Infantry on their left were able to direct a withering fire at the swarming dervishes. This must have involved inflicting casualties on their own comrades in 2nd Brigade but enabled it to reform and a moment of great danger was passed. In the course of this action two Victoria Crosses were won. Private Edwards, an Englishman serving with the Black Watch and attached as a muleteer to the Naval Machine Gun detachment, received his for defending a Gardner the crew of which had been killed, and Lieutenant Marling of the Mounted Infantry (of whom we shall be hearing a good deal more) for rescuing one of his wounded men. Considering the hand-to-hand nature of the fighting, it may seem surprising that only two VCs were awarded, but it should be borne in mind that at that time no posthumous awards could be made and we must assume that many heroic deeds were performed by men who did not survive them. From his diary we know that Marling was disappointed that the two private soldiers who helped him rescue the other did not also receive the decoration.

1st Brigade then pressed on to the village of Tamai which was in their hands by noon. Again an estimated 2,000 dervishes had been killed but at the relatively heavy cost to the British of over one hundred killed and about the same number wounded. This unusual ratio of killed to wounded reflected the nasty habit common to both sides in all the Sudan campaigns of taking few prisoners and killing off the wounded. There is no record of any British military prisoner being taken by the Mahdists. To surrender was to die, so every unwounded man cut off from his fellows either fought his way out of trouble or perished.

The Battle of Tamai. Hadendowa warriors shown trying to operate a captured machine
gun.

The Battle of Tamai. The British troops depicted are men of the York & Lancaster
Regiment.

Colonel Valentine Baker (on grey horse), before his disgrace, accompanying the Prince of Wales on exercises in England.

After Tamai and the destruction of a hostile village at Tamamieb, the desert route from Suakin to Berber lay open and a fleeting opportunity to reach Khartoum within weeks presented itself. There were, however, serious objections to the use of this route. The heat was increasing, transport animals were difficult to obtain locally and water en route was scarce. Above all, the vulnerability of thirsty and heat-exhausted men to attack from Osman Digna's still numerous, if temporarily subdued, tribesmen dominated the deliberations of the home government. The destruction of Hicks's and Baker's Egyptians was, in political terms, one thing; for the same fate to overtake a British force would be quite another.

It is interesting to observe that, with the invention of the telegraph, generals in the 1880s were under as tight political control as their successors are in the 1980s. For better or for worse the hand of government lay as heavily upon General Graham as it might have done upon General Moore in the Falklands nearly one

Private Thomas Edwards, Black Watch (*left*) and Lieutenant Percival Marling, 6oth Rifles (KRRC), both won the Victoria Cross at the Battle of Tamai.

hundred years later if an equally irresolute adminstration had been in office. Be that as it may, although Graham himself favoured a "dash" to Berber, military advice was by no means unanimous and Gladstone's government quickly decided that the risk of catastrophe outweighed the chances of success and the idea was abandoned.[7] There was to be no relief for Khartoum from that direction, particulary as Berber fell to the Mahdists in May.

The fine performance of the British troops in the savage little battles recounted above did not escape the attention of the Press. Aficionados of Victorian jingo-journalism are hard put to it to find better examples of the art than the

[7] Major De Cosson, an experienced traveller in the Sudan who accompanied Graham's second expedition in the following year, produced quite a feasible time-table for such an attempt in his book *Days and Nights of Service*. During the campaign of re-conquest in 1896/8, reinforcements of Egyptian troops, prodigious marchers, on more than one occasion tramped the 300 miles from Suakin to Berber. One British sergeant marched the whole way on foot with his Egyptian soldiers, a feat thought impossible for a European.

reports of the war correspondents who accompanied the expedition. Bluejackets who long to die for their Queen and private soldiers who make high-flown speeches of farewell to dying officers are commonplace. Most of these tales ring with improbability but doubtless there is a grain of truth in some. The Victorians, for all their hard and resolute self-confidence, were extremely sentimental. Also, more often than not, the soldiers were much attached to their officers from whom many had received the only kindness and generosity they had ever known and these feelings were reciprocated with an unselfconscious paternalism appropriate to the class structure of the time. Evidence for this lies in the innumerable occasions on which officers and men risked, and sometime sacrificed, their lives for each other in battle.

Some stories were exploited for wider purposes. On one occasion a trooper in the 10th Hussars, Private Hayes, leaping from his horse and carefully laying down his sword, squared up to an astonished dervish and proceeded to give him a sound drubbing in accordance with the Queensberry Rules. Quite why the dervish allowed himself to be dealt with in this rather unusual manner by an unarmed man history does not relate, but Hayes was awarded the Distinguished Conduct Medal for this exploit – perhaps a Lonsdale Belt would have been more appropriate. Some sections of the Press saw the chance to revive an old hobby-horse and produced a story to the effect that this same Hayes, while being congratulated by his colonel in front of the whole regiment, stepped forward and demanded the reinstatement in the army of Valentine Baker, a former colonel of the 10th. Whatever validity the tale may have had was lost on the Queen and her Commander-in-Chief, the Duke of Cambridge, who had set their faces firmly against him and Baker remained in the wilderness.

Through no fault of his own Graham had achieved little except to instil in the Mahdists (and in Osman Digna in particular) a hearty respect for this new kind of "Turk". When Graham sailed away from Suakin on 3 April, 1884, leaving only a small garrison in the town, Osman soon recovered his prestige and sway over the Eastern Sudan.

# 5 Our Only General

> "I think that the Government will ultimately, but too late, send a relieving force, not because Mr Gladstone wishes it, but because public indignation will compel him, *nolens volens*, to do so; and, little as the Prime Minister may value Gordon, the Prime Minister cares a great deal for Mr Gladstone." COLONEL FRED. BURNABY, 16 MAY, 1884.

By mid-April, 1884, many of the tribes between Shendi and Berber had declared for the Mahdi and the telegraph wire from Cairo to Khartoum had been cut. Baring has not recorded his personal feelings about this but they must have been mixed. On a previous occasion when the telegraph had been temporarily interrupted the Foreign Secretary, Lord Granville, had commented to him, "I am not sure that the stoppage of communications with Gordon for a time is the greatest of misfortunes for himself or us".

The bombardment of ever-changing demands and suggestions had ceased but the problem itself had not gone away. Most messengers from Egypt into the Sudan (and vice versa) were intercepted by the Mahdi and it had to be assumed that from then on all Anglo-Egyptian plans communicated to Gordon would be known to his opponent. Nevertheless it was not until August that the British Government finally faced up to what it must have known for several months, namely that Gordon and the Egyptian garrison could be extricated only by a substantial force of British or Indian troops. In their hearts, or at least in their heads, ministers must have wished they could leave Gordon, an insubordinate nuisance, to go to the devil – or the Mahdi – but such a dish, however well presented, would have been entirely unpalatable to the electorate. There were plenty of British troops in Egypt and surely it needed only the great Lord Wolseley and his freemasonry of imperial campaigners, the celebrated Ring, to take charge and pluck the Christian Hero from the jaws of Hell and, as the saying went, all would be Sir Garnet!

Gordon had suggested, at various times, that the Sultan might be prevailed upon to send a Turkish army to the Sudan at Britain's expense, ignoring the fact that the Turks were even more intensely hated by the Sudanese than were the

Egyptians; or that a few cavalrymen might trek across the desert from Suakin; or that some American millionaires might be persuaded to finance a relief expedition. It is doubtful if at this stage either Baring or Whitehall were paying much attention to Gordon's ideas, rather they were wondering whatever had possessed them to send him to Khartoum in the first place. Indian troops were considered, but there were thought to be political and religious disadvantages and objections from Wolseley could have been expected as this would have brought his deadly rival Roberts[1] into the game. In the end British troops were chosen with Wolseley to lead them.

Garnet Wolseley's record was one of uninterrupted success, including his lightning suppression of the recent Arabi rebellion in Egypt. From the Canadian rivers to the jungles of West Africa; from the mountains of Zululand to the Corridors of Power, he had proved himself both as a field commander and military theorist unrivalled in his generation. He was Our Only General. Like many other great British commanders he was of Anglo-Irish stock; a slight, small infantry-man, he was fifty-one when he undertook what was to be his last campaign in the field. In the years which have passed since his death in 1913 his reputation has suffered but such is the fate of most men revered and lionized in their own time.

He was a bit of a prig and his diary of the Relief campaign does not endear the reader to him. A rather shrill bitchiness comes through which, although doubtless induced by stress, and, in the end, disappointment, seems unworthy of a great leader. However, it must be said that his strictures were confined mainly to his political (and royal) superiors and his closest military subordinates and were often justified. For his men he was both privately and publicly unstinting in his praise. Indeed, as a military reformer throughout his career, he placed the interests of the private soldier above all others – except, perhaps, his own – and, rightly or wrongly, he has been credited with laying the foundations of the finest British army ever to leave England's shores, the British Expeditionary Force of 1914.

Unfortunately the rank and file have seldom gone to any great lengths to record their feelings and experiences for posterity so it is difficult to know what they thought of Wolseley. It would not be unreasonable to suppose that a largish minority of the men who served under him had never heard of him and did not know who he was. On the whole, troops are concened with their platoon and company officers and, sometimes, the colonel. The rest are brass who cause much waiting about in the heat or rain; the newspapers make more of generals than do soldiers. During the Second World War, shortly after General Leese had taken over command of the 8th Army in Italy from General Montgomery, Leese's staff

[1] Field-Marshal The Earl Roberts VC (1832–1914).

Contemporary cartoon showing Wolseley bearing the full burden of Gladstone's indecision.

car passed a platoon of infantry tramping along the road. One of the men, mildly curious, called out to the platoon commander, "Mr Jones, sir, wot 'appened to the little bloke in a beret 'oo used to chuck fags out of 'is car?" So much for the reputations of great captains!

Whatever the soldiers and the public may have felt, the appointment of Lord Wolseley to command the Relief Expedition was by no means automatic. As Adjutant-General he had War Office responsibilities and a good many enemies including the Commander-in-Chief, HRH The Duke of Cambridge, an old adversary with magnificently reactionary views.[2] It was felt that consideration should be given to senior officers already in Egypt such as General Stephenson, commanding the British troops there and General Wood, Sirdar (Commander-in-Chief) of the Egyptian Army. However, the Minister of War, Lord Hartington,

[2] He is reputed to have said "I deplore all change even when it is for the better".

The Second Cataract.

favoured Wolseley, with Redvers Buller as his Chief of Staff, and his views prevailed.

The next problem was how to get to Khartoum. As we have seen, General Graham, after his partially successful Suakin campaign, had favoured a "dash" to Berber. At the same time detailed calculations and costings were made as to the feasibility of a railway line between Suakin and Berber but a decision on this was postponed until the following year. Eventually, the longer, slower but safer Nile route, favoured by Wolseley, was chosen. Contracts were signed with Thomas Cook & Son, who operated a fleet of Nile steamers, for the transport of men and materials to Wadi Halfa. For the navigation of the river thereafter boats were built in England under the supervision of one of Wolseley's most able but also most quarrelsome officers, Colonel William Butler, and skilled boatmen were recruited in Canada (voyageurs) and West Africa (Kroo boys). For the muscle required to drag these craft over the cataracts, Egyptian troops as well as civilian labourers were to be used in addition to the British.

Before leaving England Wolseley decided that camel-borne troops would reduce considerably the time required to get an advance force of between 1,500 and 2,000 men to Khartoum as they could stirke out across the Bayuda Desert bisecting the great bend in the river with its apex at Abu Hamed. To this end and in the teeth of considerable opposition, particularly from the Duke of Cambridge, violently opposed to any innovation, he formed four camel regiments, the Guards, the Heavy, the Light and the Mounted Infantry. These units of between 400 and 450 officers and men were drawn from a variety of regiments[3] and, together with some additional infantry, cavalry, artillery, engineers and an RN Gardner Machine Gun detachment, were to make up what became known as the Desert Column, commanded by the dashing Brigadier-General Sir Herbert Stewart, a favourite of Wolseley and a veteran of Graham's recent campaign in the Eastern Sudan.

Unfortunately this scheme, logical and imaginative though it may have been, revealed many defects. The time available for training was minimal as the camel regiments had to be operational within weeks of the drafts arriving from England (only the Mounted Infantry were already in Egypt). There was little regimental spirit or cohesion between companies within the camel regiments, which was what the Duke of Cambridge had feared. Worst of all but not surprisingly, neither officers nor men had any knowledge of the camel, how to ride it, load it, feed it or water it. They did not know what it could do and what it could not, from which ignorance great losses both in numbers of animals and efficiency resulted. They chose to ignore advice based on experience and the War Office displayed neither imagination nor zoological knowledge by despatching to Egypt several rough-riding sergeants and shoeing-smiths for the camel regiments.

It should be borne in mind that there was no intention of using these troops in a cavalry role and the camels were simply to convey them from A to B where they would fight as infantry. The Heavy Regiment, drawn from the Household Cavalry, Dragoons and Lancers, had received virtually no infantry training and the only troops experienced in this type of campaigning were the Mounted Infantry, many of whom had seen active service in South Africa, Egypt and the Eastern Sudan.

One of the camel regiments, the Light, was commanded by an officer, Colonel Stanley Clarke, totally without experience or military merit, who had been appointed simply to please the Prince of Wales, a personal friend. Fortunately for his men, they were employed mainly on convoy duty and were involved in little fighting. In any case, as the short Sudan winter drew to an end, Colonel Clarke, finding the increasing heat burdensome, returned to England, doubtless to regale the Prince with his intrepid adventures.

Wolseley's strategy was for the Desert Column to be reinforced and supported

---

[3] See Appendix C.

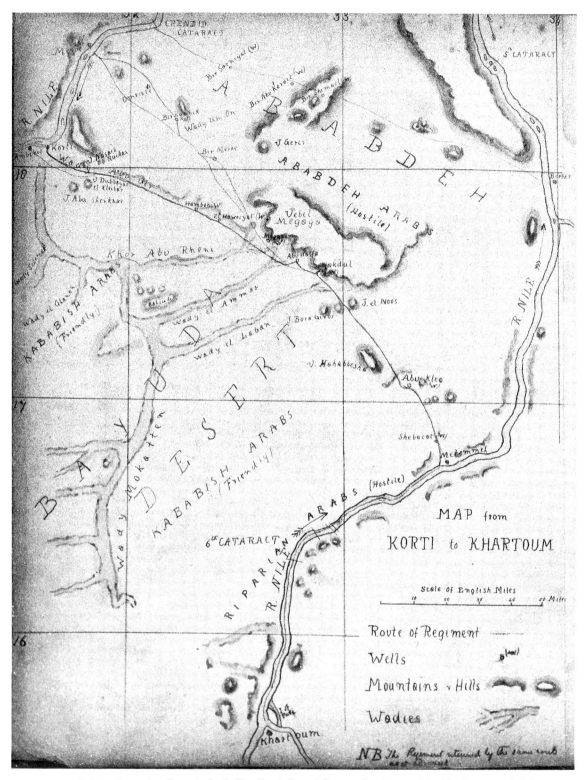

Original map by Captain L. J. Trafford, Royal Sussex Regiment. Trafford was probably mistaken in describing the Ababdeh as hostile, as, in general, this tribe remained friendly with Egypt throughout the period of the Mahdiya.

in the final phase of its advance on Khartoum by a River Column consisting of four battalions of infantry and supporting troops under command of Major-General W. Earle. The lines of communication were to be guarded by the newly re-formed Egyptian Army.

The main bodies of both River and Desert Columns reached Korti during December and early January, Wolseley himself arriving there on 16 December. The reward for the best time by river from Sarras, below the 2nd cataract, to Korti, £100 out of Wolseley's own pocket, went to the Royal Irish Regiment. The battalion had only recently arrived from India and was much admired by Wolseley, not only for the lean and fit appearance of its men but also for its padre, Father Brindle,[4] who seems to have exercised over his flock a combination of the spiritual influence of the Pope and the earthly authority of a regimental sergeant-major. The Irish did the trip in thirty-seven days while the wooden spoon, forty-nine days and the loss of most boats, went to the Duke of Cornwall's Light Infantry. The £100 prize was criticized by the Queen and, oddly enough, by the celebrated lady novelist, Ouida. British soldiers, even Irish ones, were supposed to do their duty for its own sake and not for financial reward. Wolseley, and perhaps the recipients if they knew about it, were justifiably disgusted with this criticism.[5]

At Christmas troops were still arriving at Korti. The funerals of two Guardsmen on Christmas day might have put a damper on the celebrations but plum, or rather date, pudding was served to all ranks. Wolseley and his staff enjoyed two plump wild geese and Marling of the Mounted Infantry remembered a huge camp fire and a "ripping stump speech" by a trooper in the Blues.

Bearing in mind Wolseley's subsequent tendency to blame others for the failure to reach Khartoum in time, perhaps he should have remembered the old adage about stones and glasshouses. His own journal certainly does not reflect a sense of urgency at this time and when Stewart eventually left for Jakdul wells, 100 miles into the Bayuda Desert, it was only to return a week later, a shortage of camels making it impossible for the entire column to start together. The Guards Camel Regiment having been left to garrison Jakdul, the main column finally left Korti on 8 January, 1885, composed of the following units, the Lights having been sent ahead on the previous day with a convoy of some 1,100 baggage camels:

[4] The Right Reverend Robert Brindle DSO (1837–1916) Roman Catholic Bishop of Nottingham 1901–16.

[5] Years later it was suggested that Wolseley had fiddled the result of this competition because of his partiality for the Royal Irish but it is not clear how he is supposed to have done this. However, according to his mess sergeant, Harry Heath, the Irish handed in boxes filled with sand and stones instead of the reserve rations which were supposed to be surrendered on arrival at Korti.

Officers of the Desert Column before Abu Klea.

| The Staff | 8 officers and 6 men |
|---|---|
| Heavy Camel Regt | 24 officers and 376 men |
| Mounted Infantry Camel Regt | 21 officers and 336 men |
| Naval Brigade (with Gardner MG) | 5 officers and 53 men |
| 19th Hussars (2 squadrons) | 9 officers and 121 men |
| 1/1 Southern Battery RA | 4 officers and 39 men with three 2.5″ guns |
| Royal Sussex Regt | 16 officers and 401 men |
| Essex Regt (1 coy) | 3 officers and 55 men |
| Commissariat & Transport | 5 officers and 72 men |
| Medical Staff | 3 officers and 50 men |

1. Atherton, Major W. H., 5th Dragoon Guards
2. Carmichael, Major, 5th Lancers
3. Davison, Lieut.-Col. T., 16th Lancers
4. Browne, Lieut., 16th Lancers
5. Barrow, Col. C. T., Mounted Infantry
6. Darley, Capt. J. W. W., 4th Dragoon Guards
7. Verner, Capt. W. W. C., Rifle Brigade
8. Pearse, S., Special Correspondent
9. Barn Murdoch, Capt. J. E., Royal Dragoons
10. Gough, Major, Royal Dragoon Guards
11. Wolfe, Lieut., Scots Greys
12. Wardrop, Lieut.-Col. 12th Lancers, D.A.A. and Q.M.G.
13. Hippisley, Capt. W. H., Scots Greys
14. Guthrie, Lieut. J. D., R.H.A.
15. Kincaid-Smith, Capt., 4th Hussars
16. Airlie, Major, The Earl of, 10th Hussars

17. Stewart, Capt. W., Gordon Highlanders
18. Hore, Capt. C. H., 2nd S. Staffordshire Regiment
19. Rhodes, Lieut.-Col. F. W., Royal Dragoon Guards, A.D.C.
20. Stewart, Sir Herbert, K.C.B., *General in Command*
21. Crabbe, Major Eyre, Grenadier Guards
22. Willson, Lieut.-Col. Mildmay, C.B., Scots Guards
23. Burnaby, Col. Fred., Royal Horse Guards
24. Hardinge, Lieut. The Hon. H. C., Rifle Brigade
25. Barrow, Col. P. H. S., C.B., C.M.G., 19th Hussars
26. Kane, Lieut. K. A., 1st Royal Sussex Regiment
27. Trafford, Major, 1st Royal Sussex Regiment
28. Sunderland, Col., 2nd Royal Sussex Regiment
29. De Pledge, Lieut., 19th Hussars
30. Gem, Major, Royal Sussex Regiment
31. Jones, Lieut. R. W. W., 1st Royal Sussex Regiment
32. Lyall, Lieut. C. N., R.A.

33. Wilson, Sir Charles, K.C.B., Royal Engineers
34. Herbert, St. Leger, "Morning Post" Special Correspondent
35. Stuart-Wortley, Major E., King's Royal Rifles
36. Dorward, Lieut.-Col. J. F., Royal Engineers
37. Law, Lieut. C. W. A., 4th Dragoon Guards
38. Marling, Capt. V. C., 18th Hussars
39. Poë, Major, Royal Marines
40. Hibbert, Capt. R. F., 2nd Dragoons
41. Binning, Lieut. Lord, Royal Horse Guards
42. Somerset, Major Lord Arthur, Royal Horse Guards
43. Fulvey, Surgeon, Medical Staff
44. Dickson, Lieut.-Col. J. B. B., 5th Dragoon Guards
45. Swift, Sergeant
46. Gough, Lieut.-Col. Hon. G., 14th Hussars
47. Magill, Surgeon Major, Coldstream Guards
48. Phipps, Major, 7th Hussars

49. Beech, Lieut., 2nd Life Guards
50. Dundonald, Major, The Earl of, 2nd Life Guards
51. Rodney, Capt. Lord, 1st Life Guards
52. Barleigh, Bennett, "Daily Telegraph" Correspondent
53. St. Vincent, Capt. Lord, 16th Lancers
54. Talbot, Col. Hon. R., C.B., 1st Life Guards
55. Byng, Lieut.-Col Hon. C., 1st Life Guards
56. Boscawen, Lieut.-Col. Hon. E., Coldstream Guards
57. Crutchley, Major C., Scots Guards
58. Beresford, Capt. Lord Charles, R.N.
59. Munro, Lieut., R.N.
60. Webber, Lieut., R.N.
61. De Lisle, Lieut. R., R.N.
62. Pigott, Commander, R.N.
63. "Smoke," Major Berkeley Pigott's dog

A total strength of ninety-eight officers and 1,509 men. Excluding the Light Camel Regiment convoy there were 2,228 camels and 155 horses. The Guards garrison at Jakdul consisted of nineteen officers and 365 men plus twenty-seven Royal Engineers and eleven medical staff.[6]

[6] These figures are taken from Wilson's *From Korti to Khartoum*.

# 6 "The Gatling's jammed and the Colonel's dead"

On the face of it there are superficial similiarities between Stewart's force and Hicks's but, great though the dangers were to both, Stewart enjoyed many advantages over Hicks. In the first place his troops were British regulars and, apart from some Adeni, Somali and Egyptian camel drivers and "general duties" men, numbering in all about three hundred, he was not encumbered with thousands of camp followers. Then, through careful reconnaissance and intelligence work, mostly on the part of one Major Herbert Kitchener of the Intelligence Department, Stewart was not marching off into the unknown and, above all, he knew where the water was. The season, too, was favourable, January and February being the coolest and most agreeable months in the northern Sudan, whereas Hicks had been marching in the sweltering "autumn" (September to November). Nevertheless, Stewart's task was extremely hazardous and the numerical superiority of the enemy, although difficult to calculate, was enormous.

On the other hand, in addition to the lack of training and expertise in camel management, the column suffered from another serious defect for which Wolseley himself must be held directly responsible. Stewart may have been an experienced and reasonably competent officer, although he had hardly distinguished himself as a cavalry commander in the eastern Sudan with Graham, but insufficient attention had been paid to the question of his successor in the event of his death or incapacity through wounds or sickness. The next most senior officer was Colonel Sir Charles Wilson RE,[1] Deputy Adjutant General, Intelligence, an accomplished surveyor with a largely technical and administrative background. A

[1] Major-General Sir Charles Wilson, R.E. (1836–1905).

year junior to him was the swashbuckling globe-trotter, Colonel Fred Burnaby of the Blues,[2] who had arrived in the Sudan the previous year at his own expense and in civilian clothes in time to take part in General Graham's campaign around Suakin. The huge flamboyant Burnaby was unpopular with the army hierarchy in general but not with Wolseley. He was very much his own man and his social credentials were considered less than impeccable. The Duke of Cambridge did not like him so Wolseley did. At El Teb, Burnaby had bowled over a number of Fuzzy-Wuzzys with his shotgun, exciting the admiration of some journalists but the opprobrium of others, although it is difficult to see why it should be any more or less praiseworthy to pepper a dervish with buckshot than to stick him in the belly with a bayonet. More to the point, Burnaby's position with the Desert Column was ill-defined and there was nothing in his earlier career, consisting mostly of spectacular and rather flashy individual exploits such as ballooning and a hazardous winter journey through Asiatic Russia, to confirm his fitness for senior command. Indeed, his subsequent conduct, with all its reckless gallantry, inclines one towards an opposite view.

Next in line came Lieutenant-Colonel the Hon. E. Boscawen of the Coldstream Guards, commanding the Guards Camel Regiment, who had served in the Egyptian campaign but was an unknown quantity. Leading the Naval contingent was Captain Lord Charles Beresford, very much a man of action and one to whom the giving of orders came more naturally than the receiving thereof, but as a naval officer hardly qualified to command a land operation. There must have been doubts in Wolseley's mind as to Wilson's suitability to take over command of such a dangerous operation and probably the ideal combination would have been Buller in command with Stewart as his deputy. Buller's hard campaigning experience and forceful driving personality was required in the end and it is a pity that in the beginning he was wasted on purely administrative work, which he did not do particularly well.

In the previous chapter we touched upon the question of camel management or rather the lack of it. As we have seen, nearly 3,500 camels were provided for an expedition of less than 2,000 men. In the event this proved to be inadequate, for which Buller as Chief of Staff has been blamed. However, although it must be admitted that the army's refusal to learn about camels was inexcusable it is difficult, surely, to point the finger at Buller or Wolseley himself and say that they should have realized that even this high ratio of camels to men would be insufficient. To the ignorant British the camel was the Ship of the Desert and a sailing ship at that, which, they had heard, was supposed to glide swiftly over the sand without fuel or maintenance. They were wrong.

Since October the Mahdi had been aware of the preparations and movements

[2] Royal Horse Guards.

of the Relief Expedition. He and his ansar had by this time moved from Kordofan to the Khartoum area and were laying siege to the town.

When word reached him of the concentration of British forces at Korti he sent instructions to his emirs at Berber and Metemma to oppose the advance across the Bayuda Desert and a force variously estimated at between eight and fourteen thousand men, mainly Jaalin, Dughein and Kenana tribesmen plus a few bazingers, some of them prisoners from Hicks's expedition, under Musa Wad Helu, occupied the wells at Abu Klea.[3] Meanwhile Stewart, having left the Essex company to guard the Howeiyat wells, moved on to Jakdul,[4] exchanged the Guards garrison for three companies of Sussex and set out for Abu Klea, the next wells, on 14 January. To everyone's amazement, the camels were already in a bad way. Overwork, lack of fodder and grazing[5] and general mismanagement verging on brutality were taking their toll, particularly as Stewart insisted on marching at night on the grounds that it was less tiring for the men. Wilson disagreed strongly, arguing that the men could not sleep well during the day and that the camels suffered even more at night because shifting loads could not be properly re-adjusted in the dark.

On the 16th a patrol of the 19th Hussars led by Major French[6] encountered a party of Musa Wad Helu's force guarding the pass leading to Abu Klea wells. As it was late in the afternoon Stewart decided to postpone the advance, and the fight it would probably entail, until the following morning. A zariba[7] was constructed and during the night the British were kept awake by desultory sniper fire which caused few casualties. However, as dawn broke this fire grew heavier and several people were wounded, including Major Gough, Commander of the Mounted Infantry. By 10 o'clock the inevitable square (see diagram) had been formed with the camels, some carrying wounded, in the centre. Surrounded by patrols of the Hussars and skirmishers of the Mounted Infantry, it lumbered slowly forward towards the pass.

Wilson describes the main body of the enemy suddenly appearing from a ravine to the left front of the square in a curious choice of words, as a "beautiful and striking" sight and applies Walter Scott's description of Roderick Dhu's men rising out of the heather. Such a comparison must have rather strained the imagination as the northern Sudanese desert resembles the Scottish mountains as

---

[3] This is the name given to the place by the British. The true Arabic name is Abu Tuleyh.
[4] The troops called it Jack's pool.
[5] The Bayuda Desert is not a desert in the true sense as it is covered in bushes and scrub with coarse grass in some places. Thus there was plenty of grazing for the camels, but whenever the column stopped they were tied down to prevent them wandering away or being stolen.
[6] Field-Marshal the Earl of Ypres (1852–1925).
[7] A camp surrounded by a thorn fence.

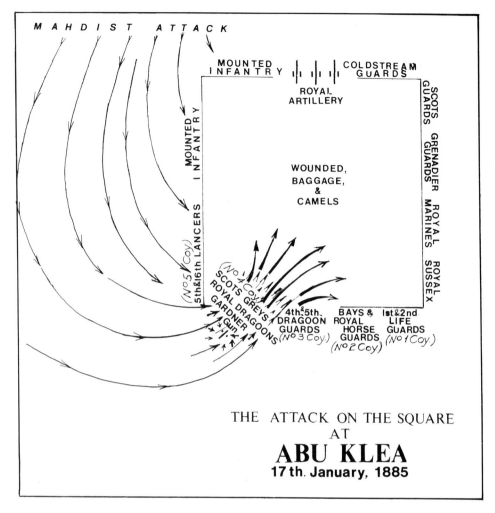

THE ATTACK ON THE SQUARE
AT
# ABU KLEA
### 17th. January, 1885

closely as a tropical jungle does an iceberg. The Mounted Infantry skirmishers (on foot) scurried back to the shelter of the square and Stuart-Wortley recounts how a small terrier belonging to an officer called Piggot challenged the advancing dervishes with furious barking and retreated back into the square only at the last minute.[8]

As soon as, and even before, the skirmishers had scrambled back into the square, their comrades on the left front opened a heavy and accurate fire with their Martini-Henrys. So withering was this fusillade that not only did dozens

[8] Lieutenant (later Major-General) the Hon E. J. Montagu-Stuart-Wortley. According to Stuart-Wortley's unpublished reminiscences the heart of this brave little beast, Smoke, a veteran of the First Boer War as well, is buried with its master in Brockenhurst churchyard.

of dervishes fall dead and wounded but the main body swung right and then sharply to its left and fell upon the Heavy Camel Regiment to the left rear of the square.

From this point until the end of the engagement, a bare ten minutes later, the confusion was total. The various eye-witness, or rather participant, accounts vary on points of detail but the blame for what followed has been seen to lie with the Heavies in general and Burnaby in particular. However, it does appear that the prime culprit, at least chronologically, was Beresford, who wanted to get his Gardner (not the Gatling of Newbolt's poem) machine gun and its crew, including himself, outside the square as obviously it could not be brought into action from the inside. Stewart seems to have given permission for this, but, bearing in mind the noise, confusion and fraction of time available for such consultation, this is by no means certain. In any case Burnaby, apparently acting over the heads of the colonel and company commanders of the Heavies' ordered numbers 3 (4th & 5th Dragoon Guards) and 4 (Scots Greys and Royal Dragoons) companies to open up and let the machine-gun through. This manoeuvre, which may sound simple, in fact involved the movement of some 200 men and took place at the moment when the initial shock-wave of dervishes hit these two companies of dismounted cavalrymen. The Gardner, as was its wont, jammed almost immediately and all its crew, except Beresford, were killed. To add to their plight, many of the troopers' rifles misfired and their bayonets buckled, probably a combination of poor maintenance and worse material. The sheer body-weight and impetus of the masses of ansar and their horses hurled the Heavies back into the Sussex on the right rear of the square and the two units became hopelessly entangled with each other and the ansar. Beresford, who had been swept back into the square by the momentum, found the press so great that he could use neither sword nor pistol.

By freakish, and indeed undeserved, chance, the dervish onslaught was stemmed, not by the troops, but by the poor, ill-treated camels tethered and uncomprehending in the centre of the square.[9] These animals and the baggage and wounded which they carried formed an impenetrable barrier between the attackers and the right flank of the square manned by the Guards, whose rear rank about faced and opened fire. Although inflicting some casualties on their own side they brought down almost every dervish who had entered the square and was sandwiched between the camels and those companies of the Heavies which had not moved.

---

[9] According to Colonel Butler (who was not present) there was another diversion as well. Apparently a box containing gold sovereigns for payment to friendly tribesmen, which had been mixed up with the ammunition boxes, was opened in the middle of the battle and an unseemly scramble for the contents ensued. A variation of this story was also recounted years later by one Private Etherington of the Royal Sussex who was present, so it is probably based on fact.

The Heavy Camel Regiment defending the square at Abu Klea.

Fighting of slightly lesser intensity had also taken place at the front of the square in the course of which the only Victoria Cross of the day was won by Gunner Albert Smith, a Cockney "striker" in the crew of a 2.5″ screw gun. Let one of his comrades, Acting Bombardier (later Sergeant-Major) Watts give his account of what he saw.

"I was a striker by trade so was No. 3 on the gun, my duty being to tighten the junction nut by hammering on the trunnion. Owing to a casualty occurring, I was promoted to Acting Bombardier and put in charge of the first line ammunition camels and Gunner Smith, also a striker, was put in my place. When the face of the square began to crumble up it was a case of 'officers to the front' and Mr Guthrie was stabbed and when Gunner Smith saw this he picked up the traversing handspike and hit the Arab who had done it over the head. The little locking stud on the handspike split his head right open and then Smith stood astride Mr Guthrie and kept the Arabs off with his handspike until the square reformed a few minutes later. I was standing within a few yards of the place and saw everything."

Lieutenant Guthrie subsequently died of his wound.

Gunner Albert Smith, Royal
Artillery, won the Victoria Cross
at Abu Klea.

Burnaby too had decided it was "officers to the front". Early in the battle and
after giving his near fatal orders, he charged out of the square on Moses, a pony
borrowed from Lieutenant Marling VC, and engaged in single combat with a
mounted dervish who was soon joined by others. Burnaby was fatally speared in
the throat but fought on and Corporal McIntosh of the Blues, unable to stand and
watch while his regimental hero fought his last fight alone, dashed from the ranks
and plunged his bayonet into one of Burnaby's assailants only to be cut down and
speared to death himself. By the time others reached him Burnaby was beyond
aid.

So passed into legend a Victorian Achilles mourned by his brother officers and
men but not, according to Wolseley, by some distinguished personages at home.
"How delighted the Prince of Wales and the Duke of Cambridge will be that poor
Burnaby is killed. His high military spirit, energy, zeal and remarkable personal

courage were not sufficient in the eyes of these Royal tailors (sic) to cover up the fact that socially Burnaby was distasteful to them and their set."

On the Mahdist side there was even greater heroism. With over one thousand dead and many more wounded in the space of less than quarter of an hour, they concluded that enough was enough – for the time being – and swaggered from the scene at walking pace disdaining to run from the continuing hail of bullets. Wilson recalls one old Emir, probably Musa Wad Helu himself, riding into the square, planting his banner in the sand and reading aloud a text from the Koran as briefly he awaited death. He was not disappointed.

Suddenly it was over and Captain Lionel Trafford of the Sussex was struck by the silence which had descended on the ghastly scene. Even these hard-bitten men were temporarily awed by the carnage all around them and subdued by the loss of so many friends in such an incredibly short space of time, 86 killed and many wounded, some of whom died later. Even more sobering must have been the narrowness of their escape from complete annihilation. A whiff of panic and all would have been lost. Had the square broken up they would have been cut down where they stood or remorselessly hunted to death through the waterless scrub. However, despite Wolseley's comment that the Heavies were "unsteady", a Victorian military euphemism for panicky, there is no evidence that this was really the case. There was some wild firing and Wilson nearly had his head shot off by the rear rank of the Guards when they turned about, but there was nothing approaching a breakdown of discipline and the general standard of marksman-ship, particularly on the part of the Mounted Infantry, must have been high to inflict such fearful casualties in such a short time. Once again, as at Tamai, the square, so dependent on rigidity to remain intact, had not been broken but had created its own gap through which a swift and fearless enemy had poured. In this case it was the Heavies and the sailors who had not been properly trained for the role they were expected to play and did not understand the theory or practice of fighting in a square.

After the battle the Desert Column occupied the wells, about four miles from the battlefied and, leaving a garrison of Sussex there, the following day, 18 January, marched on towards Metemma and the river.

This march was undertaken at night and led to great confusion, loss of camels and equipment. The native guides were unreliable even in daylight and Stewart was dependent on a local robber by the name of Ali Loda to get the column through the thick scrub and tall grass. To make matters worse, the starving camels tried to forage as they went along often getting themselves and their drivers hopelessly lost in the dark.

However, Ali Loda's guidance was reasonably accurate and by the morning of the 19th the river and fortified town of Metemma were in sight. Wilson estimated that about one hundred camels and their loads had been lost en route from Abu

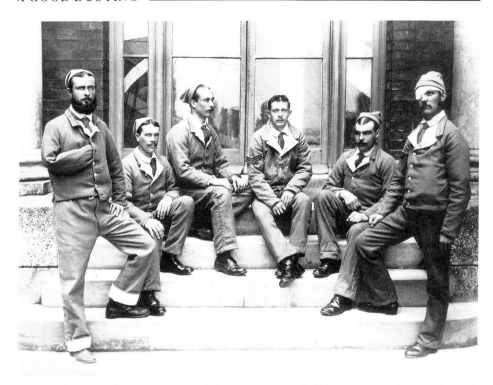

Wounded during the Gordon Relief Campaign. (l to r), Private Clarke (Scots Guards), Private Austin (5th Lancers), Private Steele (4th Dragoon Guards), Sergeant Fook (20th Hussars), Private Wagg (1st Royal Dragoons), Corporal Bower (1st Coldstream Guards), Netley, 16th May, 1885.

Klea. At about 7 a.m. they halted for breakfast, by 8 were coming under sniper fire and at some time between 10 and noon Stewart was severely wounded in the groin. The wound was mortal and although he did not die for several weeks, he was obliged to hand over command to Wilson immediately. However, he was fully conscious and able to confer with Wilson and Boscawen. They decided to prepare a zariba for the wounded and stores, continue the march to the river with a force sufficient to secure a position on the riverbank and then return to the zariba for the wounded etc. The construction of this zariba was carried out under heavy fire and fighting patrols of Guards and Mounted Infantry were sent out to keep the dervishes occupied. All the time men were falling dead and wounded. It must have been one of the worst of many bad days for the Desert Column.

Among the fatal casualties were two war correspondents, John Cameron of the *Standard*, who had had a premonition of his own death, and a free-lance journalist, St Leger Herbert. Good boots were in great demand as the rough going quickly

Death and burial of the War Correspondent, John Cameron.

wore them out and young Marling was shocked when a third correspondent, Bennet Burleigh of the *Telegraph*, suggested removing Herbert's relatively new pair for his own use. Eventually Herbert was buried in a shallow grave near the zariba with his boots still on but when Marling returned next day he noticed a pair of stockinged feet sticking out of the sand and new field-boots, albeit slit up the back, adorning the fat calves of the grave-robbing reporter.

Finally at about 3 p.m. the advance party to the river was ready to move, leaving the 19th Hussars, whose horses were completely exhausted, the remains of the Naval Brigade, who had suffered heavily at Abu Klea, the artillery, most of the sappers and half the Heavies to guard the wounded and stores in the fortified zariba.

Wilson handed over what he describes as executive command to Boscawen but progress was extremely slow as the dervishes continued their highly effective tactic of long-range harassing rifle fire. It was fortunate for the British that, just as the light was fading, their tormentors lost patience and could not restrain themselves from making one of their headlong and suicidal attacks on the square. This time, in the action which became known as the battle of Abu Kru or Gubat (a name unknown to the local Sudanese), not a single dervish reached within 50 yards of the square before being mown down by the volleys from the Guards and MI against whose side of the square the main attack was launched. This action, perhaps rather exaggeratedly elevated to the title of battle, lasted about five minutes and cost the Mahdists another 2–300 killed and as many wounded. That evening the Column reached the Nile, having been under fire almost continuously throughout the day. What Churchill has described as "the stubborn grandeur of the British soldier" had won through.

Since Abu Klea the suffering of the wounded must have been unspeakable. The Victorians, unlike later generations, preferred to draw a discreet veil over the less glorious aspects of war and contemporary accounts do not dwell upon such unpleasantness. Dragged about on camels, themselves often on the point of collapse, strapped into a swaying, bumping container known as a cacolet with little or no protection from the sun or from the chill of the night; attended, and frequently robbed, by medical orderlies who were the dregs of the army; denied most of the drugs and comforts which would be considered absolutely basic today, the chances of survival for the more seriously wounded were slim indeed. That night, Wilson remarks, "The men bore their wounds nobly and were much quieter than I expected." With the river close at hand perhaps the poor devils were slightly less thirsty than usual.

On returning the following day to the fortified zariba to bring up the remainder of the Column, Wilson was infuriated to find that the commissariat, as well as his own kit, had been looted by the Adeni camel-drivers and the British medical orderlies, far from attending to the wounded, had been making free with the

The front of the square at Abu Kru, 19 January, 1885.

"medical comforts" – mostly alcoholic. One man was completely drunk and Wilson, bitterly regretting that flogging had been abolished, had him tied to a tree in the sun outside the zariba but Stuart-Wortley observed that the culprit was in no way disconcerted by his ordeal and yelled imprecations at the dervish skirmishers who prowled around him.

The short march back to the river had to be undertaken in two journeys owing to the lack of transport and the weakness of the camels. By this time nearly all the animals were in an appalling condition. The camels had not been watered since the 14th and even the cavalry horses, tough Syrian ponies,[10] since the 17th. The camels were on very short rations and had been marching or tied down in the zariba with no opportunity to graze for days and nights on end. The horses were husbanded with professional skill by Colonel Barrow[11] and his men, but the camels were treated as though they were miraculous machines which required neither fuel nor servicing. Wilson, perhaps more sensitive than the others, was

[10] Their English troop horses had been left in Cairo.
[11] Lieutenant-Colonel P H S. Barrow, the same who had been rescued at El Teb by Q.M.S. Marshall. Barrow died in Egypt in 1886.

sickened by the open running sores on their backs and sides but most officers and men appear to have regarded their condition with callous indifference and even mirth, seemingly unaware of their dependence on the survival and welfare of these animals.

By the night of the 20th the bulk of the Desert Column had established itself in and around the village of Abu Kru, which they had found deserted by both inhabitants and dervishes, and the morning of the 21st was spent in marching round the walls of Metemma and subjecting it to a rather half-hearted bombardment with the screw guns. Wilson had done, and would continue to do, a conscientious job to the limits of his ability and experience but he must have been extremely tired and worried by this time and the lack of positive leadership was beginning to be felt. Nobody seems to have been very sure whether or not it was necessary to take Metemma. Many must have shared Marling's *cri de coeur*, "I do wish Buller was up". It is unlikely that any of the officers present had much idea how to go about storming a fortified and defended town and, mercifully, the sudden appearance of four of Gordon's steamers diverted everyone's attention from such a potentially costly operation.

Three of these steamers had been on the river for several months, but one, the *Bordein*, had left Khartoum as recenly as 15 December carrying Gordon's journal and some letters in the care of a Greek. The letters were rather vague and contradictory and do not seem to have inspired in Wilson any great sense of urgency. The commander of this flotilla on arrival at Abu Kru was one Nushi Pasha, an Egyptian, but on Gordon's written recommendation that all Egyptians, regardless of rank, should be removed from the steamers, Wilson replaced Nushi with a prominent Shaigi, Khasm el Mus, one of Gordon's most loyal and reliable lieutenants.

# 7 A Penny-steamer trip

Khasm reported to Wilson that a large force of dervishes under one Fiki (Holy Man) Mustafa was on its way from Khartoum and an attack was imminent. At the same time there was reason to believe that another enemy force had collected at Sayal, a village downstream from Metemma. Threatened, therefore, from both north and south, on the following day, the 22nd, Wilson ordered the cavalry to reconnoitre upstream and try to locate Mustafa's force while he himself would take three steamers downstream to check on the threat from Sayal. These patrols were carried out but neither force was located. Meanwhile, the "siege" of Metemma was raised and preparations for a dervish attack made.

Much blame has been attached to Wilson for this alleged waste of time, particularly as the next day, the 23rd, had to be spent refuelling (wood), revictualling and sorting out the personnel on the two steamers earmarked for Khartoum. But what was he to have done? Not to check the validity of these reports of troop movements would have been the height of irresponsibility. The extreme precariousness of the Desert Column's position must be recognized. They had been marching and fighting since the New Year on inadequate rations washed down with a few mouthfuls of filthy water daily. They had lost over one hundred men killed or died of wounds, a very high proportion of them officers, and were encumbered with large numbers of wounded, many of them critical, including the Column commander. The rather grandly named Naval Brigade, originally intended to man the steamers, had lost most of its officers, and its commander, Beresford, was partially disabled with a large boil on his behind. So short of officers was Wilson that he was obliged to promote a "gentleman" volunteer, Ingram, to the rank of lieutenant RN acting unpaid. It appears that Ingram, who had come to the Sudan ostensibly as a war correspondent, had distinguished himself fighting in the ranks at Abu Klea and Abu Kru. Furthermore, and despite the serious shortage of camels still in working condition, in order to bring up stores a stongly guarded convoy was required to return to Jakdul, thus further weakening the column numerically and in fire power. If there was to be an attack the steamers would be a useful form of mobile defence and, if the worst should come to the worst, a line of retreat for at least some of the survivors. In these circumstances it would have been extraordinary if Wilson, who was not only the commander of the Desert Column now but Chief of Intelligence for the entire expedition, had not taken all possible steps to ascertain the whereabouts of the enemy and the degree of potential threat to his own troops.

It has been suggested that he could have left everything in the hands of Boscawen and Beresford and sailed for Khartoum on the 22nd, but this does not stand up to scrutiny. In the first place it would have been absurd to set off in the steamers with a number of men who might be required for the defence of the base at Abu Kru without the reasonable certainty that there would be somewhere to come back to, with or without Gordon. Secondly, it would have been equally futile to start without taking on fuel, ammunition or food. Also the crews and soldiery had to be very carefully sorted out. Gordon was adamant in his letters that the Egyptian troops on the steamers, whom he described as "hens", were not to return to Khartoum and that only British and Soudanese troops should make the return journey. Doubtless this was good advice but to remove numbers of undisciplined men, some with their families, from the steamers and replace them with others was an operation fraught with all the semi-hysterical confusion and hubbub with which any such undertaking in the Middle East or Africa is bound to be accompanied. Indeed to set forth on such an adventure at all in two battered leaky old steamers, with both banks of the river all the way up to Khartoum probably in enemy hands, with one of the most extraordinarily polyglot collection of human beings, some of them of uncertain loyalty, ever to take part in a British military operation, hardly stamps Wilson as a hesitant wet. In fact he must have been a man not only of considerable organizing ability but of great courage and resolution, qualities for which he did not receive the recognition he undoubtedly deserved.

Even had the steamers arrived at Khartoum several days earlier than they did, there is no certainty that the town, Gordon and the garrison could have been saved. The plan was to leave two officers with Gordon to "assist" him and withdraw the steamers and their crews to await the arrival of the main force. Thus nothing would have changed except the presence of the two officers whom Gordon would not have wanted anyway (he had let Colonel Stewart go with the British and French Consuls several months before) and who could make little or no contribution to the defence of the town.

The relief of the siege depended upon the arrival of the Desert Column, small, burdened with sick and wounded, reliant upon an ever decreasing number of weak and exhausted transport animals and still several marches from Khartoum. As for the River Column which had barely started from its assembly point at Handub just above Korti, General Earle was faced with considerable natural and logistical problems, not to mention an unknown degree of Mahdist opposition, especially at Berber. His passage up river might have taken months.

On the other hand, the outcome of the battles of Abu Klea and Abu Kru having become known to the besiegers, it is conceivable that the mere sight of British troops, however few, might have caused the Mahdi to have second thoughts and withdraw back to Kordofan. Certainly those who wished to make a case against Wilson took this view.

The steamers selected for the Khartoum "trip" were the *Bordein* under Khasm el Mus and the *Talahawiya* under Abdel Hamid, also a Shaigi and a relative of Khasm's. Wilson himself and one of the two officers[1] who had been chosen to remain in Khartoum with Gordon, Captain F. R. Gascoigne of the Blues, sailed in the *Bordein* accompanied by a sergeant, a lance-corporal and eight men of C Company 1st Battalion, Royal Sussex, and Wilson's batman, Driver Sutton RE. Also on board were another prominent Shaigi, Mohamed Bey Ahmed, Sheikh Mahmud, "a great religious sheikh from Kassala", and by no means the least important, Wilson's interpreter, Mohamed Ibrahim. In addition to the Sussex detachment there were one hundred and ten Soudanese soldiers.

In the *Talahawiya* was Captain L. J. Trafford, commanding C Company 1st Royal Sussex, with a corporal and nine men.[2] The other officer to remain in Khartoum, Lieutenant the Hon E. J. Montagu-Stuart-Wortley, his batman, a Royal Naval artificer, a signaller and a contingent of eighty Soudanese were also on board.

The crews of both steamers were made up of Egyptians, Sudanese and a few Greeks, The *Talahawiya* towed a nuggar or barge carrying fifty or so additional Soudanese as well as a supply of durra (sorghum). There were also, it seems, a number of women and children, wives and families of the native soldiers and crewmen, still on board serving as catering staff. Inevitably, too, there were the ubiquitous bashi-bazooks, the usual cocktail of half-caste Turks, Albanians and other denizens of the Ottoman Empire for whom nobody ever had a good word but without whom no expedition in the Sudan was ever complete. In this case there were two bands of these scalliwags, one commanded by a Moroccan, the other by a Kurd.

Captain Trafford had selected the Sussex men, all from C Company, for their

---

[1] Originally there were to have been three but the third, Major Dickson of the Royal Dragoons, had been wounded earlier.

[2] See Appendix D.

steadiness and marksmanship. It seems that he chose well, as no less than four received the Distinguished Conduct Medal[3] for their roles in the perilous adventure to come. Wolseley had stipulated that the British troops on arrival at Khartoum were to wear their red coats, for it was in this highly unsuitable garb that the Empire had been won and held and he believed the psychological effect on the Mahdists might be decisive. Unfortunately the red coats of the Sussex had been left somewhere along the way and they had to borrow some red jerseys from the Guards, many of which would have completely enveloped the borrowers had they ever worn them, a point about which there is some diversity in the various eye-witness accounts.

The steamers finally got away at 8 a.m. on 24 January. At this point in his reminiscences Stuart-Wortley blames Beresford for the delay in departure, remarking that it was his influence which caused Wilson to spend the two previous days on reconnaissance, revictualling etc. According to Stuart-Wortley, Beresford hoped that if enough time was wasted his boil would have improved sufficiently to enable him to accompany and, indeed, take charge of the expedition. Stuart-Wortley goes on to say that when subsequently Wilson was blamed and castigated for his failure to reach Khartoum in time, Beresford should have spoken up for him and at least made some attempt to share the blame. Whatever the truth of these assertions and whatever influence Beresford may have had upon Wilson, we have seen that the days in question were spent in activities which were both prudent and unavoidable in the circumstances and the difference which an earlier departure might have made is highly questionable anyway.

No medical officers or even orderlies were taken but a herd of milking goats was, adding to the indescribable stench which rose from the holds of the steamers where the wives and slave girls of the native soldiers cooked durra-cakes and suckled their screaming babies. From these foetid depths emerged large numbers of rats and other vermin which kept Wilson awake at night by scuttling over his balding pate.

Fiki Mustafa's force, although undetected by the earlier cavalry reconnaissance, was soon sighted but showed no fight. The only fuel available for the steamers' boilers were the sakiehs (water-wheels) along the banks and parties were landed from time to time to break these up and bring them on board. The British officers and Sussex men had great difficulty in concentrating the minds of their Soudanese allies on this arduous and insalubrious task and only frequent recourse to the kurbash could tear them away from looting and feasting on any edible beast which might be so unfortunate as to cross their path.

Reaching the sixth cataract which included the exceptionally hazardous and easily defended Shabluka Gorge on the 25th, the *Bordein* struck a rock from which

[3] See Appendix D.

it was dislodged on the following day with great exertions only to run onto a sandbank. Surprisingly, there was no opposition mounted from the cliffs of the gorge and, the *Bordein* having been eventually dislodged from the sandbank, the little flotilla steamed through into open water. At about this time the first news of the fall of Khartoum was shouted from the bank but not believed by its would-be rescuers. Again parties were landed for wood and, after much lashing from which even the native officers were not spared, induced to return on board without their loot.

On the morning of the 28th, Khartoum was sighted and the steamers soon came under heavy fire from the village of Halfiyeh and a little later from Tuti Island. At first they thought the town was still holding out as the fire from Tuti appeared to be aimed at Khartoum opposite. The steamers' nine pounder brass cannons went into action, their sweating half-naked crews working like demons and the Sussex men making "good practice" with their Martini-Henrys. Soon the little ships were being bombarded with every form of weapon from every direction, from Khartoum, from Tuti, from Omdurman Fort, but fortunately the standard of Mahdist marksmanship and gunnery was low and there were few casualties and little damage. Slowly it began to dawn on Wilson and his companions that no shot was being fired to assist them and, with sinking hearts and straining eyes, they searched through their binoculars for the Egyptian flag which they knew should be fluttering over the Governor-General's Palace. It was not. The siege was over. Khartoum had fallen.

But what of Gordon? Wilson had an agonizing but clear decision to take. To try to land his tiny force in the teeth of these colossal odds in the vague hope that Gordon might still be alive and holding out somewhere would be suicidal. Their chances of getting back to Abu Kru were slim enough and the longer they waited the more dervish reinforcements would be marching north from Khartoum to ambush the river banks and attack the Abu Kru depot. He must go about and run downstream as fast as his funny little ships could carry him and his demoralized force.

Now another danger faced Wilson. Khasm el Mus was stunned by the realization that Khartoum had fallen and that his family and all his wordly goods were in the hands of the Mahdi. When he recovered would he remain loyal or decide to throw in his lot with the winner? And if he turned his coat who would turn with him? Could the two dozen or so Englishmen survive the defection of the black troops, bashi-bazooks and, most serious of all, the steamers' crews?

As soon as the steamers turned about a pall of despair descended upon the Soudanese and muwaledeen.[4] They had lost everything, wives, families, slaves and possessions. Knowing the Egyptians as they did, even if they survived, it

---

[4] Egyptians born in the Sudan.

would be pointless to look in that direction for compensation. On the other hand, defection to the Mahdi might mean immediate slaughter or a lingering death in a foul dungeon.

Luckily for Wilson, as for many others in his sort of predicament, some people rose unexpectedly to the occasion. One such was Wilson's Egyptian interpreter,[5] Mohamed Ibrahim, who kept his head and his nerve, bolstering the morale of his companions and acting as an invaluable source of information to Wilson as to the intentions of Khasm and the others over the next few days.

By four o'clock they were out of range of the Mahdist guns and Gascoigne and Stuart-Wortley, in the absence of any professional medical assistance, turned their hands to patching up the wounded. Miraculously the injuries were few and minor and none of the British had been hit. The only really serious moments had been when a burning shell-fuse had landed on the *Talahawiya* but this had been thrown overboard by Drummer Gilbert. Similarly, a blazing fragment of wood had fallen among the ammunition boxes on the *Bordein* and was disposed of by a Soudanese soldier whom Wilson would have liked to recommend for the Victoria Cross but native troops in the Egyptian service were not eligible for British decorations.

That evening, to nip trouble in the bud, Wilson, through the imperturbable Mohamed Ibrahim, harangued the assembled captains and helmsmen (apparently there were several of each on each steamer) and offered them bonuses of £100 and £50 respectively if they reached Abu Kru safely. Next day, however, the *Talahawiya* struck a rock and sank, leaving just enough time for its personnel and most of its stores to be transferred to the *Bordein*. The various captains and helmsmen, who, not surprisingly, had been giving contradictory orders to each other, were suspected of sabotage but nothing seems to have been proved except the futility (or perhaps inadequacy) of Wilson's proffered bonus.

Later the same day, the 29th, one Fiki Abdel Rahman hailed the *Bordein* from the bank and sought audience with Wilson and Khasm. He was allowed on board, bringing with him one of the Mahdi's more or less standard letters with which he endeavoured to persuade his enemies to surrender and embrace the true faith with promises of safe-conduct and leniency. Wilson, who on this occasion seems to have shown some lack of common sense, at first declined to reply but Khasm, realising the extreme danger through which they must pass in "shooting" the sixth cataract, both from the river and the dervishes, decided upon a ruse. Despite Wilson's objections, Khasm told Abdel Rahman that he would surrender to Fiki Mustafa, *below* the cataract, if the Mahdi would send him a personal safe-conduct. Wilson suspected that Khasm would do exactly as he said he would. Also his rigid code of honour was offended by the idea of being party to a deception, a luxury

---

[5] Of the British only Stuart-Wortley spoke any Arabic.

of conscience which someone in his position could ill afford. However, he must have come eventually to this conclusion himself, or perhaps he was persuaded by his less fastidious juniors and Mohamed Ibrahaim, as he agreed to Khasm's reply with the rather meaningless stipulation (probably never translated to Abdel Rahman) that the British should not be associated with it. Also by this time Wilson's confidence in Khasm was returning. It was becoming clear that Khasm did not fancy his chances of survival if he surrendered to the Mahdi and, furthermore, morale boosting rumours, doubtless manufactured by the indespensible Mohamed Ibrahaim, were circulating to the effect that the British had taken Metemma and that huge reinforcements from Korti were pouring across the Bayuda Desert.

In any case, Khasm's trick seems to have worked as, on the next day, 30 January, the *Bordein* negotiated the sixth cataract and Shabluka Gorge unopposed, despite being temporarily stranded on a sandbank. However, on the 31st their luck ran out when, on emerging from the rapids and approaching Wad Habeshi where Fiki Mustafa's gun battery was known to be, the *Bordein* was severely holed by a rock and started to sink. The crew managed to lay her on a sandbank adjacent to the island of Mernat. Fortunately they did not come under fire and were able to evacuate the ship without much loss of equipment or stores except for some of the officers' kit which was looted by the native troops. Wilson recounts a curious incident which occurred when the ship struck. One of the soldiers, a Shilluk,[6] seized a small child and threw it overboard. It is not clear why he did this or if the child was drowned but Wilson theorized that the Shilluk may have been attempting to propitiate some river god. The Sussex men were unimpressed by any possible religious significance "and the savage was at once made prisoner and tightly bound".

Steamerless, Wilson was faced with the bleak alternatives of staying on Mernat Island until help could reach him from Abu Kru or attempting to march the remaining forty odd miles through hostile country. Extraordinarily, at first he seems to have opted for the latter course which almost certainly would have led to the desertion en route of most of his native troops and the annihilation of the British contingent. On this occasion, however, the indiscipline (or perhaps good sense) of the Soudanese and bashi-bazooks came to his rescue when they simply refused to move and, "in spite of a little kurbashing", sat down to cook and eat their suppers.

Bowing to the inevitable, Wilson now prepared defensive positions on Mernat Island as best he could and despatched Stuart-Wortley in a rowing boat with four British soldiers[7] and eight natives to Abu Kru for help. This forty-mile journey

---

[6] A large Nilotic tribe of the southern Sudan.

[7] In his unpublished reminiscences written about forty years later, Stuart-Wortley mentions the four British soldiers as being two Riflemen and two Essex. With the passage of time he [continued

was a little epic of its kind. Leaving at quarter to seven in the evening the boat slid silently past the battery at Wad Habeshi just as the moon rose and the gunners on the bank could be heard discussing whether or not it was a boat they could see. Stuart-Wortley and his men held their breath and, as a little bit of extra insurance, a pistol to the helmsman's head to discourage any thoughts of betrayal. Some shots were fired at the boat but missed and every now and again throughout the night they would pass a dervish position, their hearts in their mouths. They were not challenged again and the greatest hazard of all, that of running onto a rock or sandbank in the dark, was avoided.

On arrival at Abu Kru in the small hours of the morning Stuart-Wortley found Beresford more or less in charge, his boil having been lanced. No time was wasted in preparing another of the steamers, the *Safiya*, for action and, manned by Royal Naval personnel as well as some native sailors with a fighting contingent of about twenty Mounted Infantrymen under Lieutenant Bower KRRC, she sailed at 2 p.m. with Beresford himself in command. The indefatigable Stuart-Wortley, determined to miss nothing, sailed with her.

Meanwhile on Mernat, Wilson's problems remained serious. The not unexpected desertion of Khasm's cousin, Abdel Hamid, raised the tension and Wilson had Khasm himself and the other potential deserters closely watched by Mohamed Ibrahim and the Sussex men. He tried to arrange his defensive positions in such a way that everyone could keep an eye on everyone else. He felt he could rely on the bashi-bazook whose brutal tax-gathering activities in pre-Mahdist Sudan had not endeared them to the local population, particularly the riverain tribes, and whose best chances of survival lay with the British. Not infrequently Wilson and Khasm received visits from Shaigi notables and once, remarkably, from the Mahdist commander Fiki Mustafa. Wilson's feelings about these visits were mixed. On the one hand he wanted to obtain as much intelligence as possible from any source but on the other he feared the visitors would attempt to suborn Khasm. With hindsight it seems unlikely that having recovered from the initial blow to his morale Khasm ever had any intention of deserting. The Shaigieh as a tribe, and Khasm's family in particular, had been allied since the days of Mohamed Ali's conquest of the Sudan to the Turko-Egyptians, an alliance which had alienated them from some of the other major tribes. By the standards of the time and place Khasm was a well-informed man who probably understood the British position in Egypt and the world and realized that the British connection

must have confused Essex with Sussex! As for the Riflemen one may have been his batman but there is no explanation for the other.

(Right)   Wilson watching the arrival of the *Safiya* at Mernat Island.

was a profitable one to hold on to. His resolve was also strengthened by a visit from his sister who had managed to travel from Halfiyeh to advise her brother not to surrender. Wilson rewarded her with £110 so that she might attempt to ransom other members of the family held in Khartoum.

It took the *Safiya* four times as long to cover the distance against the current as Stuart-Wortley's rowing boat had taken going with it and it was not until late on 3 February that her approach was spotted by some of Wilson's look-outs. Remarkably, the stranded force had escaped attack partly due to their being on an island and partly thanks to the unwarlike disposition of Fiki Mustafa. The *Safiya*, however, was not so lucky and came under heavy fire, was hit in the boiler and had to defend herself vigorously for many hours while Chief Engineer Henry Benbow RN carried out emergency repairs aided by a heavily greased and equally heavily paid youth who actually clambered into the boiler itself. Eventually, after great difficulties and under continuous fire, in the course of which Captain Gascoigne and his runner, Private Paine, particularly distinguished themselves, Wilson managed to embark his entire force on the *Safiya* and steam for Abu Kru, arriving there on the evening of 4 February.

This daring adventure, had it been successful, would have made Wilson and his men national heroes. That the two steamers had survived the one-hundred-mile journey through largely enemy-held territory to Khartoum is remarkable enough. That almost the entire force had returned eleven days after its departure, albeit without its steamers, is nothing short of astounding. Few lives had been lost and Wilson had managed to hold together a force which by all reasonable expectations should have disintegrated. That he was coolly and bravely supported by the three young British officers and the unflappable Sussex men is axiomatic but great credit must also go to Khasm el Mus and the native troops and sailors who remained loyal to Gordon, even after his death, despite every temptation to do otherwise.

Wilson set off for Korti immediately to report to Wolseley. His reception was chilly. He was to be the scapegoat. In his report to the War Office Wolseley was damning.[8] Never again was Wilson to be employed on active service.

---

[8] The Duke of Cambridge supported Wilson – if only as a reaction to Wolseley's condemnation.

# 8 The Siege

It is difficult to date the start of the siege of Khartoum precisely but the town was in ever-increasing danger after the defeat of Hicks in November, 1883. As we have seen, Gordon and Stewart arrived in February, 1884, an event which gave morale a considerable, if temporary, boost. Gordon assumed both civil and military command from his acting predecessor Colonel De Coetlogon,[1] who, despite Hicks's low opinion of him, had done much in the previous few months to strengthen Khartoum's defences.

Perhaps the first significant move by the Mahdists in the area was the occupation of Halfiyeh a few miles north of Khartoum on the east bank of the main Nile in March, 1884. However, more important was the fall of Berber to the Emir Mohamed el Kheir in May of that year which effectively severed Gordon's lifeline to Egypt and virtually eliminated the Suakin – Berber route as an option for any rescue expedition. A final blow quite shortly before the fall of Khartoum itself was the surrender of Omdurman Fort commanded by Faragallah Pasha, a Soudanese officer, who afterwards took service under the Mahdi and became known as Faragallah el Omdurmani.

During the summer of 1884 Khartoum was invested on all sides by the Mahdists but well-planned sorties by the garrison were successful in easing the pressure from time to time and enabling supplies to be brought into the town. Although there was a steady trickle of refugees and deserters leaving the town throughout the period of the siege, the possibility of evacuating the garrison and its dependents as a whole rapidly diminished. Gordon himself had no intention of

[1] De Coetlogon returned to Cairo a few days after Gordon's arrival in Khartoum and, in due course, became commandant of the Alexandria police. He was the only European of all those attached to Hicks's army, of which he was the HQ staff officer in Khartoum, to survive into the twentieth century. He died in 1908.

Contemporary cartoon depicting (l to r) Granville and Gladstone leaving Gordon to his fate in Khartoum.

leaving except as part of a total evacuation and the not entirely unwelcome prospect of martyrdom was never far from his mind. He encouraged, but did not order, Stewart, Power and the French Consul Herbin with an escort of nineteen Greeks to leave by the steamer *Abbas* on 7 September, 1884. They ran aground near Abu Hamed some days later, were tricked into accepting the hospitality of one Suleiman Numan Wad Qamar and massacred.[2]

As the largest European community in Khartoum, and, indeed, in the Sudan as a whole, was and is today Greek, this may be an opportune point at which to glance at a curious and rather irritating theme which runs through many of the British accounts of life and events in the Sudan during this period.

Few of these observers have a good word for the Greeks, mostly traders, whom they seemed to have regarded with a sneering contempt. As these Greeks were often hardy, brave and resourceful, qualities much admired by the Victorian British, it is difficult to account for this attitude. How had the heroic image of the Greek palikari (guerrillas), so beloved of Byron and the English romantics of the

[2] The fate of all the Greeks is uncertain. Some may have escaped.

1820's, become so tarnished by the 1880's? Perhaps because they had hammered their swords into cash registers and it was fashionable in British upper-class circles to despise trade although, of course, inter-marriage with the *nouveaux riches* was all right provided they were *riche* enough.

As well as those already there, many Greeks followed the Anglo-Egyptian armies into the Sudan from Egypt performing the role for which the NAAFI was constituted half a century or so later. These intrepid men with their camel-loads of goodies followed the drum through the harshest and most dangerous conditions, setting up shop wherever the army had a moment to stop and put a hand into its pocket for a bottle of beer, some tooth powder or a tin of sardines. Marling records a caravan of Greeks trekking ahead of the Desert Column to reach Khartoum before the troops. Far from finding this enterprise admirable he describes them as "extraordinarily pushing fellows" who would "take any risk to make money" and drily observes, almost with satisfaction, that "the Mahdi bagged the lot and cut a right hand and a left foot off each of them."

Some took part in active military operations. Hicks's Surgeon-General, George Douloglu, was a Greek and perished in Kordofan. At least one Greek officer, Lieutenant Mosconos, served with Baker's Gendarmes and was killed at El Teb. According to H. C. Jackson in his book *Osman Digna* four Greeks stood, fought and died with Consul Moncrieff near Tokar, but their names are not recorded. Gordon was not generally well disposed towards the Greeks but is exceptional in his praise for "Leonidas",[3] the Greek Consul in Khartoum, "who," he wrote in his journal, "has behaved worthy of his ancestor of Thermopolae".

In the end it did not matter what others may have thought of them. The Sudan Greeks survived the Mahdi, his successor, the Condominium and a number of post-independence Sudanese governments and are thriving to this day.

During the siege the Mahdi tried on at least two occasions to use captured European go-betweens to open negotiations with Gordon. Both these men, Guiseppi Cuzzi, an Italian and former British consular agent at Berber, and George Kalamatinos, a Greek merchant, had embraced Islam after capture, thus rendering themselves quite unacceptable to Gordon, a point which the Mahdi probably did not appreciate. As Gordon refused to meet either of them we do not know what form any discussions might have taken but it is unlikely that their briefs would have extended beyond offers to spare Gordon's life should he renounce Christianity. On the other hand, it is just conceivable that some proposal acceptable to Gordon might have been made which could have led to the extraction of the Khartoum garrison under flag of truce. However, this is pure speculation and neither the previous nor subsequent behaviour of either the Mahdi or Gordon should lead the reader to imagine that any such arrangement

---

[3] His real name was Nicolas Leontides and he was killed during the sack of Khartoum by the Mahdists.

would have had much chance of success in practice. Presumably the Mahdi decided upon, or at least sanctioned, these initiatives in the mistaken belief that Gordon might be influenced by fellow Europeans rather than by native emissaries. Also we may assume that both Cuzzi and Kalamatinos spoke English, a language entirely unknown to the Sudanese at that time, and that the Mahdi was aware of Gordon's lack of Arabic and his interpreters' unreliability.

As well as these attempts at verbal negotiation there were intermittent and inconclusive exchanges of correspondence between the Mahdi, his principal followers and Gordon. Although these two religious fanatics had a certain amount in common there is little sign that either understood the psychology of the other. Gordon's letters contain clumsy bombast and some attempts at heavy and ironic humour, both of which would have been quite lost on the Mahdi. In contrast the Mahdist letters, although consisting largely of the usual demands for surrender and conversion, are better written and make better sense. All in all there is little doubt that the Mahdi won the battle of words as well as deeds.

The siege, although it took place towards the end of the nineteenth century, was very much a mediaeval affair – long-drawn-out and punctuated with sorties by the defenders; flamboyant exchanges of letters and even gifts[4] between flamboyant opponents; whispers of treason among the besieged followed by the execution of suspected traitors; starvation and disease; the eating of cats and dogs and eventually the sacking and destruction of the city; the butchery of many of its innocent citizens and the distribution of the women to the victors as slaves and concubines.

Towards the end there is evidence[5] that Gordon ceased to take much interest in the proceedings and sat in his room chain-smoking while his secretary represented him at meetings with the leading citizens and officers. His hair turned completely white – perhaps his always precarious reason had finally snapped – but, whatever he did or did not do and whatever his mental condition, the outcome was a foregone conclusion. One feels a deal more sympathy for the unfortunate members of Gordon's staff than one does for Gordon himself. They had no wish to die.

Perhaps unbeknown to them, there was a brief moment of hope for Khartoum. The outcome of the Battle of Abu Klea on 17 January, although announced by the Mahdi to the mass of his followers as a great victory, caused serious consternation in his inner councils and there was talk of lifting the siege and withdrawing to Kordofan. However, as the days passed without signs of British movement upstream from Metemma, the decision was taken to attack without further delay.

In the small hours of the morning of 26 January the main assault went in at the south-western corner of the defences where the mud ramparts had been eroded

[4] The Mahdi sent Gordon a complete dervish outfit.
[5] The Journal of Bordeini Bey, a leading Khartoum merchant, quoted in Wingate's *Mahdism and the Egyptian Sudan*.

by the flood-waters of the White Nile. In overall command was Wad Nejumi. There was some resistance but most of the troops were too debilitated by hunger and despair to put up much of a fight. Also by this time many of the officers had come to the conclusion that whatever future they had lay with the Mahdi and were not inclined to jeopardize their slim chances of survival by leading a hopeless defence. Months earlier two senior officers had been shot on Gordon's orders, probably quite unjustly, for suspected treachery and, in June, 1887, a battalion commander, Hassan Bey el Bahnassawi, who had escaped to Egypt after the siege, was court-martialled for "having treacherously delivered up his post to the enemy" – that post allegedly being the sector of the defences where Nejumi's main attack went in. The Egyptian Government was very eager to obtain a conviction as it was something of a test case. Any officer or soldier against whom such a charge could be proven would forfeit his back-pay and pension rights, a highly desirable outcome for an impecunious Egyptian Treasury. Doctored plans of Khartoum's defences, showing Bahnassawi's position two miles from where it was in reality, were used by the prosecution in evidence against him, but, luckily for him, the President of the Court, Major Quirk,[6] a British officer in the Egyptian Army, summed up in his favour, and he was acquitted. Bahnassawi's superior officer, Farag Pasha, was also suspected of treachery but as he was killed soon after surrendering to the Mahdists the opportunity to bring him to trial never arose.

There are a number of different versions of the heroic legend of Gordon's death. One, and the most generally accepted, has him standing at the top of the Palace steps offering no resistance to his killers and another that he was cut down near the Palace gates. But perhaps the most persuasive is that recounted by his head cavass (attendant), Khalid Agha Orphali. According to Orphali, an ex-soldier or bashi-bazook of Syrian origin, Gordon and he put up a spirited resistance in the Palace, killing and wounding a number of Mahdists before Gordon himself was killed and Orphali incapacitated by wounds from which he later recovered, Orphali, a rascal who had given Gordon a good deal of trouble, was an unreliable witness but his account rings true. It is hard to imagine Gordon, a fighter to his fingertips, allowing himself to be slaughtered without taking a few of his assailants with him.

Whatever the circumstances of his death, it has been suggested that the Mahdi wished him spared and was angry at his killing. But the Mahdi was shrewd and the likelihood is that he preferred him dead. Why should the English come for a dead man?

When the dreadful severed head was brought to Slatin for identification, the little Austrian murmured an epitaph for this strange man: "A brave soldier who fell at his post; happy is he to have fallen; his sufferings are over".

---

[6] Major Quirk's daughter, Eugenie, subsequently married the late Field-Marshal Earl Wavell.

# 9 Failure and Withdrawal

"Our only general, he had ten thousand men.
He led up the Nile, and he led them down again."
*The Egyptian Red Book*, 1885

With the fall of Khartoum and the death of Gordon the British Cabinet was faced with a new quandary. Its objective, to rescue Gordon, incidentally one which had never been acceptable to its intended beneficiary unless coupled with the evacuation of the garrison, was no longer attainable. But precipitate withdrawl would be interpreted in Egypt, the Sudan, the world at large and, above all, at home as defeat. Gladstone's administration was shaky (it fell in June, 1885) and the news of Gordon's death was received in Britain with horror and dismay. It was very important therefore to the government that the Relief Expedition itself should not be seen to have suffered a reverse. The British taxpayer, through his elected representatives, denied the army proper pay, food and equipment but nevertheless expected it to win on all occasions and in all circumstances. Usually it did.

So the policy was to be business as usual in the Nile valley, and, in order to give further evidence of its resolve to set the Sudan to rights, the Liberal Government ordered General Graham, with a powerful British, Indian and, for the first time in imperial history, Australian force, to return to the eastern Sudan and inflict further exemplary punishment upon Osman Digna and his Fuzzy-Wuzzys. With the approach of summer, campaigning on the Nile could continue only for another few weeks and then the troops would have to be withdrawn into summer quarters. The Mahdi could wait until autumn to be crushed. This was the party line, but, as one of Gladstone's successors was to say nearly a century later, even a week is a long time in politics and between March and September something would turn up to enable the government to bring the whole wretched business to a face-saving conclusion.

This policy, suitably wrapped up in the bold phrases which politicians use when

Major-General Sir Redvers
Buller, V.C., a celebrated
member of the "Wolseley
Ring".

they intend to scuttle, caused Wolseley some surprise and mixed feelings. He had
been convinced that with Gordon dead the whole thing would be called off
without further delay. Now he saw that he might still have the chance to avenge
Gordon and cover his army with glory during the following winter. On the other
hand he dreaded the effect on his troops of over-summering[1] in the shattering
heat of the northern Sudan.

This decision led to new orders and counterorders being issued to Earle, whose
River Column had started upstream from its collection point at Handub on 24
January, and to Buller who had marched from Korti with the Royal Irish, followed
by the West Kents, to take over command of, and to reinforce, the Desert Column
at Abu Kru on 31 January. However, when the dismal news from Khartoum

[1] There are said to be three seasons in the northern Sudan – hot, very hot and unbearably hot. The
last of these starts in April.

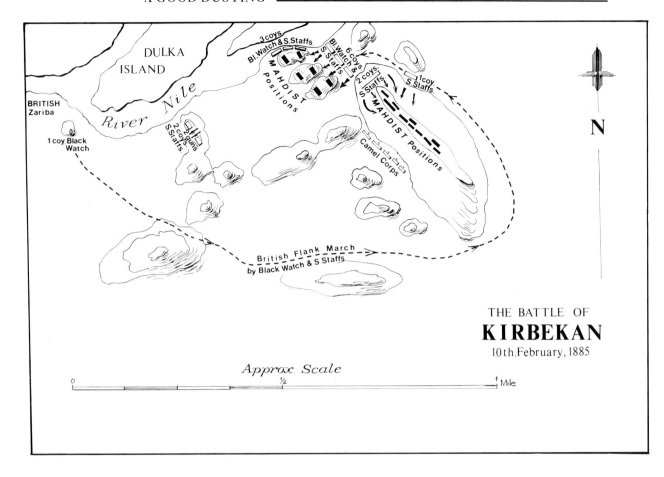

DULKA
ISLAND

3 coys.
Bl.Watch & S.Staffs.
MAHDIST Positions
Bl. Watch
& S.Staffs
6 coys
& 2 guns

BRITISH
Zariba
River Nile
2 coys
S.Staffs
1 coy. Black
Watch

2 coys.
S.Staffs.
1 coy.
S.Staffs.

2 guns
2 coys.
S.Staffs.

MAHDIST Positions

Camel Corps

N

British Flank March
by Black Watch & S Staffs

THE BATTLE OF
**KIRBEKAN**
10th.February, 1885

*Approx. Scale*

0                    ½                    1 Mile

reached Wolseley on 4 February he ordered Earle and Buller to halt where they were where they were (Buller was at Jakdul), pending further instructions from London. On the 6th he received the government's surprise decision to carry on and so ordered his column commanders to resume their advance in the hope of securing Abu Hamed, Berber and Metemma before the summer. In one of his messages Gordon had been insistent that Berber should be taken and not by-passed as an undefeated Mahdist force there would be dangerous to the Relief Expedition both in advance and withdrawal. Also, possession of Berber would be crucial to any force crossing the desert from Suakin to the river.[2]

Earle encountered a dervish force consisting mainly of Manassir and Robatat tribesmen at Kirbekan on 9 February, occupying positions of some strength in

---

[2] It seems that 10,000 umbrellas were ordered to protect any such force from the sun on the line of march. A delightfully comic picture is conjured up.

Major-General W. Earle, commanding the River Column. Killed at Kirbekan 10th February, 1885.

(*Left*) Lt.Colonel R. C. Coveny, Black Watch. Killed at Kirbekan 10 February, 1885.
(*Right*) Lt.Colonel P. Eyre, South Staffordshire Regiment. Killed at Kirbekan 10 February, 1885.

rocky outcrops on the right bank of the river. An outflanking movement was reconnoitred by the versatile Colonel Butler of boat-building fame, now commanding the cavalry (one squadron 19th Hussars) and a contingent of Egyptian Camel Corps. This manoeuvre was found to be feasible and on the 10th an attack from the rear by the Black Watch and South Staffords, advancing for the first time in the campaign in open order as opposed to square or column formation, swiftly dislodged the defenders. Some dervishes trying to counter-attack were shot down by steady and accurate rifle fire, the remainder being winkled out of their positions at bayonet point to the accompanying skirl of the pipes. This was the only action fought by the River Column and, although British casualties were light, Earle himself was killed, largely through his own careless-ness, when, peering through the window of a hut he had already been told was occupied by the enemy, he was shot through the head and died within a few minutes. As Colonels Coveney and Eyre[3] of the Black Watch and South Staffords

[3] Eyre had the rare distinction of commanding a battalion of the regiment he had joined as a private soldier.

respectively were also killed, the casualty ratio of senior officers to other ranks, at three to nine, was extraordinarily high. Four officers and forty-four men were wounded, several of whom died later.

Command devolved upon Brigadier-General Henry Brackenbury,[4] an officer, according to Wolseley, of extreme ugliness but high efficiency. Rarely in British military history could so many senior officers, including generals, have lost their lives in a campaign where overall battle casualties were so light on the British side, bringing to positions of active command such officers as Wilson and Brackenbury whose talents lay in staff work and administration. But Brackenbury was to have less opportunity than Wilson to show his mettle as a unilateral decision by Buller to withdraw the Desert Column from Abu Kru caused Wolseley to order the River Column back as well. This order was received by Brackenbury on 24 February when he was within 26 miles of his first objective, Abu Hamed. Bitterly disappointed and frustrated, the River Column arrived back at Handub on 4 March, having vented its spleen on the property of the murderers of Colonel Stewart and his party near Hebbeh, destroying their houses, water-wheels and date palm groves.

Meanwhile Buller had tramped across the Bayuda Desert with his Irishmen in eleven days (152 miles in 73 marching hours) despite being halted at Jakdul for four of them while London and Wolseley made up their minds what to do. Arriving at Abu Kru on 11 February the massive Devonian was a welcome sight to all ranks. Very much a soldiers' general, at this stage of his career he was still a decisive and forceful character. He discovered quickly that the transport and convoy system was on the verge of collapse owing to the parlous condition of the remaining camels. He decided, notwithstanding his orders to take Metemma and advance on Berber to link up with the River Column, on immediate withdrawal. There was no point in the first part of the operation if the second part was beyond the capacity of his force. To withdraw upon prepared positions where stores and water were available, Abu Klea, Jakdul, Howeiyat and finally Korti, was one thing but to march off into the blue towards Berber with exhausted men and dying camels was quite another.

The withdrawal itself was no picnic. Encumbered by wounded and harassed by skirmishers, most of the men were now on foot and not a few fell out on the line of march. A number of these were picked up by the indomitable Roman Catholic padre, Father Robert Brindle, who borrowed a horse and let them ride until they had recovered sufficiently to continue marching. Those of his flock whom he suspected of swinging the lead were threatened with excommunication if they failed to keep going. However, the Royal Irish managed to complete the return journey in only 67 marching hours. There were a number of incidents en route

---

[4] Wolseley thought he had Greek blood, in his eyes a serious blemish.

Contemporary cartoon depicting (l to r) Wolseley, Gladstone and Granville.

which illustrate the tension and weariness from which the Column was suffering by this time. Early in the march the Mounted Infantry fired on the Light Camel Regiment by mistake and, later, Major Gough, the cavalryman commanding the Mounted Infantry, was suspended by Buller for halting his men without orders. Gough had been wounded earlier in the campaign and clearly was suffering from what would nowadays be recognized as battle fatigue but at the time he was described simply as being "quite off his head".

The last of the Desert Column finally reached Korti on 16 March. The democratic Buller dined that evening with some young Mounted Infantry officers and took some cheek from one "Bimbash" Stewart, a wild Gordon Highlander, celebrated for his ability to acquire his brother officers' kit of which he had none of his own and for his daring proposal of marriage to the beautiful daughter of Nubar Pasha, the Prime Minister of Egypt.[5] However, a dig in the ribs was too much for

[5] Stuart-Wortley was present at a Cairo dinner party where the same young lady chided Bimbash for his lack of French to which the unabashed Highlander replied that he would learn if she would become his "maitresse". It seems that both this offer and that of marriage were declined.

Buller who thrust out a huge paw and toppled the overebullient Scot head over heels into the sand. Marling, who was present, reports "lashings of fizz" on this occasion.

For all its short-comings the Desert Column had done its best and more. It had ridden, marched, dug wells, built forts and zaribas, sweated, thirsted, steamed, fought and, in many cases, died for nothing. The Column had lost fourteen officers and one hundred and fifteen men killed in action, twenty-three officers and two hundred and twenty-three men wounded, a number of whom died later (Sir Herbert Stewart had died on the return journey). In addition, perhaps another hundred had died of disease or exhaustion and the health of many must have been permanently impaired leading to premature death. The Heavies had suffered most. They had borne the brunt of the dervish charge at Abu Klea and, largely as a result of their lack of infantry training, had lost sixty-seven officers and men killed in action and another thirty from other causes.

Complete figures for animal losses are not available but out of the five hundred camels with which the Mounted Infantry had started the campaign only ninety-five returned to Korti and they were emaciated wrecks worth roughly £2 each as compared with the original cost of £15.[6] Presumably the survival rate in the other camel regiments was no better. In sharp contrast to their condition was that of the cavalry horses. Proper care and husbandry had kept losses from disease and exhaustion to a minimum. Out of three hundred and fifty horses with which the 19th Hussars had started the campaign only twelve died from disease, twenty were killed in action and thirty-seven had to be destroyed for other reasons, giving a remarkable survival rate of approximately 80%.[7]

Wolseley, who, it must be said, never seemed to have a real grip on the campaign himself, is less than generous to his senior colleagues in his journal – "I hate the sight of Sir C. Wilson" – but no word has he in criticism of his men. To his wife he wrote: "As I look back at the events of the last four months my mind dwells upon one bright spot only, namely the splendid conduct of the private soldier: he is a splendid fellow . . . and now that I grow old I feel as if they (sic) were my own sons". And the younger officers shared this view. Thus Marling – "I take my hat off to Tommy every time . . . I'll back the British soldier against anyone in the world."

It should be remembered that these troops were not the leathery veterans of the old long-service system but the post-Cardwell "seven and five" men (seven years with the Colours and five on the reserve), many of them quite young. Their conduct was an exoneration of a much-criticized system of recruiting which Wolseley had supported ardently, so he had every reason to be proud of his "sons".

[6] Marling's Memoirs.
[7] The Marquess of Anglesey's *History of the British Cavalry, Vol. III.*

Given the reluctance of the British Government to intervene in the Sudan and its delay in doing so, was the failure of the Gordon Relief Expedition inevitable? The answer is probably yes. Even had the camels been better managed and available in larger quantities, even had Wolseley taken personal command of the Desert Column, even had Sir Herbert Stewart or Burnaby survived, there was simply not enough time to reach Khartoum in sufficient numbers to save the city and Gordon from the Mahdi. The greatest chance of success and equally the greatest chance of disaster would have been in the choice of the Suakin-Berber route, but, as we have seen, this was rejected at an early stage largely through fears of a Hicks-style catastrophe. But a more interesting, if purely hypothetical, question is what would have happened if Khartoum had been reached in sufficient numbers to raise the siege. What then? Gordon would not have agreed to leave without the foreign civilians, the Egyptian troops and the dependents of both, to say nothing of the bashi-bazooks and loyal blacks, an unruly swarm several thousand strong (or weak). How would Wolseley have dealt with such a massive problem? Where would he have found the transport and the food for this horde? Would he have "arrested" Gordon and whisked him away by steamer, leaving the rest to their fate? Most unlikely. Would he have attempted to destroy the Mahdists in one great battle outside Khartoum as did Kitchener fifteen years later? Most probably. But much less probable is it that the shrewd Mohamed Ahmed would have allowed his forces to be drawn into such a death trap. By then he would have learnt what Osman Digna was to put into words years later when arguing against just such a confrontation with Kitchener, "By God, the English . . . they cannot be defeated without deceit!"[8] Had the Mahdi played his hand coolly and resolutely – and there is no reason to assume that he would not – the consequences of the Relief Expedition actually relieving Khartoum might have been considerably worse than its failure to do so. Although all such speculation is idle, it is quite conceivable that a Wolseley Relief Expedition would have had to be mounted!

In the light of the American attempt to rescue the Teheran hostages in 1980, even today the problem would be one to stretch the ingenuity of the military planners. Helicopters seem to be as perishable in the desert as camels and in some respects the logistical aspects of such an operation would be as formidable as they were one hundred years ago.

[8] *Karari* by Ismat Hasan Zulfo.

# 10 Postscript in the East

The second British expedition to the eastern Sudan had three main objectives, two military and one political. Militarily it was to ensure the security of the port of Suakin and the eastern flank of Wolseley's force on the Nile by breaking the power and authority of Osman Digna and to construct a railway from Suakin to Berber, a grandiose plan the contract for which had been let to a British company, Messrs Lucas and Aird. Politically, its purpose was to reassure a restive electorate (and Monarch) that the government was not "soft" on the Sudan. Osman Digna's reputation as a leading slave merchant lent support to the expedition from the Left which otherwise might have seen it as just another manifestation of aggressive imperialism.

The force, again commanded by General Graham, consisted of two British Infantry brigades, 1st Guards Brigade (one battalion each Grenadiers, Coldstream and Scots[1]) commanded by Major-General A. J. Lyon-Fremantle, 2nd Brigade (East Surreys, Berkshires, Shropshire Light Infantry and Royal Marine Light Infantry) under Major-General Sir John McNeill VC, one Indian Infantry Brigade (15th Sikhs, 28th Bombay Infantry and 17th Bengal Infantry) commanded by Brigadier-General J. Hudson, elements of four cavalry regiments (5th Lancers, 19th & 20th Hussars, 9th Bengal Cavalry) under Colonel H. P. Ewart, four batteries of field artillery (one of them Australian,) a Horse artillery battery, a Royal Naval Gardner Machine Gun detachment and various support troops including a balloon detachment. Later an Australian infantry battalion arrived as well.

These troops were served by a host of "followers", mostly Indian but including Adenis, Somalis, Sudanese, Egyptians, Cypriots and Maltese. From India came

[1] It should be remembered that the Irish and Welsh Guards are twentieth century creations.

"a Corps of dhooly bearers, five hundred strong, with one hundred Lushai dandies"[2] (stretcher bearers with covered hammocks carried on poles) and from England, or more probably from Ireland, came a number of bowler-hatted railway navvies employed by Lucas & Aird at the enormous wage for the time of twelve shillings per day. Staff planners slipped up by billeting these gentlemen next to a padre whose vocabulary was widened by the experience.

Private Frank Ferguson, a young trooper in the 20th Hussars, complained in a letter to his parents that, whereas he and his mates did not receive even their ration of lime juice, "it was all right for the officers with champagne, ice, soda-water, potted tomatoes and peaches and potted strewed steaks, Liebeg's extract and a thousand different kinds of stuff . . . and yet they begrudge us a drink of water with salty corned beef".

By the middle of March, 1885, most of the force had assembled at Suakin. Some of the British line infantry and other troops had come from Egypt but the Guards Brigade arrived quite unacclimatized straight from England. Operations started on 19 March with an advance upon the hill and wells at Hashin, about eight miles west of Suakin, whence several irritating little night raids had been made on the British encampment. In the course of one of these alarms a Scots Guards sentry, Private McGuinness, bayonetted and killed a fellow guardsman, Private McGreary, mistaking him for a Fuzzy-Wuzzy, not, one would think, an easy error to make, even in the dark. Might one have been a supporter of Celtic and the other of Rangers?

On the next day the cavalry attempted some ill-advised charges against groups of the enemy in which they suffered a number of quite unnecessary casualties and which earned Colonel Ewart a rebuke and adverse report from General Graham. With the possible exception of Colonel Barrow, who commanded the 19th Hussars contingent with the Desert Column, British cavalry officers either could not or would not learn that the only roles their arm could usefully play in the Sudan were those of reconnaisance and dismounted action with their carbines, occasionally livened with a cautious pursuit of an already broken enemy. Agile dervishes concealed behind bushes or rocks had the advantage of surprise over charging cavalrymen. Horses were hamstrung or otherwise brought down, their falling riders then being unable to defend themselves for a few vital seconds.

In due course the hill and wells of Hashin were secured by 2nd Brigade against little resistance but, as the Brigade was withdrawing, leaving one battalion (East Surreys) as a temporary garrison, the dervishes opened fire on the Guards Brigade, which was covering the retirement, killing Captain Dalison of the Scots Guards[3] and two guardsmen. According to Drum-Major Albert Noble, the

[2] Official History.
[3] See Appendix E for Captain Dalison's servant's letter to his widow.

Guards Brigade square had opened to allow in some Indian cavalry, a dangerous moment as Tamai and Abu Klea had proved. However, on this occasion the dervishes contented themselves with shooting at the square rather than charging it. A Private McLaughlin was hit in the leg and Drum-Major Noble was in the process of bandaging the wound when Dalison, who, as battalion transport officer, had had a slight altercation with the adjutant over a missing mulecart, collapsed on top of Noble with a bullet through the chest. He refused a drink of water and died almost immediately.

As was the case with the campaign as a whole, the attack on Hashin seems to have lacked any strategic purpose. But Private Ferguson, never prone to understatement, was determined that his parents should appreciate that Hashin, his first aciton, had been a considerable affair in which at least two thousand dervishes had perished, adding with ghoulish satisfaction that "the sun has made them (the bodies) frizzle, the fat is boiling on them." Four days later the East Surreys were withdrawn and the well reoccupied by Osman's men, who, as in reality they had suffered few casualties, were far from discouraged and believed that they had forced the "Turks" to withdraw. The most likely explanation is that Graham was under great political pressure to inflict a bloody defeat upon the Mahdists which would go down well at home. Therefore he was determined to take them on wherever he could find them and, with the heat increasing daily, time was not on his side.

Two days later, with this in mind and presumably hoping to repeat the performance of the previous year, Graham ordered General McNeill, with the Berkshires, Marines, the Indian Brigade and a squadron of the 5th Lancers, to march in the direction of Tamai to the south believing this to be Osman's headquarters, insofar as he had one. The heat was tremendous and the going, through dense mimosa scrub, hard. A halt was ordered and at about 2 o'clock on the afternoon of 22 March, while some of McNeill's men were constructing a zariba and others were eating their lunch, a cavalry scout rode in to report large numbers of the enemy in the vicinity. Perhaps not too hurriedly, preparations to receive an attack were begun and a second cavalry patrol report had hardly left the lips of its bearer when a screaming horde of some five thousand Fuzzy-Wuzzys swept like lightning into the half-constructed zariba from the south-west, driving before them the remaining cavalry pickets, large numbers of transport animals and their drivers and overwhelming the Bengal Infantry who broke and fled.

The battle of Tofrik or McNeill's zariba, as it became known, had, like Tamai and Abu Klea before it, all the makings of a catastrophe. However, the half-battalion of Berkshires[4] to the right (west) of the Bengalis stood firm and checked, but could not stop, the onslaught which swept through the central area of

---

[4] For their conduct in this action the Berkshires were awarded the prefix Royal.

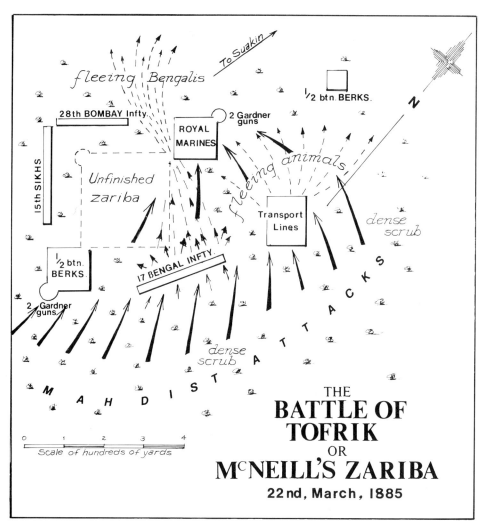

THE
**BATTLE OF
TOFRIK**
OR
**MᶜNEILL'S ZARIBA**
**22nd, March, 1885**

the zariba and hit the Marines at its northern corner. It is not clear if the sailors with them were able to bring the Gardners into action – there are conflicting accounts – but the crews of these machine guns suffered severely and their commander, Lieutenant Seymour RN, was killed. The fire discipline of the Marines seems to have been highly effective, with the front rank shooting outwards and the rear rank dealing with those dervishes who had broken into the centre of their part of the zariba.

The other half-battalion of Berkshires was caught in the open to the east of the zariba, but, by forming square with a speed acquired only through constant practice, and volleying steadily, survived not only the charging enemy but also the stampeding transport animals with only one man wounded. Camels, horses and mules careered madly in all directions and in clouds of dust for nearly twenty minutes, pursued by frenzied tribesmen cutting, slashing and hamstringing. A few of the Somali camel-drivers had old-fashioned bayonets with which to defend themselves, the others nothing and suffered accordingly. In the confusion and poor visibility probably as many drivers and animals were killed by British and Indian rifle fire as by the enemy.

Gradually the momentum of the attack died away and Osman's men moved off slowly, defiantly refusing to run, some returning alone to offer another challenge, inviting certain death. At least one thousand of them had been killed as well as about one hundred and thirty British and Indian soldiers and over one hundred and fifty drivers. Some seven hundred and fifty animals were killed, maimed or missing.

"McNeill's zariba" was the last and, in terms of British casualties, the most costly action of the two eastern Sudan campaigns. Nor had it been any more satisfactory for Osman Digna. Once again his followers lost confidence and started to drift away from him. He could not make them fight again and Graham could not find them. So, for a while, the sweating British wandered through the scrubby desert burning a few huts and losing a few more men, mostly from heat exhaustion. The campaign was ending with neither a bang nor a whimper, it was just fizzling out.

Fortunately for everyone in Whitehall and the Sudan, during that same month, March, the Russians had been making threatening noises on their border with Afghanistan and, in due course, occupied an Afghan village. Here was the opportunity for which the British Government had been waiting. It would not be difficult to convince the public that another round in "the Great Game" was about to be played and both attention and troops could be withdrawn from the Sudan. Gordon was dead but punishment had been inflicted upon his killers and enough was enough. Wolseley's men were ordered back to Dongola and Graham's to England and India.

Apart from the loss of life, £3 million had been been wasted in one month in the eastern Sudan (more than the total cost of the campaign of reconquest a decade or so later) of which £865,000 had been spent on building eighteen and three-quarter miles of railway which was never used, the only beneficiaries being Messrs. Lucas and Aird and the local tribesmen who tore up the line and used it for their own purposes. What they made of a Pear's Soap advertisement which miraculously appeared painted on a rock within sight of the railway, we do not know, but no doubt from that time "they have used no other".

Even if troops had been needed to deal with the Afghan crisis, which they were not, Graham's men would not have been of much immediate use. So debilitated by the climatic conditions around Suakin were the men of the Guards Brigade that they were sent, after a spell in Alexandria, to the Troödos Mountains in Cyprus for seven weeks. Ostensibly they were being held in readiness for Afghanistan, but it is more likely that the authorities at home did not relish the prospect of a brigade of Her Majesty's Household troops returning to public duties looking like the inmates of a workhouse. Khaki[5] had not been issued until the thermometer had risen over the 100°F mark and the men, presumably in their red coats, had been marching, building zaribas and clearing scrub, in a part of the Sudan where, to the present writer's knowledge, even the local Beja dock-workers occasionally die of heat exhaustion. Of the 1st Coldstream, during a campaign lasting barely six weeks, fourteen officers and men had died and well over a hundred had been invalided home or to Egypt, in addition to the few killed or wounded in action. The 2nd Scots Guards were reasonably satisfied that the maximum number of men sick on any one day was a mere sixty-four. In all, some 25% of the total strength of the force went to hospital during the campaign of whom less than half returned to duty before the withdrawal. Nine or ten men, including Sergeant-Major Alan Strachan of the Scots Guards, died in Cyprus of typhoid contracted in the Sudan.

By the end of June, 1885, a bitter and frustrated Wolseley had left the Sudan, never to return. Gladstone had fallen from office and the Mahdi was dead. The world, but not Lieutenant F. R. Wingate, lost interest in the Sudan.

---

[5] This is the first record of khaki being issued to the Brigade of Guards, except to those serving in the Guards Camel Regiment.

# Entr'acte

# 11 The Khalifa and his Army

When the Mahdi died, probably of typhus, on 22 June, 1885, the mantle of office descended upon his lieutenant, the Khalifa Abdullahi. The Mahdi himself had indicated his desire that Abdullahi should succeed him but when the moment came this was opposed by the Mahdi's family, known as the Ashraf (Descendants of the Prophet), who favoured another of the three Khalifas,[1] Mohamed Sherif, the Mahdi's son-in-law. However, with the backing of the third Khalifa, Ali Wad Helu, and most of the other Mahdist notables. Abdullahi prevailed.

His master, although reputedly of a gentle and pleasant demeanour, had been a man of revolution and war leading a warrior people in an expansionist jehad.[2] Cairo, Mecca, Jerusalem, Istanbul and even Rome were to be conquered and the infidels converted or put to the sword. Or so he said. Probably he was much too intelligent to believe his own rhetoric. Under Abdullahi there was no overt change in policy but his rule was characterized by isolationism rather than the reverse. Throughout his reign he was busy consolidating and maintaining his power base at Omdurman, surrounding himself with his fellow Baggara and, in particular, his own clan, the Taisha, never once leaving the immediate vicinity of his capital. The one attempt to invade Egypt in 1889 was half-hearted and little more than a means of disposing of the pious and popular Jaali Emir, Abdel Rahman Wad Nejumi, but the campaigns in Abyssinia are less simply explained.

Apart from the traditional antipathy between the Moslem Sudan and Christian-dominated Abyssinia, territorial and frontier disputes had been a feature of relations between Abyssinia and Egypt in pre-Mahdist days. Egypt had

---

[1] There were to have been four Khalifas but the Mahdi offered the fourth to the Senussi, the great religious leader in Libya, who did not deign to reply and the fourth appointment was never made.
[2] Holy war.

occupied Bogos, that is to say roughly what is now Eritrea, and in the 1870s had suffered a number of defeats in their attempts to expand their Ethiopian possessions. However, in 1884, with evacuation of the Sudan in the face of the Mahdist onslaught becoming increasingly inevitable, an Anglo-Egyptian mission led by Admiral Sir William Hewett, VC, assisted by Mason Bey, the American governor of the Egyptian-occupied port of Massawa, visited King Yohannes at Adowa and ceded Bogos to him in return for his help in extracting the Egyptian garrisons from the area. The majority of the inhabitants thus handed over to Yohannes' tender mercies were Moslems and it is conceivable that the Mahdists felt that their co-religionists should be liberated from his oppression. More practically, they were concerned about the effect of British and, later, Italian, influence in Abyssinia. Also British and Egyptian money and arms had formed an important part of the Hewett deal and the Mahdists had little doubt against whom these were likely to be used.

Politics on the Abyssinian frontier were further complicated by the strongly anti-Mahdist sentiments of some of the Sudanese tribes in the area, such as the Shukria and Beni Amer, and their shifting alliances with the Habash,[3] which were at once a danger and an affront to the Mahdiya. A serious challenge too came from the Khatmiya sect centred around the border town of Kassala and led by the powerful Mirghani family. But perhaps most important of all, successful campaigns led to the acquisition of booty, livestock and slaves, particularly much sought after Abyssinian girls, and even unsuccessful ones kept the Khalifa's large and unruly army occupied and his ambitious emirs out of mischief.

As for Abdullahi himself, unlike his predecessor, there was nothing very remarkable about him; the pages of history are liberally peppered with his type and he is by no means a rarity today. Ruthless, suspicious and ignorant, but far from stupid, he possessed all the instincts necessary for survival in such circumstances, above all the ability to play both ends against the middle. Nevertheless, it is remarkable that he survived for so long, particularly as he presided over a period of unparalleled catastrophe for the Sudanese people as a whole. It has been estimated that the population of the Sudan during the period 1883 to 1899 was reduced by 75 to 80%, or from eight million to about one and a half million. The actual figures should be regarded with caution as no census was taken either before or immediately after the period in question; however, there is no doubt that depopulation had taken place on a massive scale.

In mitigation of the Khalifa's conduct of affairs it must be said that, unlike the giants of destruction of the twentieth century, he did not set out to destroy large sections of his own people deliberately. Executions, though frequent, seldom expanded into massacres. The constant warfare with Abyssinia and, to a lesser

[3] Arabic for Abyssinian or Ethiopian.

extent, with the Anglo-Egyptians accounted for several hundred thousand deaths but the great killer was hunger. In the past the Egyptians and their bashi-bazooks had taken a good deal more than their share but had had the sense not to kill the geese which laid the golden eggs, but during the Mahdiya crop failures, and sometimes the failure even to plant a crop, culminating in the great famine of 1889, were aggravated by the depredations of the Khalifa's armies and fellow tribesmen. At his behest, in some important agricultural areas, the Baggara, a nomadic people with little knowledge of or interest in cultivation, had displaced the riverain tribes with disastrous results. At the same time the Khalifa actively discouraged foreign trade, which he associated with spying and treason, and severe restrictions on exports to the Sudan were imposed by the Anglo-Egyptian authorities. However, there is evidence that by 1891 the Khalifa was emphasizing the importance of agricultural production and liberalizing trade. To the latter end he made good use of entrepreneurs such as the Jewish merchant Ben Zion Koshti, known as Basiyuni in the Sudan, who was able to arrange commercial transactions with Egypt through his contacts at Suakin, which remained in Anglo-Egyptian hands throughout the period of the Mahdiya.

Nineteenth-century Mahdism, as preached by its founder, would be described today as Moslem "fundamentalism" and perhaps its closest living relative in political terms is the Khomeini régime in Iran. Bigotry and intolerance, the killing-off of opponents, economic decline and the waging of wars as a diversion from internal problems, although by no means exclusive to them, were and are features of both régimes. The rise of the Mahdi was greeted by western liberals, including Gladstone, as a struggle for freedom. Perhaps it was, but similar ecstatic cries welcomed the overthrow of the Shah when in reality both the Sudanese and the Iranians had jumped out of the frying pan into the fire.

On the other hand, exaggerated denunciations of the Mahdiya and the Khalifa's role in it, understandably propagated by those whose job it was to bring about its downfall, have led to a reaction in more recent times. Several writers since the Second World War have sought to portray Abdullahi in a more generous light. To the extent that he was trying to create something out of nothing, with a certain amount of success, they have a point. It should be remembered that the Sudanese state was in its cradle. Before the Mahdi there had been no such thing, only the tribes, some sedentary, some nomadic, exploited rather than ruled by the Turko-Egyptians, forming loose alliances, breaking them and forming others. In terms of civil and military administration the Khalifa was starting from scratch and basing the constitution, if it may be so termed, of the new state upon a hotch-potch of tribal tradition, the Koran, the written and verbal instructions of the Mahdi and the legal code of the former Turko-Egyptian government. That it did not work very well is hardly surprising. That it worked well enough to endure for thirteen years after the Mahdi's death must say something for his successor, and who

A typical "ansar" infantryman of the Khalifa's army. He was a good deal more formidable than he looked. This one was a PoW. Note patched "jibba" or smock.

better to say it than Winston Churchill, an eye-witness of the events which led to the downfall of that successor:

"Of the Khalifa himself it is difficult for me to write, since he gave us no opportunity of discussing matters. His house exhibited several signs of cleanliness and refinement, and the loyalty of his people – unquestionably displayed – gave him some claims to be considered a fair ruler according to his lights and theirs. He did not, even in the crash of his authority, massacre his prisoners, and when found they did not look ill-fed. It has been said that he was cruel. If that be so, he may yet find companions in other and more scientific nations."

The Khalifa's army, like many others, fell into two categories, part-time "Territorials" and Regulars. All adult males were soldiers or potential soldiers who either volunteered or were pressed into service as and when required. The Mahdi called them his ansar (helpers). The pay was low, five Egyptian piastres per month if they were lucky, but there was loot to be had, although most of this was supposed to be surrendered to the Beit el Mal (treasury). They carried no firearms but were equipped with a sword and several spears. The fighting unit was the *rub* (literally, quarter) which might vary in strength according to the standing and prestige of its leader from about eight hundred to several thousand. The *rub* was divided into *muqqadamiyas*, again varying in size from company to platoon strength. To each *rub* was attached a squadron or troop of cavalry, usually Baggara. These too were Territorials and provided their own horses.

There were two Regular components of the army, the *jehadiya* and the *mulazimin*. The former were black riflemen, usually soldiers of the Egyptian Army taken prisoner in the early years of the Mahdiya or more recently recruited slaves (bazingers). They were armed for the most part with rather elderly Remington .43 rifles and gave fire support to the ansar. The *mulazimin* (literally, lieutenants) were the household troops of the Khalifa from whom were selected his personal bodyguard. These could be either northern Sudanese tribesmen or blacks from the south; they received ten piastres a month and rations (as did the *jehadiya*) and lived in barracks. Some were armed with Remingtons and others with huge elephant guns. As for numerical strength, estimates vary considerably, particularly for the Territorials, but at the time of his escape from Omdurman in 1895 Slatin gave the Intelligence Department of the Egyptian Army the following strengths of the various components of the Omdurman garrison.

| *Mulazimin* | blacks (southerners) | 4,000 |
|---|---|---|
| | Arabs (northerners) | 5,000 |
| Horsemen | (all Arab) | 3,000 |
| Camel Corps | (presumably all Arab Territorials) | 6,350 |
| Sword and spearmen | (ansar) | 32,300 |
| *Jehadiya* | (blacks) | 3,000 |

A total of some 53,650 men. Clearly this was the main concentration of forces at that time, as it had been reported to Wingate, Director of Egyptian Army Intelligence, as early as 1891 that the Khalifa had decided the final destruction of any invading Anglo-Egyptian army would take place at Kereri, a plain a short distance to the north of Omdurman.

Training, apart from religious instruction which was thorough and continuous, was limited. Most tribesmen were already expert in the use of sword and spear and shortage of ammunition sharply curtailed musketry practice, resulting in a very low standard of marksmanship among the *jehadiya* and *mulazimin*. Indeed, in battle the rifle was usually fired from the hip and kneeling or lying down to take aim was discouraged. The artillery, such as it was, seems to have been more or less the preserve of Egyptian PoWs and was for some time commanded by an Egyptian artillery officer, Yusef Bey Mansour. There was no special training for officers, whose effectiveness depended entirely upon their natural qualities of leadership and tactical sense.

The officer hierarchy is impossible to define and the lines dividing civil, military and religious duties are blurred. Yakub, the Khalifa's favourite brother, appears to have acted as a sort of Chief of the General Staff and the Khalifa's playboy son, Osman Sheikh el Din, as commander of the *mulazimin*. Hamdan Abu Anga, himself of slave origin, was regarded as leader of the *jehadiya* until his death in 1889. However, the Khalifa maintained direct control over his own bodyguard and the Omdurman garrison. The senior emirs, such as Wad Nejumi and Osman Digna, may be equated to generals but some other emirs commanded nothing larger than a *rub* of battalion strength. Nevertheless, every emir was entitled to his own standard, a symbol of both his courage and piety. Below the emirs came *rasmiyas* (chiefs of a hundred men) and *muqqudams*, roughly the equivalents of company and platoon commanders. There were no NCOs as such.

In the latter years of the Khalifa's reign many of the leading emirs were very young men, most of the Mahdi's Old Guard having disappeared from the scene in one way or another. These youngsters were headstrong, quarrelsome and inexperienced and Kitchener's advance into the Sudan in 1896–98 was greatly facilitated by the lack of co-operation between them. In the absence of any hard and fast order of seniority, they frequently disputed each other's decisions and wasted valuable time denouncing each other to the Khalifa, hundreds of miles away in Omdurman, while seeking his intervention on their own behalf.

From all this it may be seen that the Sudanese were as ill-prepared for the juggernaut which was to roll over them in the 1890s as the Egyptians had been for the whirlwind which swept them out of the Sudan in the 1880s.

# 12 An Army Reborn

Until the end of 1882, when its reconstruction and retraining was undertaken by the British, service in the Egyptian Army had been a form of slavery. Conscripted by ballot mainly from the fellahin (peasantry), length of service was indefinite and the men were seldom released until their health had broken down and then without pension or gratuity. The pay was negligible and always in arrears.[1] Of leave, for obvious reasons, there was none and a conscript might spend his entire military career, and thus most of his active life, in the same remote garrison in the Sudan. The officers, Turkish, Circassian and Egyptian, with a few foreign "technical advisers", mostly American veterans of the Civil War, were, on the whole, corrupt, lazy and totally indifferent to the welfare of the men.

It is not surprising that the potential recruit and his family would go to almost any lengths to avoid his conscription. Officially a payment of £E100, the average fellah's income for many years, could be made to the government in lieu of military service. For those who could not afford this other grounds for exemption were available. The village *omdah* or headman could issue a certificate to the effect that a young man was a *wahidani*, the sole support of a widowed mother or orphaned family. A sheikh of the Muslim religion or a Coptic priest could certify that he was a religious student, altar boy or verger. Needless to say, such certificates were seldom, if ever, granted without bribery and even these lesser payments, usually about £E20, were beyond the resources of the majority. Thus self-mutilation and voluntarily induced disease were often resorted to. Parents would partially blind

---

[1] In the Sudan the troops were often paid in lengths of cloth rather than cash by officials who misappropriated the soldiers pay. These the men were obliged to sell to merchants for a fraction of their official value who then sold them back to the government officials at a profit and so the process continued, everyone profiting except the soldier.

their male children, cut off their trigger fingers and, in some extreme cases, larger limbs. One peculiar quirk of the system was that men of military age (19–23) resident in Cairo or Alexandria were exempted, possibly through official fears of serious rioting during the recruitment process.

All this was hardly conducive to the maintenance of an effective force with which to police a remote and turbulent empire. Nonetheless, the fellah conscript was not entirely devoid of military qualities. He was amenable to discipline, keen on drill, possessed of immense powers of endurance and, when decently led, capable of a steadfast, if not heroic, fighting performance. Men like Gessi, Tewfik the Cretan and Slatin had found it possible to use Egyptian troops successfully against slavers and tribesmen. They had led by example and from the front.

After the suppression of Arabi's rebellion, under a Khedivial decree of 20 December, 1882, the British took over responsibility for the formation and training of a new Egyptian Army. This suited both parties. The Khedive could be assured that another military *coup d'état* would not be attempted against him[2] and the British, with the Egyptian Army under their control, could reduce the number of relatively expensive British troops to be kept in Egypt.

Conditions for the conscript were almost immediately improved, although it was impossible to cure the endemic corruption of the recruitment system itself. Length of service was reduced to four years with the colours, four with the police, and four on the reserve. However, as the situation in the Sudan deteriorated, this was later increased to six, five and four years. A regular pay scale was introduced, a recruit receiving £E3.60 per annum (plus rations) rising to £E18 for a Warrant Officer. If this does not sound overgenerous, at the time it compared quite favourably with the wages of a labourer, who had to buy his own food, or a domestic servant.

Early in 1884 an attempt was made to recruit an Albanian brigade but the nucleus of the first batallion mutinied and the idea was abandoned. However, in addition to the native Egyptians there were also a number of black Sudanese troops in the army. These were mainly slaves or the descendants of slaves derived from the same sources as the *jehadiya* in the Khalifa's army. Although difficult to train, these troops had great fighting qualities and by the 1890s had become the backbone of the Egyptian infantry, playing a decisive role in the campaign to reconquer the Sudan. They were long-service men and provision was made for the maintenance of their wives and children. Several of them were commissioned, among them El Kaimakam (Lieutenant-Colonel) El Mas Bey Mursi, a Dinka, who served forty-three years with the colours, in every battle against the Mahdists

[2] "What," wrote Baring, "could be more perfect (from the point of view of the Khedivial government) than the presence in Egypt of a thoroughly disciplined force, commanded by young men who took no interest in local politics and who occupied themselves exclusively with polo and cricket?"

The 12th Soudanese parading in ceremonial uniform. This battalion was formed in 1888 and the mounted officer leading the parade is probably its first commanding officer, El Kaimakam Besant. Later the battalion was commanded by El Kaimakam C. V. Townshend who achieved fame as "Townshend of Kut" at Kut el Amara in 1915/16.

from Ginnis to Um Dibaykarat and in many punitive expeditions until his retirement in 1915.

Originally it was intended that Colonel Valentine Baker should be appointed Sirdar (Commander-in-Chief) of the Egyptian Army and he had resigned his senior position in the Turkish Army, much to the irritation of the Sultan, specifically to take up this post. However, when news of this reached Queen Victoria she did not conceal her displeasure, letting it be known that she did not wish British officers to serve under a man who had been convicted of a sexual offence.[3] No doubt with a sigh, Her Majesty's ministers were obliged to look round for another candidate and Major-General Sir Evelyn Wood VC was appointed in Baker's place, the latter having to content himself with the command of the Gendarmerie at a lower salary and with even less promising human material to work with.

Initially twenty-five British officers and a similar number of NCOs were selected for service with the new army, which was to consist of two infantry brigades, one of which was to remain for the time being under Turkish and

[3] The Queen also disapproved of his brother, the explorer Sir Samuel Baker, his insatiable appetite for the young ladies of the southern Sudanese tribes having been reported to her. Also it was rumoured that he had bought his beautiful Hungarian wife in a Turkish slave-market.

The band of the 12th Soudanese in ceremonial uniform.

Egyptian officers, of four battalions each, a cavalry regiment, and some artillery, about 6,000 men in all. The Egyptian service was an attractive proposition, particularly for British officers with small private means and little social influence. The pay, at £450 per annum for subalterns, was good, promotion automatic as all officers stepped up at least one rank on joining and none ranked lower than *bimbashi* (major).[4] Also there were considerable opportunities for active service, but the mortality rate, mostly from disease and accident, was alarmingly high. However, this hazard in no way daunted potential applicants whose military record had to be impeccable, standards of horsemanship, musketry and other martial arts high and knowledge of spoken and written French (the language of the educated classes in Egypt) above average. Furthermore, they were required to pass an examination in colloquial Arabic within six months of joining. A higher examination could be taken after a year but few officers passed this, notable exceptions being the future Sirdars Kitchener and Wingate, and most contented themselves with basic "*bimbashi*" Arabic which just about enabled them to converse with their men. Their contracts were for two years renewable, and married officers were usually ineligible. Most of the British NCOs were borrowed from the regiments currently serving in Egypt. The work done by these men was of equal, or even greater, value to that of the officers although their positions were anomalous. Theoretically subordinate to the native commissioned officers, in practice they took orders only from their British superiors, a system which required a good deal of tact on all sides but appears to have worked without too much friction and, in due course, several of these men were themselves commissioned.[5]

Wood and his officers were presented with an immediate non-military problem

[4] See Appendix F.
[5] Kipling wrote a poem about these NCOs called *The Pharoah and the Sergeant*. See Appendix L.

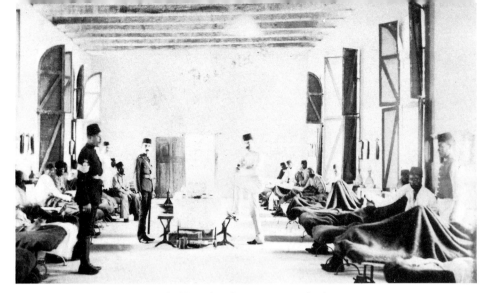

An Egyptian military hospital. Note headgear worn in bed.

almost as soon as they had taken up their new duties. In the summer of 1883 there was a severe outbreak of cholera in Egypt affecting not only the civilian population but also the Egyptian and British troops. The Egyptian Army medical service, which had been almost non-existent, was still in its infancy, and such medical staff as there were appeared more concerned with avoiding infection than nursing their patients. Stuart-Wortley observed one Egyptian doctor examining the cholera victims from a distance through binoculars! As all the British doctors and nurses were fully occupied in the British military hospitals, the "Egyptian" officers found themselves in the unaccustomed role of medical orderlies and succeeded in nursing many of their men back to health. At the outbreak of the epidemic a newly joined young Gunner officer, Lieutenant Reginald Wingate,[6] was appointed director of the cholera hospital, the first and perhaps the most dangerous of many appointments which this capable and ambitious officer was to hold in Egypt and the Sudan over the next thirty-five years. Also prominent in this humanitarian activity was a madcap Shropshire Light Infantry subaltern, Chamley Turner. Turner, it seems, was a man who enjoyed every kind of risk to his own safety, no matter the nature of the peril. He would frequently dose himself with the same concoctions he had prepared for his patients, taking it from the same glass. Not surprisingly he contracted the disease himself, but recovered, only to drown in the Nile while on a camel-buying mission in Upper Egypt.

The cholera epidemic, unpleasant though it undoubtedly was, did much to create confidence and even affection between the Egyptian soldiery and their new officers. Indeed the officers became so closely identified with their men in these early days that they almost lost their own. After the battle of Ginnis in December, 1885, one of the first in which the new Egyptian Army took part, the commander

---

[6] General Sir Reginald Wingate, Bart, GCB, DSO (1861–1953).

of the Egyptian artillery, Joscelin Wodehouse,[7] charged into the enemy camp shouting "Don't let the English get the flags!" and feverishly collected up all the dervish banners he could find as trophies for his own and other Egyptian units. This feeling was intensified by the mocking and contemptuous attitude adopted towards the Egyptian Army by the other British officers (and Other Ranks) serving in Egypt, an attitude which regrettably endured through the Second World War and thereafter until Britain's final withdrawal from Egypt. Colonel Andrew Haggard (brother of H. Rider Haggard), one of the first twenty-five British officers to join the Egyptian Army in 1883, recounts in his book *Under Crescent and Star* that when some British troops panicked at a false alarm during the night following the battle of Tamai it was reported in the newspapers that "a slight scare took place among our troops last night". He adds wryly that, had this occurred among the "Gyppies", it would have been described as "the horrible demoralization of those cowardly Egyptians".

Although Egyptian troops were used almost entirely on Line of Communications duties in the Gordon Relief Expedition, small numbers served satisfactorily at both Kirbekan and Ginnis. By the end of 1886 all British troops had been withdrawn from the frontier with the Sudan and replaced by Egyptians and Soudanese. In 1889, under Sir Francis Grenfell, who had by then replaced Wood as Sirdar, the New Army fought its first major action at Toski in Upper Egypt against the invading Mahdists and won almost without the aid of British troops.[8] It had passed the test. Haggard wrote: "The young soldiers of the present army are well fed, well paid and well clothed. They get a periodical furlough to see their friends; are allowed . . . to travel by train or steamer at greatly reduced rates; are given medals for active service; and if discharged from the service on account of wounds or sickness, they are sent home with a gratuity and a complete set of clothes . . . Malingering by self-mutilation has entirely ceased. The young soldiers themselves . . . have frequently behaved with distinguished bravery in the field."

When, in March, 1896, the decision was taken to invade and reconquer the Sudan, ostensibly on behalf of the Khedive, the establishment of that worthy's army stood at 658 officers, 14,420 men, 18 field guns and 3,048 animals, made up of eight squadrons of cavalry, one battery of horse artillery, two field batteries, one Maxim battery, four companies each of Egyptian and Soudanese Camel Corps, ten battalions of Egyptian infantry and six of Soudanese, one transport battalion and one railway battalion. After thirteen years of careful training, one major action (Toski) and a number of skirmishes on the Frontier and around Suakin, the new Egyptian Army had come of age.

[7] General Sir J. H. Wodehouse, GCB, CMG, (1852–1930) was a famous name on the Sudan Frontier for several years. Particularly fluent in Arabic he was a strong candidate for the Sirdarship but was passed over in favour of Kitchener.

[8] One squadron of the 20th Hussars took part and one British soldier was killed.

# 13 The Happy Warrior

Peacetime soldiering was, is, and probably always will be, a tedious occupation. During the long period of relative peace between the end of the Crimean War and the beginning of the Second Boer War young officers who sought adventure and advancement were many and the opportunities few. Unless your regiment was fortunate enough to be earmarked for some minor imperial peacekeeping role or punitive expedition, in theory you languished at Aldershot, the Curragh or one of the many garrisons around the Empire. In practice the better-off spent little time with their regiments, officers' leave being lengthy and frequent.

When a smallish balloon went up, as it did in Egypt in 1882, every string was pulled by every officer with the slightest ambition and influence to get himself appointed to the staff of one of the numerous generals, who, by dint of much jostling, snarling, toadying and backbiting, had been given a command. In those days very senior officers frequently commanded relatively small units. The suppression of Arabi's rebellion, although involving only two divisions of infantry and one of cavalry, apparently required no less than four lieutenant-generals, six major-generals and a host of brigadier-generals. Colonel Butler estimated there was one general to every nine hundred men. Often infantry companies and cavalry squadrons were commanded by lieutenant-colonels, many of them past their prime.

By the usual *jeux d'influence*, the well-heeled and well-connected Lieutenant the Hon E. J. Montagu-Stuart-Wortley of the 60th Rifles wangled the job of orderly officer to one Colonel Owen Lanyon, commandant of the base depot at Port Said. Lanyon did not know and did not want Wortley and made this plain from the outset. This suited them both as Wortley, a 25-year-old veteran of campaigns in Afghanistan and South Africa, had no desire to remain a "base wallah" in Port Said. After a few weeks there, during which time he conducted a fiery interview with the great Ferdinand de Lesseps, the violently anti-British constructor of the Suez Canal, he succeeded in achieving a transfer to the staff of the Heavy Cavalry Brigade and took part in its successful charge at Tel el Kebir (13 September, 1882), a rare experience for an infantryman.

At the cessation of hostilities Wortley joined the Egyptian Army as Military Secretary to Colonel Valentine Baker who was temporarily in command of what remained of it. His duties included assisting Baker in the selection of officers for the Hicks expedition, including Hicks himself. Unfortunately his reminiscences do not describe in any detail the process of selection except to say that Hicks's name was picked out of a hat. Several applicants sent photographs of themselves with their applications, one such being a Swiss, doubtless of high military qualification but unlovely aspect. Here Wortley's schoolboyish sense of humour got the better of him and he replied refusing the application and offering the advice, "When next you apply for an appointment, do not send your photograph." This was not well received and a complaint found its way through diplomatic channels to the GOC Egypt and Wortley's knuckles were severely rapped. Perhaps later the Swiss officer thanked his lucky stars and Wortley's somewhat immature sense of fun for his failure to obtain what would have been a fatal appointment.

As we have seen, Baker specifically resigned his command in the Turkish Army in order to take over and reconstruct the new Egyptian Army but the British War Office, influenced by the Queen and the Duke of Cambridge, refused to confirm this appointment and Sir Evelyn Wood became the first Sirdar of the Egyptian Army. Baker was fobbed off with the Gendarmerie, a motley collection of time-expired soldiers and policemen and the criminal riff-raff of Cairo and Alexandria, who were cut to pieces or put to flight at the first (so-called) Battle of El Teb.

Wisely, Wortley had not followed Baker into the Gendarmerie but remained in the Egyptian Army as Wood's ADC. His reminiscences of Egypt and the Sudan, written not long before his death in the 1930s and never published, make happy and carefree reading. He was a man who would risk his life as readily as he would play a practical joke or lend a fiver to a friend. His Cairo flat near the Ezbekiyeh Gardens, a fashionable residential district before the development of Zamalek and Garden City, was a centre of that riotous but usually harmless jollification which was so much a feature of the British military presence in Egypt for over sixty years. The cost of living was incredibly low, much "fizz" was consumed and any consequent damage to persons or property could be put right for a few piastres. Indignant neighbours watched as, on the occasion of an all-night farewell party for Hicks's staff, "hounds" hunted the "fox" up and down stairs and on and off balconies to the piercing strains of the horn and high-pitched shrieks of "Gornaway!" and the rest.

We seldom find him upset or disconcerted but when, with his chief, Wood, he

Major the Hon Edward Montagu-Stuart-Wortley.

was called upon to inspect the troops earmarked for Hicks's expedition, they were both horrified. Some were old and had already served thirty years in the army, others were partially maimed or blinded by self-inflicted wounds and all were tied together with logs like slaves. When Wood protested to the Egyptian Minister of War, that worthy laughingly replied that as they were so old and lame they would not be able to run away.[1]

With the capture of most of Kordofan and the western Sudan by the Mahdi, the British military authorities began to take the threat of a Mahdist invasion of Egypt by the Dar el Arbain (the forty-day route), the ancient caravan trail from El Fasher in Darfur to Assiut in Upper Egypt, seriously. In the summer of 1884 Wortley, together with Colonel Colvile[2] of the Intelligence Department, was instructed to carry out a reconnaissance of part of this route in some strength using local Bedouin tribesmen as guides and escorts. With about 550 Jawazi Bedouin the two officers advanced south from Assiut into the desert, preceded, Wortley tells us, by "wailing minstrels". Only three days later they arrived at the oasis of Khargeh, having covered one hundred and fifty miles, a remarkable achievement.

Eventually, three weeks after leaving Assiut, they reached the Selimah Oasis well inside the Sudan and some five hundred miles from their starting point. On at least one occasion the entire expedition nearly died of thirst, but the two Englishmen were not quite reduced to consuming their last two dozen pints of champagne or removing their blue silk smoking jackets. Wortley was proud to think that anyone finding their skeletons might remark, "these fellows did themselves well up to the end!".

Turning east they reached the Nile south of Wadi Halfa covering sixty miles in fourteen hours. Wortley believed they had proved that a hostile force could not reach Egypt by this route but it is not clear on what he based this conclusion, nor were his superiors convinced. However, what he had established was his own ability as a desert traveller and a natural leader of unruly irregular native forces. Also, he produced a serious report on the selection, feeding, loading and general management of camels, which, had it been adopted by the Relief Expedition, might well have improved its speed and efficiency as well as reducing losses and preventing at least some of the appalling and unnecessary suffering of those wretched beasts.

By the time Wortley had returned to Assiut the Relief Expedition was under way and he joined up with it as though just back from a short ride in the English countryside. But General Wood was not prepared to leave it at that and ordered

---

[1] Stuart-Wortley's impression of these men conflicts with that of Hicks, who found them in good physical condition on arrival in the Sudan.
[2] Later the Official Historian of the Gordon Relief Expedition.

him to return to Selimah with a party of "Friendlies" from the Garareesh tribe, of whom Wortley had little opinion, and there to set up an outpost. Presumably Wood, with some justification, was still concerned that a Mahdist attack on Egypt might be launched from that direction. It is true that, when it came in 1889, Wad Nejumi's attempt to invade Egypt did not take that route but peaceful caravans still used it, the Intelligence Department recording the arrival at Assiut from western Darfur in 1887 of a caravan 1,500 camels strong.

Unwilling to spend the rest of the campaign hundreds of miles from the "sharp end", Wortley arranged for a few of his Jawazi friends to "attack" the outpost and fire a few shots over the heads of the Garareesh who instantly fled never to be seen again, thus, willy-nilly, relieving Wortley of his unwelcome command.

Continued service with the Egyptian Army would have condemned him to an L of C role throughout the campaign, so, with his usual dexterity, he succeeded in arranging a transfer back to the British Army, Wingate having replaced him as Wood's ADC, and, as we have seen, was selected as one of the officers to remain in Khartoum with Gordon until relief came. After the withdrawal of the Relief Expedition he did not return to the Egyptian Army and resumed other more normal duties. His health was not always good and, as was the fashion among the fashionable, he resorted frequently to various French and German spas whence he would be summoned at short notice when it looked as though something exciting was going to happen. Thus in the campaign of re-conquest he was recalled for service on the gunboats in 1897 and to command the "Friendlies" in 1898. Although he received greater and more formal rewards for his services, perhaps he set as much store by a signed photograph of the old slaver, Zubeir Pasha, which was accompanied by the following address in Arabic:

"This has been presented as a token of remembrance and regard by Zubeir Rahma Pasha, the Abbaside, to his honoured friend His Excellency the Mighty Officer Stuart-Wortley, who commanded the military division on the eastern bank which took part in the conquest of Omdurman, the rout of Abdullah el Taisha and the destruction of his armies with the help and by the powers of this zealous hero. Moreover, at this action there was in his company my son, Misara, to whom His Excellency vouchsafed high thanks and noble commendation."

Wortley personified all that was engagingly paraxodical about the late Victorian and Edwardian upper classes. Unhindered by complexes and accepting privilege as a right, he and his kind could "walk with kings nor lose the common touch". He was as much at home around a camp fire with the Bedouin camel drivers as in a great society drawing-room; as Military Attaché in Paris[3] or on a diplomatic

---

[3] His term at the Paris Embassy coincided with the suicide in a hotel there of his former Egyptian Army colleague, Hector MacDonald. A loyal friend, he wrote to the Press complaining of the tasteless way in which this tragic hero's death had been reported, while most other members of the military establishment preferred to distance themselves from the sordid affair. See last chapter.

mission to the Grande Porte, he blended as easily with the rich and powerful, of whom he was one, as with the wild Jaalin irregulars before Omdurman. Resolute yet easily bored, reliable yet casual, brave to the point of recklessness yet shrewd and resourceful, he had more than his share of luck and in a lifetime of campaigning was never once wounded. Warfare to him was an attack on a zariba sword in hand, a charge of heavy cavalry or a night journey in a leaky rowing-boat with the enemy on both banks, not the organized slaughter of the Great War. His world perished on the fields of Flanders and the heights of Gallipoli. If he did not quite fulfil his early promise perhaps it was because he could not be bothered. He retired in 1919 as a Major-General and died in 1934. If he is in Paradise, how dull he must find it! Unless, of course, he is allowed an occasional donkey race along the corridors of some celestial Shepheard's Hotel or a long camel ride across an ethereal desert with a few pint bottles of 'fizz' clinking in his saddle-bag.

# 14 The Prisoners

In earlier chapters we have glimpsed a few of the Europeans who were captured during the rebellion which swept the Sudan in the early 1880s. For the sake of simplicity they may be divided into three categories; officials of the former Egyptian Government, missionaries and civilian residents. There were one or two others who do not fit into any of these categories and we shall come to them later.

Among the first to be taken, in 1882, were the members of the Roman Catholic Mission, priests, nuns and laity, at Dilling in the Nuba Mountains of Kordofan. The best known of these was Father Joseph Ohrwalder, an Austrian in his thirties who eventually escaped from Omdurman in 1891. His book *Ten Years' Captivity in the Mahdi's Camp* was translated into English from the German by a Syrian and then edited by Wingate, Director of Intelligence of the Egyptian Army. When it was published in 1892 its harrowing tale re-awoke European interest in the Sudan and aroused strong feelings of indignation against the Mahdiya, or to be more accurate, against the Khalifa's rule. Whatever embellishments Wingate may have added to the story for propaganda purposes, there is no doubt that Ohrwalder and his colleagues suffered severe hardship and deprivation, particularly in the early days of their captivity in the Mahdi's temporary camps. Few would challenge his descriptions of the squalor and filth of these camps in which several of the missionaries died. The Sisters fared a good deal worse at the hands of their captors than did the priests, although they seem to have escaped sexual violation. The Prophet Mohamed had laid down some quite definite rules regulating the treatment of Christian clergy but these had not been extended to their female equivalents, perhaps because they represented a concept beyond the scope of his experience and imagination.

However, once they had settled in Omdurman all physical ill-treatment ceased and at least one of the Sisters married a European, presumably in order to avoid compulsory enrolment in a harem. To scratch a living both priests and nuns took up various trades. Ohrwalder made ribbons and his Italian colleague Father Rossignoli worked in a cookshop. The women sewed. Occasionally one of the priests would conduct a furtive Christian rite; a prayer whispered over a grave, a secret Christian wedding of two Greeks or an unobtrusive baptism. It is possible that an official blind eye was turned to this, the Mahdists having long since given up any attempt to convert the missionaries.

They were intrepid escapers and Ohrwalder took with him two nuns[1] and a black slave-girl when he left. Fathers Bonomi and Rossignoli also escaped, Bonomi from El Obeid in the early days and Rossignoli from Omdurman in 1894. Rossignoli's escape led to the imprisonment and chaining of the lay brother Rognotto with whom he had been sharing a house. This we learn from Sister Grigolini who had married Dimitri Kokorembos, the "emir" or leader of the Greek community in Omdurman, and who managed an intermittent correspond-ence with Ohrwalder in Egypt in the hope of being extricated herself. This seems to have been the only occasion on which such punishment was meted out to one of the religious fraternity.

These escapes were organized jointly by Wingate and the Papal representatives in Cairo and implemented under contract by daring and resourceful Ababdeh tribesmen from the frontier. Sometimes these men had to cope not only with the Khalifa's spies and patrols but also with the eccentric behaviour of their clients. Rossignoli's rescuer, Abdullah Mohamed Omar, seems to have had a particularly bad time. In the first place the priest was only a substitute for the prisoner whom Wingate really wanted and therefore a less valuable prize and, moreover, according to Abdullah's account, Rossignoli became temporarily deranged in the course of the journey, announcing to anyone who would listen that he was a fugitive.

Of the "politicals", undoubtedly the Mahdi's, and even more so the Khalifa's, star prize was Rudolf Slatin. Young as he was,[2] the Austrian was an important Khedivial official, clever, apparently co-operative and possessing a knowledge of the outside world which Abdullahi and most of his emirs lacked. From almost the first days of his surrender Slatin seems to have fascinated the Khalifa and in due course became his confidant and adviser. There is little doubt that Abdullahi was shattered and even hurt by Abdel Kader's (Slatin's Arabic name) flight from Omdurman in 1895. Slatin's book *Fire and Sword in the Sudan*, although, like Ohrwalder's, carefully edited by Wingate, remains the single most important

---

[1] One of these nuns, Sister Elisabetta Venturini, had nursed Gessi during his last illness in Khartoum in 1881. After the Mahdiya she returned to Khartoum where she died in 1937.
[2] He was 27 in 1884.

source of first-hand information about the Mahdiya. Subsequently his unique knowledge of the Sudan and its peoples was invaluable to the Anglo-Egyptian Condominium which he served as Inspector-General, a hybrid of Ombudsman and deputy governor-general, for many years until the First World War.

And yet it is with a slight feeling of scepticism that one regards Slatin's career. He seems to have been too many things to too many men. His ability to survive should not be held against him but, in an age when the Christian faith had a stronger hold on most of its adherents than it has today, his more or less voluntary conversion to Islam was particularly rapid and painless. Perhaps his Jewish origins made the transition easier. Then he seems to have ingratiated himself with the Khalifa with consummate ease and maintained the semi-confidence of this suspicious potentate, something achieved by no one else except perhaps his brother Yakub for over a decade. Could any one have bluffed their way through for so long? The Khalifa was no fool and Slatin must have rendered services of genuine value to him to retain his privileged position, otherwise he would have been relegated to the same scrapheap as the other Europeans.

After his escape and during the campaign of re-conquest, his desire for the personal destruction of his former master was implacable and all-consuming. Lord Edward Cecil,[3] a sour but vivid diarist, disliked and despised Slatin, but was struck by his hatred of the Khalifa and recorded him as saying, "I hope he (the Khalifa) will not have never a good moment – no never!" However, Cecil's opinion of most people, particularly foreigners, was low and his description of Slatin as "an ass but only a poor foreigner" is at least partially inaccurate. Foreigner he may have been but ass he was not!

During his years as one of Abdullahi's *mulazamin* his efforts to escape were not overstrenuous, doubtless to the frustration of Wingate and his other well-wishers. It is true he was closely watched but while it would be foolish to suggest that he was contented with his lot, clearly it was far from intolerable and improved rather than deteriorated as time passed. Although his hours of duty were long and required constant and doubtless extremely boring attendance at the mosque, they were seldom arduous, once his novitiate days of running beside the Khalifa's horse were over. He was provided with money, housing, food, servants and women and, above all, he was "in the know". In almost every way he was incomparably better off than the other Europeans from whom he seems to have distanced himself and who, so far as we can tell, did not place much trust in him.

The incentives to make the long, hard and dangerous journey to Egypt were not great but in 1895 he took the shrewd calculated risk which laid the foundations of his future career.

Slatin's fellow provincial governor, the young English sailor Frank Lupton,

---

[3] One of Kitchener's ADCs and a son of the Prime Minister, Lord Salisbury.

who surrendered in Bahr el Ghazal Province and was eventually brought to Omdurman, sadly lacked the Austrian's cunning and adaptability. Although Slatin found him work in the steamer repair yards and later Ohrwalder suggested a soap-making partnership, Lupton fretted at his confinement in the Khalifa's squalid capital and pined for the open sea. Prematurely aged and white-haired he weakened steadily and died in 1887.

Guiseppe Cuzzi, the former British Consular Agent at Berber, who had attempted to negotiate with Gordon, survived by one means or another in Omdurman throughout the Mahdiya. Despite being described by Rossignoli in 1894 as old and decrepit while still in his early fifties, he lived on for another twenty-five years.

Of the civilian residents we catch few glimpses and it would be intriguing to know more about their lives. The majority, and there were not more than a few dozen in all, were Greeks, some of whom may have had no particular desire to leave. Without money or knowledge of another country, for those who had been born and brought up in the Sudan there was little to choose between going and staying and it was much easier to stay. Indeed it may be inaccurate to describe these people as prisoners at all, except in the sense that everyone is a prisoner in a place which is difficult to get out of. Khartoum and Omdurman were then, and are today, surrounded by thousands of square miles of nothing and more than one twentieth century expatriate has been heard to describe the place as an "open prison". It should be borne in mind that even had the authorities been co-operative the difficulties of travel in the Sudan at that time were immense and even today they are considerable.

Prominent among these civilians was one George Stambouli, or Istambouliya, a leading Christian Syrian merchant of El Obeid who had embraced Islam and was appointed emir of the European prisoners in the early days of the Mahdiya. He seems to have been a generous and benevolent man and was largely responsible for the survival of the missionaries. At first he was allowed to keep his wealth but the Mahdists were as greedy and jealous of the possessions of others as most human beings and eventually it was all confiscated. We last hear of him working in the Khalifa's mint. We know nothing of his subsequent history but it is to be hoped that fate dealt kindly with this decent man.

A few others appear in the footnotes of history. An Italian bricklayer, Pietro Agati, built the Khalifa's house (which stands to this day) and never left the Sudan. From Rossignoli we hear of the widow and children of Franz Klein, a Hungarian tailor murdered in the sack of Khartoum, surviving in Omdurman in 1894.

Some bold (and foolish) spirits entered the Sudan during the Mahdiya. Of these the weirdest was the Frenchman, Olivier Pain. Describing himself as a journalist he appeared at the Mahdi's camp near El Obeid in 1884 with an imaginary offer of submission from the French Government. The Mahdi and his advisers were understandably suspicious and rejected his fictitious overtures. Soon he became ill and, as the great Mahdist host was on the move, fell off his camel unconscious and may have suffered the unspeakably horrible fate of being buried alive.

A tragi-comic figure, remembered by Ohrwalder and Neufeld, was a Bohemian known as Joseppi[4] who in 1889 wandered drunk out of Wadi Halfa where he was employed in a Greek bakery. His declared intention was to reach Suakin, hundreds of miles away across an almost waterless desert, equipped only with a violin, but he was soon picked up by a dervish patrol and taken to Omdurman. There he received the usual cordial welcome afforded to strangers and was flung into prison for two years, barely surviving this ordeal. Eventually released, he wandered off again and disappeared. However, in due course, word reached Omdurman that this pathetic tramp had died of starvation at Rufaa on the Blue Nile.

In complete contrast to most of the others was Carl Neufeld, a German merchant based at Assouan, who entered the Sudan on a combined trading and espionage mission in 1887. He had close connections with the British, having served as an interpreter with the River Column in 1884/5 and taught Arabic to a number of British officers. Betrayed by a double agent acting as a guide, he was seized and taken to Omdurman where, stubbornly refusing to foreswear his Christian faith, he was in and out of the dreaded Saier and Um Hagar,[5] frequently flogged and almost continuously in chains until his release after the Battle of Omdurman in 1898. The Sudanese did not know what to make of Neufeld. Above all they admired courage and fortitude and the tough German possessed more than his share of both but his religious defiance had to be punished. Nor would he tell them what they wanted to hear, often mocking their army and most other aspects of the Khalifa's rule. That he survived is nothing short of a miracle – perhaps it was one, a reward for his faith, although one is inclined to think that his resistance was due more to bloody-mindedness than religious fervour. It is more likely that sheer guts, an iron constitution and the devotion of his slave-girl Hasseena pulled him through. Surprisingly, he bore less resentment against the Khalifa than did Slatin, who had been treated very much better, and on his release told the reporter Bennett Burleigh that Abdullahi was not really a bad fellow! On his return to Egypt his reception was mixed. He had not wanted to escape, it was said. He was happy with his native wives and concubines. He had made the gunpowder which had killed British and Egyptian soldiers. In

[4] In his novel *The Four Feathers* A. E. W. Mason based the character assumed by Harry Feversham for his journey into the Sudan on Joseppi.
[5] The "Saier" was the Omdurman gaol (named after the head gaoler) and the "Um Hagar" (Mother of Stone) the dungeon within that gaol – a sort of Sudanese Black Hole of Calcutta.

other words, he was a fraud. There does not seem to have been much substance to these accusations. It was true that Abdullah Mohamed Omar had brought Rossignoli out instead of Neufeld but this was due to the latter being loaded with chains, making movement much more difficult and greatly increasing the chances of recapture. He may have tried to make some gunpowder but he had little or no scientific knowledge and the results were probably of no value to the Khalifa's war machine. A Greek who had attempted the same thing had been blown sky-high.

On the whole Neufeld, who may have lacked charm, was shabbily treated by the press and the German authorities but he wrote a moderately successful book *A Prisoner of the Khaleefa*, continued his life of merchant adventuring and is thought to have died in about 1918.

How should we sum up the Khalifa's attitude towards his European "guests"? Slatin apart, he did not show them any particular favour, nor, generally speaking, did he treat them especially badly. He regarded them with suspicion but then so he did nearly everyone else. The probability is that he was indifferent to their presence most of the time but could see no advantage in letting them go. There was always the possibility that he might be able to make use of them in some way in the future.

Remove Slatin, and perhaps Ohrwalder, from the picture and the Europeans in Omdurman during the Mahdiya lose all historical significance but remain of great human interest.

# 15 On the Frontier

The last British troops were withdrawn from Dongola to Wadi Halfa in mid-June 1885; the Gordon Relief Expedition was dismantled and replaced by the Frontier Field Force made up of both British and Egyptian troops under command of General Grenfell who had replaced Wood as Sirdar in March of that year. An early attempt to invade Egypt by the Mahdists under Wad Nejumi was expected but there was quarrelling between him and Mohamed el Kheir, the Mahdi's Governor of Dongola Province, and dismay at the premature demise of the Mahdi himself on 22 June.

Under Grenfell the first of a series of field commanders on the Frontier was Wolseley's faithful henchman, Brigadier-General William Butler, who had skilfully commanded the rearguard of the retreat from Dongola. Butler's most southerly outpost was a fort at Kosheh about one hundred miles from Wadi Halfa and several more such posts were dotted between the two along the railway line which ran from Wadi Halfa to Akasha. These were subjected to frequent but small-scale attacks and bombardments by the dervishes whose objective was the destruction of the line. On one such occasion at Ambigol Wells, Lieutenant Annesley of the West Kents noticed that the crops of the sandgrouse, which he flighted regularly at dawn, were empty. From this, Butler records, Annesley deduced that some unusual disturbance in a normally uninhabited area of desert had disrupted the birds' feeding habits. This warning enabled him to prepare for and repel a dervish attack.

During this period the first British decoration for gallantry was awarded to an Egyptian officer when Bimbashi Hassan Radwan[1] of the Artillery received the

---

[1] Ironically, this officer had fought against the British in Arabi's rebellion and had been taken prisoner at the battle of Tel-el-Kebir!

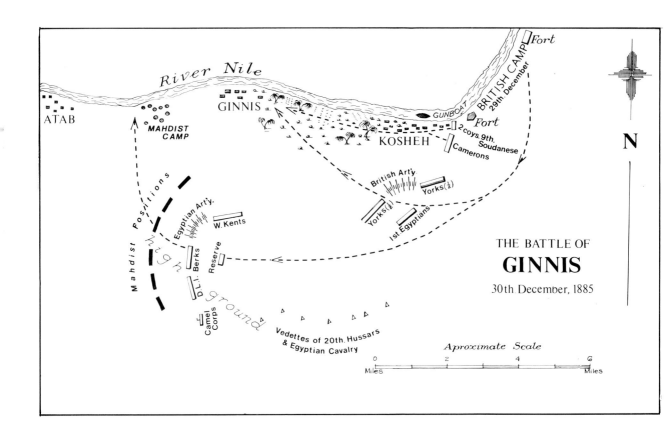

The Battle of
**GINNIS**
30th December, 1885

DSO for his part in the defence of Kosheh fort where he was severely wounded. Later, a Sudanese officer of the Camel Corps, with the confusingly similar name of Mulazim (Lieutenant) Said Radwan, received the same decoration for a series of exploits including a spectacular hand-to-hand sword fight with a group of dervishes. Butler, who happened to witness this contest, was struck by its medieval flavour as the Mahdists hacked and slashed at their fellow-countrymen with their double-handed, double-edged Crusader swords. Radwan was wounded in several places and fell, but this gave the men with Butler a clear field of fire and they were able to pick off his opponents before Radwan could be cut to pieces.

A native of Kordofan, probably a Baggari, Said Radwan had a sad and rather mysterious end. Suffering from advanced tuberculosis he set out from Cairo to Tripoli in 1892 and was never seen again. An enigmatic letter from Kitchener to Baring baldly states that Radwan "was struck off the strength of the Egyptian Army" in that year.

Much of the fighting on the Frontier at this time was of a hand-to-hand nature, one patrol of the Cameron Highlanders killing fourteen dervishes with the bayonet, losing one officer (a Lieutenant Cameron) and one soldier killed, as well

Generals Stephenson and Grenfell observing the progress of the Battle of Ginnis. The Pyramid in the background seems to have been known locally as El Zubr El Kelb, the Dog's Penis!

as two officers severely wounded in the process, including Bimbashi Archibald Hunter[2] of the 9th Soudanese of whom we shall be hearing a good deal more. Hunter, an expert in this type of semi-irregular warfare, asked for and gave no quarter. A crack rifle shot, he had been a musketry instructor at Hythe. Later, even as a senior commander, he was reputed to have picked off six dervishes with his Winchester rifle and was inclined to turn a blind eye to the post-battle activities of his Soudanese.

During the last week of December, 1885, preparations were made for an attack on a dervish concentration in and around the village of Ginnis and at dawn on 30 December two brigades of infantry under General Stephenson,[3] with supporting

[2] General Sir Archibald Hunter GCB DSO, King's Own Royal Lancaster Regiment. (1856–1936).
[3] General Sir Frederick Stephenson GCB, Scots Guards (1821–1911), who was in command of the British Army of Occupation in Egypt at the time.

troops, marched from Kosheh fort to take the high ground overlooking Ginnis from the south. This assault was spearheaded by Butler's brigade consisting of the Berkshires (of McNeil's zariba fame), the West Kents and the Durham Light Infantry, with elements of Egyptian artillery and Camel Corps and a detachment of the 3rd Egyptian Infantry battalion. Brigadier-General Huyshe's brigade (Yorkshires, Camerons and Egyptians) was in support. The forward troops were sharply engaged on a ridge and the Camel Corps on the left (the scene of Said Radwan's sword-play) were particularly hard-pressed but disciplined rifle fire and effective gunnery soon forced the dervishes from the ridge and enabled Ginnis to be occupied. For once, the cavalry, 20th Hussars and Egyptians, erred on the side of caution and for reasons known only to their commander, Colonel Blake, failed to pursue the retreating Mahdists. Only Wodehouse and his Egyptian gunners dashed forward, but, as has been recounted earlier, their main preoccupation was to seize the Mahdist standards as souvenirs.

However, Private Ferguson of the 20th assured his parents at home, there had been a vigorous pursuit, whatever they may have heard to the contrary. Anyway, the Hussars must have taken at least one prisoner as Ferguson's troop adopted a child, presumably orphaned in the battle, and took him back to Cairo as a mascot. Later, perhaps irritated at being dressed up as a jockey by the cavalrymen, this enterprising youngster transferred to the infantry and went to India with the Durhams!

Meanwhile six companies of Camerons and two of 9th Soudanese, covered by the gunboat *Lotus*, had been allotted the task of clearing the village of Kosheh and the cultivated land and palm groves along the river bank to the east of Ginnis. In the course of this operation they were reinforced by Bimbashi Haggard's 1st Egyptians who became involved in one of the infrequent instances of house-to-house fighting in the Sudan. Some dervishes holding out in a row of connecting mud houses had defied the efforts of a company of Camerons to dislodge them. To Haggard's obvious pride, his Egyptians were ordered to try where the Highlanders had failed. The fighting in and around these houses lasted for several hours and over seventy of the stubborn defenders were killed, several by Ombashi (Corporal) Mohamed Daoud whose bayonet work was commended by Haggard. However, an Egyptian officer and several men were killed and Haggard himself narrowly escaped death when a timely shout from his orderly room clerk, Private Warburton, seconded from the Durhams, saved him from a sniper's bullet. When darkness fell some Mahdists were still hanging on grimly and it was not until next morning that the Camerons, noses rather out of joint and aided by an artillery pounding, managed to finish the job.

In the battle as a whole Anglo-Egyptian losses had been slight with only one British officer, Lieutenant Soltau of the Berkshires, losing his life. In the 1880s it was not considered good form for officers to take cover under fire and Soltau was shot through the head while standing behind his men as they lay firing over the top of the ridge above Ginnis. Butler remembered Soltau's spaniel being lifted from the edge of his master's grave as though dead itself – "a sight to make strong men turn aside".

It is no surprise to find Stuart-Wortley ("Wortles" to his friend Haggard) at this battle sitting on his horse drawing on his white kid gloves and discussing the prospects of a "good bag". Wortles, it seems, had returned recently to Cairo from Constantinople where he had been attached to Sir Henry Drummond Wolff's special mission to the Grande Porte and had decided to slip away to the frontier for a little relaxation from his arduous diplomatic duties.

In historical terms, the Battle of Ginnis, although fought by the Frontier Field Force, may be regarded as the last action in the Gordon Relief campaign. It is an extraordinary but incontrovertible fact that the British had won every battle and yet lost the war. The outposts between Wadi Halfa and Akasha were judged to be untenable and by the early summer of 1886 all troops had been withdrawn to Wadi Halfa.

The main purpose of the Drummond Wolff mission to Turkey, referred to above, had been to legitimize the British occupation of Egypt but at the same time the opportunity was taken to discuss the Sudan and vague ideas of a negotiated settlement with the Khalifa were mooted. To this end two Turkish officers, El Lewa (Major-General) Shudi Pasha, a brigade commander in the Egyptian Army, and Mukhtar Pasha, the Turkish Commissioner in Egypt, were sent to Wadi Halfa to await any peace overtures which might be forthcoming from Omdurman. They waited in vain.

Meanwhile the remaining British troops on the Frontier were suffering unacceptable losses from heat and disease. It was only as a result of Butler's urgent representations to Cairo and London that they were withdrawn from the inferno of Wadi Halfa to Assouan. On 25 April, 1886, Butler had recorded a temperature of 122°F in the mens' tents and twenty-two soldiers had died in a fortnight. At Assouan it was little better, eleven officers and men dying in one day, 13 June. During this summer a youthful battalion of the Dorsets, recently arrived at Assouan, earned the cruel sobriquet of "the Dying Dorsets" by losing approximately one third of its entire strength without seeing a shot fired in anger. It was not only these unacclimitized youngsters who died miserably on this dreary garrison duty. "Baby" Martin, the grumpy giant who had missed the Hicks expedition through illness, and Brigadier-General Huyshe, also fell victims to this devastating heat. Morale had slumped to zero, and the presence of the troops was pointless as they would have been incapable of fighting. Butler's own health collapsed and as his increasingly strident demands for the complete withdrawal of British troops had not enhanced his popularity with the War Office, he was relieved of his command in July, 1886, and given a spell on half-pay. But his persistence was to save many lives as all but a handful of British troops were withdrawn to Lower Egypt before the following summer. In due course Butler's outstanding services on the Nile were rewarded with a K.C.B.

Thereafter responsibility for frontier security rested solely with the Egyptian Army and for two and a half years following the action at Ginnis military activity in the area was restricted to raids by small groups of dervishes and punitive counterraids by fighting patrols of the Egyptian Army. The bulk of the Khalifa's forces was committed elsewhere and the Anglo-Egyptian authorities were preoccupied, for the time being, with financial rather than military matters.

# 16 The Spy-Master

During the Gordon Relief campaign the Egyptian Army, such as it was at that time, had played a largely administrative role on the lines of communication, but its Sirdar, Sir Evelyn Wood, accompanied by his ADC, Reginald Wingate, had commanded the final stages of the withdrawal to Korti of the Desert Column. That task completed, disillusioned and ill, Wood resigned the Sirdarship and left for England, followed by Wingate, who met and fell in love with Kitty Rundle, the sister of one of his brother officers in the Egyptian Army. He proposed and was accepted but life at home was expensive and a subaltern's pay a pittance. Neither Wingate, youngest of the eleven children of respectable but impoverished Lowland Scots parents, nor his fiancée, had private means. There was nothing for it but to return to Egypt where the pay was good, advancement rapid and the new Sirdar, Sir Francis Grenfell, willing to re-employ this ambitious and energetic young officer. Marriage, discouraged for British officers of the Egyptian Army, would have to wait a while.[1]

His first appointment after his return to Cairo in 1886 was as Assistant and Military Secretary to Grenfell, but by early 1887 he had progressed to the dual role of Assistant Adjutant-General for Recruiting and Intelligence. Soon the latter was to take preference over the former and in 1889 he was appointed Director of Intelligence.

One of his earlier duties in 1887 was to receive four Baggara delegates bearing letters from the Khalifa. These were addressed to Queen Victoria, the Sultan of Turkey and the Khedive, but, far from setting out his negotiating position, long awaited by the two Turks at Wadi Halfa, the letters imperiously demanded that

---

[1] They were married in 1888.

The "Founding Fathers" of the Anglo-Egyptian Sudan. Wingate and Slatin (in cart) at Balmoral in 1910.

the Sultan and the Khedive return to the true ways of Islam and that the Queen be converted to it. The penalties for non-compliance were, needless to say, death and destruction. It is interesting, if vain, to speculate on the Khalifa's motives for sending these absurd documents. He was not a stupid man and there is no evidence that he possessed a sense of humour, so we cannot assume either that he expected the recipients to obey his instructions or that he wrote with his tongue in his cheek. Perhaps Slatin inveigled him into writing them in order to make him appear ridiculous to the civilized world. Perhaps the Khalifa himself felt that if the letters were answered, even with outright rejection, any reply would raise him to a level of equality with these legitimate heads of state. Whatever he and his advisors had in mind the letters were ignored and their bearers allowed to return to Omdurman. However, a reply of a sort was made when Colonel Chermside, commanding on the Frontier, attacked a dervish force at Sarras, 35 miles south of Wadi Halfa. On 28 April, a few days after the letters had been received in Cairo, Chermside's patrol-in-strength, which included some of Gordon's bashi-bazooks who had come down in the steamers with Khasm el Mus two years before, defeated and killed the Mahdist Emir Nur el Kanzi. At one stage the Egyptian infantry were subjected to a wild dervish charge which a few years before would have routed them utterly, but now, properly trained and led, they withdrew

Na'um Bey Shuqair one of
Wingate's most valued
assistants.

steadily, contesting every yard of ground until reinforced by the 9th Soudanese
who advanced and drove the enemy into the river, killing most of them. It was at
this point that Nur el Kanzi was killed in hand-to-hand combat with Sergeant
Thomas Healey, a Cameron Highlander attached to the 9th Soudanese, an
exploit for which Healey was awarded the second of his three Distinguished
Conduct Medals.

Wingate soon gathered round him a small staff of skilful intelligence analysers
and interrogators. His right-hand man was a Syrian Christian, Milhem Bey
Shakoor, who played an important role in negotiations with would-be and actual
rescuers of the Omdurman prisoners. But perhaps the most able of "Wingate's
People" was another Syrian, Na'um Bey Shuqair,[2] a professional intelligence

[2] Both Shuqair and Shakoor came from the Lebanon which was then part of Syria. In 1905 Shuqair
wrote *El Tarikh el Sudan*, a history of the Sudan in Arabic.

officer who remained in the British service throughout the First World War and until his death in 1922.

Wingate and his assistants quickly built up a network of spies throughout the Sudan. These were designated and referred to with rather engaging naïvety as Secret Agents Numbers One, Two, Three etc. To our generation, steeped in the incomprehensible convolutions of modern spy fiction, this may indicate a lamentable ignorance of "trade craft", a feeling reinforced by the information that Secret Agent No. One, a certain Abdullah Ali, was "blown" and arrested in Omdurman. Grisly must have been his fate.

For all that, a vast wealth of information was fed back to Wingate's office in Cairo, much of it worthless (that the late Mahdi's harem had included thirty Egyptians, thirty Jaalin and forty-five Abyssinians and negresses); some misleading (that the great Senussi of Libya might be in a position to overthrow the Khalifa, which was not at all the case); but much was worthwhile material such as who was in and who was out of the Khalifa's favour; the strength of the Omdurman garrison and the dispositions of the provincial forces; the relative shortage or availability of durra, its price etc., all of which enabled Wingate to keep tabs on developments, political, social, military and economic, throughout the Sudan.

The goodwill of certain northern tribes, such as the Ababdeh, Bisharin and Kabbabish, whose trading activities with Egypt had been seriously disrupted by the Sudan's UDI, was assiduously cultivated by Wingate and the Anglo-Egyptian command on the frontier. Most spies and agents were well-paid and trusted members of these tribes whose trading ventures into the Sudan, cover for their intelligence gathering and prisoner-rescuing tasks, were subsidized by the Intelligence Department. Sometimes quite elaborate contracts were drawn up by Wingate or one of his Syrians with these men, guaranteed by independent merchants in Cairo or Alexandria, as Arabs put not their trust in government departments. The name of one such guarantor, Girgis Brahimsha, defies ethnic analysis unless there is such a being as an Indian Copt.

It has been suggested that Wingate's tentacles extended also into Khedivial and ministerial circles in Egypt itself. For obvious reasons there is no extant evidence for this but it would be strange were it otherwise. Baring needed to be abreast of the Byzantine intrigues of Egyptian domestic politics so that he knew which string to pull and when and where to crack the whip.

Sometimes the interests of Wingate's department extended beyond the borders of both Egypt and the Sudan. He was able to make use of the old slaver Zubeir Pasha's erstwhile lieutenant, Rabeh, who was challenging the authority of the French in the Chad region. Rabeh was really just a brigand but he had ambitions and on the principle that one's enemy's enemy is one's friend, Wingate considered him worthy of support. Precisely what he was able to do for him over such vast distances is obscure but there is no doubt that Rabeh was regarded by the French as an instrument of British policy in the region. However, it is more likely that Wingate hoped to steer Rabeh in the direction of Darfur, an old stamping ground of his former master, thus to harass the Khalifa in the far west of his domain. Eventually Rabeh was killed by the French near Kouori in Chad in 1900.

Usually Wingate was bogged down with paper work in Cairo – his nickname among the Egyptians was Abu Hibr, Father of the Ink – but on occasion he would travel to the frontier or to Suakin for an event of particular importance. Such was the case in the summer of 1889 when reports indicated a northerly movement of a Mahdist force under the famous Emir Abdel Rahman Wad el Nejumi, who had led the final assault upon Hicks's army and had breached Gordon's defences at Khartoum.

Nejumi's advance is interesting from more than one aspect. Firstly, it was the only ostensibly serious attempt by the Khalifa to invade the land of Egypt. It has been suggested, probably with justification, that it was simply an excuse for the Khalifa to dispose of the revered and popular Nejumi, a Jaali, and therefore a potential enemy of the Baggara and rival to the Khalifa himself. Be that as it may, and there is no evidence that Nejumi had any such ambitions, this disastrous expedition turned out to be the Mahdist equivalent of the Hicks debacle. Nejumi's tatterdemalion army, a mixture of many tribes and by no means all volunteers, linked up with that of his second-in-command, Abdel Halim, at Sarras at the end of June, 1889. Numbering some 13,000 souls, including many women and children, short of transport and supplies of every kind, kept away from the river by gunboats and an Egyptian "flying column" under the experienced Wodehouse, Nejumi tramped through the desert to the west of the Nile, by-passing Wadi Halfa and hoping to strike the river again at Bimban, about twenty-five miles south of Assouan, losing men and animals by death and desertion every day. Desperate for water, part of his army attacked the village of Argin just north of Wadi Halfa and was repulsed with heavy losses by Wodehouse. Although urged by Abdel Halim, who had been wounded at Argin, to abandon, or at least postpone, the invasion, Nejumi pressed on and after frequent skirmishes with Egyptian patrols was finally brought to battle at Toski,[3] about sixty miles north of Wadi Halfa. Here Nejumi was killed and his army, by then no more than about three thousand strong, destroyed by the Egyptian Army virtually unaided by British troops.[4]

The most interesting aspect of Nejumi's campaign, however, is the tremendous propaganda build-up both it and its leader were given by Wingate, who turned it

---

[3] Arabic scholars prefer Tushki. The village and battlefield are now deep beneath the waters of Lake Nasser.
[4] One squadron of 20th Hussars took part and one British trooper, Private Washbrook, was killed and five others wounded.

into a "media event". Astonishingly, Wingate, although Director of the Egyptian Army Intelligence Department, arranged for himself to be appointed Reuter's special correspondent in Upper Egypt, for which service, incidentally, he received an honorarium of sixty guineas. Today such a conflict of interest would be unthinkable and General Dormer, commanding British troops in Egypt, was disapproving, but Wingate's chief, the Sirdar Sir Francis Grenfell was more indulgent. David Rees, Reuter's man in Cairo, had smoothed Wingate's path by arranging to send Grenfell, a keen fight-fan, the full *New York Times* account of the Kilrain-Sullivan heavyweight championship contest. More seriously, Grenfell realised that Wingate's motives for placing himself in this invidious position were political rather than financial. The intention was to ensure that this pathetic exhibition of military incompetence and foolhardiness on the part of Nejumi and his master the Khalifa was presented to the world as a genuine threat by a barbaric power to overwhelm a nation struggling towards modern civilization under British tutelege. The main thrust of his ploy was aimed at British public opinion and to this end he arranged for Grenfell (who took personal command at Toski) to write a special report on the battle for *The Times* under his own name while he, Wingate, prepared a hand-written memorandum for the Queen in which Nejumi is depicted as a kind of hybrid of Salah el Din and Alexander the Great![5]

To an extent Nejumi's threat to Egypt had been taken seriously by the British authorities who had reinforced the Army of Occupation with a number of battalions from various Mediterranean garrisons, but they were not used and merely served as an insurance against the eventuality, never entirely absent from the minds of their British officers, that the fellahin conscripts, given the right (or wrong) circumstances, might just cut and run. There was also the faint possibility that the Mahdist expectation of a popular rising in Egypt in support of the invasion might be something more than wishful thinking. But a mountain had been deliberately made ouf of a molehill in order to convince all concerned that the Khalifa's Sudan was a danger to Egypt, to British prestige and ultimately to the British Empire.

Before moving on to a description of the Battle of Toski itself, let us catch a last glimpse of a relic of happier days for the Mahdist cause. "Old John Colborne", wrote Reuter's man David Rees to Wingate, "has turned up (in Cairo) looking like a second rate Jupiter in reduced circumstances . . . much cleaner than of yore . . . with a clean stick-up collar and a new blue and white tie." The game old hack was trying to get up-river in time for the battle but does not seem to have made it. Within a year he was dead and thus within seven years of the ill-fated Kordofan expedition of all Hicks' European staff only De Coetlogen was still alive.

The battle which Colborne missed was fought in the hottest season of one of the

[5] Appendix G.

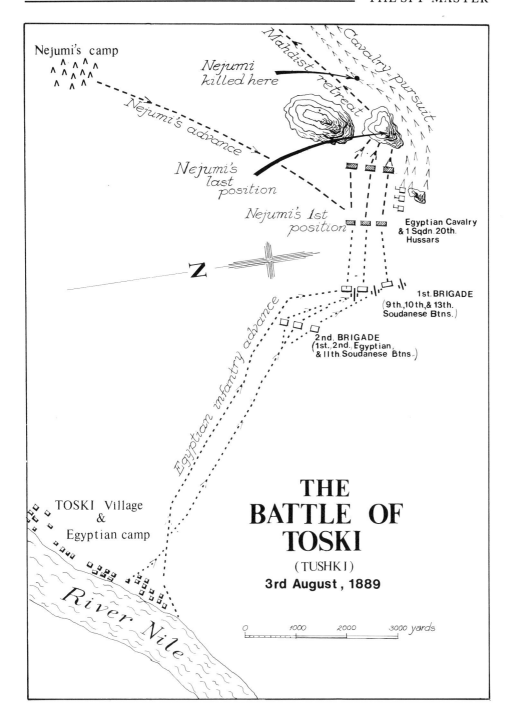

Nejumi's camp

Cavalry Pursuit

Mahdist retreat

*Nejumi killed here*

*Nejumi's advance*

*Nejumi's last position*

*Nejumi's 1st position*

Egyptian Cavalry
& 1 Sqdn. 20th.
Hussars

Z

*Egyptian infantry advance*

1st. BRIGADE
(9 th., 10 th., & 13th.
Soudanese Btns.)

2nd. BRIGADE
(1st., 2nd., Egyptian
& 11th. Soudanese Btns.)

TOSKI Village
&
Egyptian camp

**THE
BATTLE OF
TOSKI**
(TUSHKI)
**3rd August, 1889**

*River Nile*

0    1000    2000    3000 *yards*

hottest places in the world. Nevertheless the terrain suited Grenfell who could manoeuvre his cavalry and artillery over the hard, smooth sand, charging and pounding the dervishes at will. At dawn on 3 August, 1889, a mounted reconnaisance in strength under Colonel Herbert Kitchener (one squadron 20th Hussars, three squadrons Egyptian cavalry and one company Camel Corps) observed the enemy breaking camp a few miles to the west of the village of Toski where the bulk of the Egyptian forces was bivouacked. By this time Nejumi's army had dwindled to about three thousand fighting men, outnumbered by the Egyptians with six battalions of infantry, plus the cavalry and Camel Corps and several batteries of artillery. It was clear to Grenfell that Nejumi wished to avoid battle in the open desert, where he knew that superior Egyptian fire-power could be brought to bear with devastating results, and was heading for rocky, broken ground further to the north. Determined to prevent this and risking the absence of the British Brigade (2nd KOSB, 1st Welsh and 2nd Royal Irish Rifles plus an artillery battery and some Mounted Infantry) which was on its way from Assouan, Grenfell ordered Kitchener to head Nejumi off and at the same time sent to Toski for the infantry and gunners. These troops, under Wodehouse with Hunter as second-in-command, reached the battlefield at about 10 am and took up positions in the path of the enemy's advance which had been checked by Kitchener. Nejumi could either retreat into the desert and away from the desperately needed Nile water or attack. True to his character and creed he chose the latter course and his ansar hurled themselves with magnificent but futile courage at the Egyptian and Soudanese battalions.

No machine-guns appear to have been used in this battle but the Egyptian Army had been re-equipped late in 1885 (at about the time of the Battle of Ginnis) with the Martini-Henry .450 replacing the old Remington with which the Khalifa's *jehadiya* were armed, and these they used with steady discipline and good effect. Also it was ideal artillery country and the quick-firing Maxim-Nordenfeldts and heavier Krupp cannon tore great gaps in the Mahdist ranks. At about noon the Sirdar decided to go on to the offensive and ordered Wodehouse to advance. In an assault on a strongly defended hillock, the 1st Egyptians and 13th Soudanese suffered most of the Egyptian Army's casualties. Hunter, to be found as usual in the thick of the fight, was wounded by a spear thrust in the arm, and elsewhere on the battlefield Lieutenant Cotton of the 11th Soudanese was shot through the chest and severely wounded. Driven from this hillock, its defenders made repeated counterattacks until virtually their last man had been shot or bayonetted. Now all over the battlefield the ansar were in full-scale retreat, pursued by the cavalry, but the ceasefire was sounded at about 2pm, as the horses and their riders were near to collapse through heat and thirst.

Nejumi himself had been wounded more than once in the battle and his bodyguard tried to remove him from the field on a camel. However, they were

Desert in the Toski area of upper Egypt now flooded by Lake Nasser.

attacked by a troop of Egyptian cavalry and all but one died defending their master. The dead bodies of Nejumi and his five-year-old son were found among those of his brave housecarls.

Wingate's tribute to this tragic hero in the form of a Memorandum to Queen Victoria (see Appendix G), although written with a political objective, reflects a genuine admiration for the man in stark contrast to the almost universal dislike and contempt felt in Anglo-Egyptian circles for the Khalifa. Even the prosaic Baring was moved to make romantic comparisons. Many years later he wrote, "(Nejumi) was at once the Peter the Hermit of the Mahdist crusaders and the Prince Rupert of the dervish cavalry," and then, allowing his imagination to develop this theme, goes on to find in this "savage warrior" characteristics in common with a Homeric hero or "a Beowulf of Anglo-Saxon times". Fortunately we have Private Ferguson, whose squadron was the only British unit to take part in the Battle of Toski, to balance these effusive outpourings. Nejumi, he wrote home, had murdered Gordon with his own hand while the Christian Hero was at prayer. However, Ferguson, now in his fifth year of service in Egypt and the Sudan, conceded that Nejumi was a good enough soldier and had defeated King John of Abyssinia![6]

There is a happy footnote to the Nejumi saga. On the day following the battle a year-old baby boy, the great man's youngest son, was brought into the Egyptian camp. This infant was raised by the British nurses at Kasr el Aini Hospital in Cairo and in due course became a member of the entourage of the Egyptian Royal Family.

[6] Nejumi was not involved in the Abyssinian campaign, nor, so far as we know, was he involved directly in the death of Gordon.

Wingate, in his book *Mahdism and the Egyptian Sudan*, is at pains to explain the arrangements for the re-settlement in Upper Egypt of the many less exalted prisoners and deserters, mostly camp followers. Only the emirs and *muqqadams* were removed to Cairo for imprisonment and interrogation (conducted by Milhem Shakoor) and only one prisoner, the Omdah (headman) of a village who was considered to have behaved treacherously, was executed. One learns this with relief as among Wingate's papers at Durham University the researcher may come upon the pencil scribbled draft of a telegram or memorandum reading thus, "As regards prisoners I cannot authorize what you propose but if they become an actual danger you must take any steps you think necessary but I should deeply regret your proposal being carried out." There is no indication by whom it was written or to whom it was sent.

Another area which from time to time required Wingate's on-the-spot attention was Suakin. This Egyptian enclave on the Red Sea coast had been under intermittent siege since 1883. Garrisoned by Egyptian and Soudanese troops, usually with a Royal Naval presence in the harbour or roads, the authorities there had reached a *modus vivendi* with many of the neighbouring tribes and some trade through the port continued virtually throughout the period of the Mahdiya. Occasionally Osman Digna would feel constrained to make his presence felt and with increasing difficulty would persuade or bully the Hadendowa and some other related Beja tribesmen to make a nuisance of themselves by attacking "friendlies", robbing caravans or even firing on government troops. On such occasions[7] Wingate would arrive at Suakin to mastermind an anti-Digna excursion. The most notable clashes took place in December, 1888 and February, 1891.

On the first of these Osman Digna determined to press home an attack on Suakin and brought reinforcements of Baggara and Jaalin from Omdurman for this purpose, giving him a strength of some four to five thousand combatants. In order to match this the Governor of Suakin, Colonel Holled-Smith, asked Cairo for reinforcements which he received in the shape of two British battalions, KOSB and Welsh, a squadron of 20th Hussars, two Soudanese and one Egyptian battalion. Additionally, two extra Royal Naval vessels were despatched from the Mediterranean to Suakin.

Desultory skirmishing around Suakin continued from September until mid-December when the Sirdar himself arrived to take charge of operations. Osman's main force had dug itself in at a place called Gemaizeh,[8] just outside the

---

[7] In one of the minor actions at a place called Handub on 17 January, 1888, Kitchener, commanding a force of policemen, "friendlies" and a few cavalry, received his only wound in action when he was shot in the face, putting him *hors de combat* for several weeks.

[8] This means wild fig tree in Arabic. A single *gemaizeh* stood among the Mahdist trenches.

Kitchener (seated) with a group of British officers of the Egyptian Army and an Egyptian cavalry trooper (second from the left). This photograph was taken after the Battle of Gemaizeh in 1888 at which, presumably the young officer on the left was wounded.

Suakin defences and on 20 December the Anglo-Egyptians attacked them there. Showing less than their usual gusto for a fight, the dervishes were dislodged from their trenches by artillery fire and the advancing infantry. A charge by the 20th Hussars completed the job and the once formidable Fuzzy-Wuzzys departed hastily, leaving some five hundred dead behind them, while the Anglo-Egyptian casualties amounted to about fifty of whom only six were killed.

The second and more decisive occasion came in February, 1891, when Baring, with Lord Salisbury's grudging permission, decided to reoccupy Tokar, district capital of a rich agricultural area naturally irrigated by the flood waters of the Baraka river and described by Baring as "the granary of the eastern Sudan". This would be the deepest incursion into the Mahdist state since Ginnis in 1885. The military had long urged that this step was necessary if the pressure on Suakin was

A group of Mahdist prisoners, taken at the Battle of Gemaizeh in 1888. In the centre is Osman Digna's nephew Musa who appears to have a black eye! The other prisoners are *Jehadiya*.

to be eased permanently by denying readily available food supplies to Osman Digna. Hitherto Salisbury had opposed the move as he feared the soldiers would get the bit between their teeth and he would find them leap-frogging deeper and deeper into the Sudan, involving the British Government once again in an adventure with an unpredictable outcome. However, a potentially embarrassing upsurge in the slave trade along the coastal strip controlled by Osman and confidence that Baring had enough grip on the military to prevent them going too far, persuaded the Prime Minister to allow the expedition to go ahead. Also the British public was diverted by home affairs and would hardly notice. "We are thinking of nothing but strikes and the later cantos of the epic of Kitty O'Shea," wrote Salisbury to Baring, but drew the British Agent's attention to the point that "if they (the soldiers) were allowed full scope, they would insist on the importance

Ansar prisoners held at Wadi Halfa.

of garrisoning the moon in order to protect us from Mars." Perhaps he was premature rather than fanciful!

In any case the expedition was highly successful and the ruins of Tokar, long abandoned by the Mahdists, easily reoccupied. The troops employed were two battalions of Soudanese and one of Egyptians with four guns and two troops of cavalry, commanded by Colonel Holled-Smith. No British troops, apart from the British officers and NCOs of the Egyptian Army, were involved, but naval support was provided by HMS *Dolphin* which assisted in the shipment of the force to the small port of Trinkitat. A sharp fight took place at the village of Afafit near Tokar and one of Holled-Smith's staff officers, Captain Barrow, was killed. The most spectacular individual exploit was the rescue of a wounded Egyptian officer by Captain J. R. Beech, commander of the cavalry. Seeing the Egyptian attacked by three dervishes Beech galloped forward and killed two of them with his sword. The third fled but was cut down by other cavalrymen. By a strange coincidence Beech's own life had been saved under similar circumstances by an Egyptian trooper two years before. This officer had an unusual career. Originally a vet, he was commissioned in the 21st Hussars (later Lancers) and in 1887 accompanied an official of the British Legation in Cairo, Gerald Portal,[9] on a mission to King Yohannes of Abyssina in the course of which he risked his life to deliver letters from Queen Victoria to the king and was awarded the CMG. Later he won the DSO at Toski but his eventual demise was unspectacular. In 1908 he caught cold at a Yeomanry camp in Lincolnshire and died of pneumonia.

The reoccupation of Tokar and the outcome of the fighting at Afafit were decisive. Osman's prestige in the area, shaky for many years and kept alive by fear rather than conviction, finally collapsed and "Egyptian" government was reinstated throughout the Tokar district. Despite the ease with which this had been achieved, another five years were to elapse before the British Government would authorize any further significant occupation of the Khalifa's territory.

[9] Portal has left an interesting account of this journey, *Mission to Abyssinia*.

# 17 A Three-Cornered Contest

Italy had joined the scramble for Africa rather late in the day and Abyssinia was one of the few remaining areas of the continent to which the other European powers had not yet laid claim.

Before the Mahdiya, a part of northern Abyssinia, then known as Bogos and now as Eritrea, was under Egyptian occupation and contained a number of Egyptian garrisons, the most important of these being at Senheit (Keren). The port of Massawa had been Turkish for centuries and was leased to Egypt by the Sultan.

With the collapse of Khedivial authority in the Sudan these garrisons became untenable and, as we have seen, in 1884 the Hewett mission arranged for King Yohannes[1] of Tigre to assist in the evacuation of the Egyptian troops and their families to Massawa. In return Bogos would be ceded to him, together with large quantities of rifles and ammunition. Remarkably the agreement was honoured and the majority of the evacuees reached Massawa and eventually Egypt, thanks to the skilful handling of the local "authorities" by an exceptionally resolute and resourceful Egyptian officer, El Bimbashi Saad Rifaat. At about the same time, under British supervision, the town and province of Harar was handed over to the son of the local ruler who had been originally dispossessed by the Egyptians. Having withdrawn from the interior, the Egyptians had no further use for Massawa and the British arranged for it to be handed over to their Italian allies, a first step towards the Italian colonization of Eritrea and eventually their short-lived conquest of the whole of Ethiopia in 1936/7.

The Mahdi and, after his death, the Khalifa regarded these manoeuvres with

---

[1] Often referred to as John.

annoyance and alarm. At first they knew little about Italian ambitions in Abyssinia and, for the reasons described in a previous chapter, concentrated their military attentions upon the Abyssinians themselves. In the bloody history of a bloody continent there have been few bloodier conflicts than the intermittent warfare between the Khalifa of the Sudan and King Yohannes of Tigre. Between 1885 and 1889 hundreds of thousands of Sudanese and Abyssinians were slain, including, of course, many non-combatants. The numbers were uncounted and uncountable; indeed our knowledge of details of the various battles is sketchy.

For the first time two large African armies confronted each other equipped with fairly reliable firearms. Both were equally brave and steeped in the same warlike traditions. On the whole the Sudanese got the better of it, penetrating deep into Abyssinia, looting, killing and burning churches. So vast were the numbers of slaves, cattle and beasts of burden, captured after, for example, the Battle of Gallabat in 1889 that the price of a slave-girl fell to two or three Egyptian dollars (50p–75p) and that of a donkey to 2 piastres (2p).

However, perhaps fortunately, both leaders faced considerable problems in prosecuting their quarrels with each other. Apart from the normal difficulties of keeping large tribal forces from wandering off home with their loot or to lick their wounds while their services were still required, King Yohannes, although claiming sovereignity over the whole country, in reality exercised very limited control outside Tigre, especially over his main vassal, King Menelik of Shoa, who eventually succeeded Yohannes and became the founder of modern Ethiopia. Both Yohannes and the Khalifa were constantly diverted by internal problems. Thus their campaigns would peter out after a spectacular victory by one side or the other.

While these two African powers hammered at each other, the Italians were quietly edging their way up from the coast into the mountainous interior of Eritrea, a tendency not unobserved by Yohannes. In 1887 his liegeman Ras Alula ambushed an Italian column marching to the relief of an outpost and killed four hundred and fifty men at a place called Dogali. The British, who saw an outbreak of general hostilities between Italy and Abyssinia as an advantage only to the Khalifa and, perhaps more importantly, to the French who would seize any opportunity to strengthen their position in the Red Sea area, decided to mediate. Mr Portal of the Foreign Office and Captain Beech were sent from Cairo via Massawa bearing letters to King Yohannes from the Queen and the Prime Minister (Salisbury) as well as rich gifts of a technoligical nature including a telescope and a modern rifle. Yohannes was tickled to death with these, confiding in Portal that he would now be able to shoot an approaching enemy before the target even knew that he had been observed.

In effect the Queen and Salisbury called upon Yohannes to desist in his resistance to Italian encroachment, a plea which understandably he rejected.

Portal and Beech had some difficulty in extricating themselves from his hospitality and, in common with nearly everyone who has ever travelled in Ethiopia from the earliest times to the present day, found that every petty squire and official en route felt it incumbent upon himself to place in the traveller's way every tiresome obstacle which human ingenuity can devise. However, the mission cannot be described as unsuccessful as there was no immediate outbreak of fighting between the feuding parties; indeed an uneasy truce held between the two for many years.

The first major hostilities between the Mahdiya and Abyssinia broke out following the surrender of the Egyptian garrison at Kassala to Osman Digna in July, 1885. Believing, probably correctly, that the Abyssinians, encouraged by the Anglo-Egyptians, had designs upon Kassala themselves, Osman attacked Ras Alula at Kufit in September and was heavily defeated. Returning to Kassala in rage and disappointment, he accused the leading citizens of plotting with the Ras and executed a number of them, including the former governor, the *sirsawari* (commander) of bashi-bazooks and a Greek merchant, Stelios Apostolidis.[2] Alula did not follow up his advantage and shortly after this the belligerent Osman returned to his native haunts around Suakin and a relative peace descended upon the frontier only to be shattered when in 1887 another feudal magnate, Ras Adal, later known as Tekle Haimanot, King of Gojjam, defeated the Mahdists somewhere between Gedaref and Gallabat. This alarmed the Khalifa who sent two armies to deal with this new threat, one under Yunes el Dikaym and another, some months later, under the famous commander of the *jehadiya*, Hamdan Abu Anga, a Baggari of Mandala[3] or slave origin, an experienced soldier and popular with his men. However, Yunes was jealous of him and resentful of being subordinated to a slave. The Khalifa's instructions as to overall command seem to have been ambiguous and the piqued Yunes became entangled in a plot involving one Adam Mohamed, who claimed to be Jesus. All such claims appeared threatening to the Khalifa and he ordered the execution of Adam and his followers and the return to Omdurman of Yunes.

Thus Abu Anga was left in sole charge on the frontier and in January, 1888, marched into Abyssinia, defeated Ras Adal in a huge battle on the plain of Debra Sina and entered Gondar, in the heart of the country and a town of considerable importance, on 23 January. After a fortnight of burning and looting he returned to Gallabat loaded with booty, slaves and hostages including the children of Ras Adal. This remarkable expedition, so deep into hostile and unfamiliar territory with a climate insalubrious to the Sudanese, was perhaps the high-point of the Khalifa's military achievement, although, of course, he took no part in it himself.

---

[2] This is the only recorded instance of a European being deliberately executed throughout the period of the Mahdiya.

[3] The Mandala were the helots of the Taisha Baggara.

After it, Yohannes, probably seeking a purely temporary respite, sued for peace. This was rejected by the Khalifa but the heavy rains of the Abyssinian wet season discouraged active campaigning for a time and in January, 1889, Abu Anga died. A number of different causes of death have been suggested but the most probable explanation is that he accidentally poisoned himself with a concoction intended to relieve his indigestion.

Confident now of victory, Yohannes prepared a vast army which included the feudal levies of both his most powerful *rases*,[4] Alula and Adal, and attacked Gallabat on 9 March, 1889. The Mahdist army, now under Zaki Tamal, another Mandala and former subordinate of Abu Anga, defended prepared positions. A great battle raged for hours and the defences of Gallabat were penetrated but at the moment of victory Yohannes was mortally wounded and Abyssinian morale collapsed. Their retreat was swiftly followed up by Zaki who, in addition to the vast numbers of slaves and animals which so depressed market prices, seized the body of the King and Queen Victoria's letter to him delivered by Portal and Beech eighteen months before. The Royal head was severed and, with the letter, despatched to Omdurman and thence to Wadi Halfa as an awful warning to those who would challenge the power and authority of the heirs to the Mahdi.

Once again hostilities lapsed as both sides were preoccupied elsewhere and famine was raging throughout the Sudan. Zaki was ordered south to deal with a rising of the Shilluk tribe, which he suppressed with vigour and ferocity, while the Abyssinians were busy deciding, by not entirely peaceful means, who should succeed Yohannes.

In due course King Menelik of Shoa emerged as the new King of Kings but Zaki's fortunes were reversed by the jealousy of his rivals who accused him of plotting with the Italians and denounced him to the Khalifa. His end, in 1892, was particularly nasty, walled up in a cell to suffocate or starve, but few tears need be shed over this brutal ruffian. In a small way, he was to the Khalifa as Beria was to Stalin. At his master's behest he had tortured and murdered several members of the Mahdi's family, the Ashraf, and other senior men who had incurred the dictator's displeasure. Following his suppression of the Shilluk, he had exiled thousands of that tribe and their cousins the Dinka to the north. Many died en route and many others of starvation and misery in and around Omdurman. Of course it was not on account of these atrocities that Zaki fell from grace, rather it was that envious eyes had been cast upon the wealth and voluptuous harem he had accumulated during his years of power. In his downfall too there is a Stalinist similarity in that (according to Slatin) seven of his brothers and a sister, together with a number of faithful retainers, went to their deaths with or shortly after him.

To return to Abyssinia, the first clashes between the Mahdists and the Italians

---

[4] Abyssinian feudal barons.

occurred in the early 1890s during Mahdist raids into Italy's new colony of Eritrea.[5] After the Battle of Agordat in December, 1893, in which a dervish force was defeated by the Italians, it was reported to Wingate, perhaps with some exaggeration, that the Khalifa now regarded Italy as a greater threat to his own empire than the Anglo-Egyptians. Following this success the Italians decided to attack and occupy Kassala, a move which they hoped would have the effects of pacifying their frontier with the Sudan and pleasing their British friends. Thus in July, 1894, the Governor of Eritrea, General Baratieri, in a brief campaign of perhaps surprising competence and using a force consisting almost entirely of Eritrean native troops,[6] occupied Kassala, which was only feebly defended by the Mahdists.

Meanwhile Menelik, who in his days as Yohannes's vassal had received strong Italian support, having won overall supremacy with their backing, under French influence was changing his attitude towards Italy. The Italian ambassador to his court, Count Antonelli, believed that through Menelik Italy could achieve a protectorate and a trading monopoly over the whole of Abyssinia. But he had underestimated his man and Menelik had other ideas. Soon he was challenging Italy's policy, repudiating a treaty negotiated by Antonelli and disputing the border between Abyssina and Eritrea. Two successive governors of the colony had disagreed so violently with Antonelli's pro-Menelik policy that they had resigned and eventually on 1 March, 1896, Baratieri, a hero of Italian unification, allowed his hopelessly outnumbered and poorly trained troops to be drawn into battle with a huge and, for once, united Abyssinian army near Adowa. Baratieri's approximately eighteen thousand men (ten thousand five hundred Italian and the remainder Eritrean) were opposed by an army variously estimated at between eighty and one hundred and twenty thousand. By a series of extraordinary blunders Baratieri managed to isolate his brigades from each other and in conditions entirely favourable to Menelik, they were cut to ribbons. Nearly seven thousand Italian and Eritrean troops were killed and several thousand taken prisoner. To everyone's surprise there was no general massacre of prisoners but some of the Italians were castrated and a number of Eritreans mutilated. However, many more died of the hardships and deprivations of their captivity and only seventeen hundred of the Italians ever returned to their homeland after payment of a large ransom.[7]

---

[5] The colonization of Eritrea had gathered pace after the death of King Yohannes in March, 1889, and it was officially proclaimed as 'The Colony of Eritrea' on 1 January, 1890, by decree of the King of Italy.

[6] Italian – led Eritrean troops fought well against British, Indian and Sudanese forces when Eritrea was invaded in 1941. See Appendix H.

[7] For the most detailed English language description of the Battle of Adowa and the circumstances surrounding it see G. F. H. Berkeley's *The Campaign of Adowa and the Rise of Menelik* (1902).

Baratieri, who had escaped from the battlefield, was court-martialled but, although all the main charges against him were proven, he was acquitted, a remarkable feat of judicial dexterity on the part of the Court.

Adowa was one of the great, perhaps the greatest, disasters to European arms and prestige in the history of the colonization of Africa against which such minor hiccoughs as the annihilation of the 24th Regiment at Isandhlwana in the Zulu War pale into insignificance. In any case, this humiliation forced a peace treaty upon the Italians which maintained Abyssinian independence for the next forty years but, paradoxically, led to a reaction on the part of Italy's ally, Britain, which had the opposite effect upon the Sudan.

# PART TWO
## Re-Entry

# 18 Invasion

On 18 March, 1896, a battalion group of the 13th Soudanese with cavalry, Camel Corps and artillery support marched from the frontier post at Sarras and occupied Akasha on the 20th. Appropriately, the advance was lead by an officer who had served with the Desert Column of the Gordon Relief Expedition, Major R. J. Tudway of the Camel Corps,[1] formerly a subaltern with the Essex detachment of the Mounted Infantry Camel Regiment.

It was a long, long way to Omdurman . . .

Baring, now Lord Cromer, had never been in a hurry to reoccupy the Sudan. He was by instinct and inheritance, if not by profession, a banker and thus almost invariably gave priority to financial and economic considerations. The pressure exerted upon him by Sir William Garstin, the Under-Secretary (effectively Minister) at the Egyptian Ministry of Public Works, for the construction of a dam at Assouan weighed more heavily with him than the pleas for military initiatives against the Khalifa urged by Kitchener and Wingate. So long as it remained a vaccum under Abdullahi, the Sudan represented little threat to Egypt or to British interests. He believed that eventually the problem, such as it was, would solve itself, or at least alter in such a way as to enable the Sudan to be brought back into the Egyptian fold without much expenditure of blood or treasure. The Khalifa

---

[1] The Egyptian Camel Corps by this time was very different to Wolseley's Camel Regiments of 1884/5. In the intervening years every aspect of camel management had been studied and perfected. By 1896 the establishment of the Corps had risen to eight companies, four Egyptian and four Soudanese, of approximately one hundred men each with one British officer for every two companies, in addition to the commanding officer. Only good quality Bisharin camels were used, except in an emergency, and officers and men treated their animals with the same care and consideration as cavalrymen did their horses.

Major-General Sir Herbert Kitchener.

would die or would be overthrown; the riverain and northern tribes would weary of Baggara hegemony and seek an accommodation with Egypt, which meant with Great Britain. Meanwhile, the only danger lay in the possible exploitation of the Sudan situation by some other European Power for its own ends.

In general his masters in London agreed with him and the Foreign Office kept a wary eye on three potential rivals in north-east and central Africa – the French, the Belgians and the Italians. The complicated machinations and diplomatic manoeuverings on the subject of the Khedivial provinces on the Upper Nile will not be dealt with here; suffice it to say that it was the French who presented Whitehall with the most formidable challenge in the area. In 1882, France, by an extraordinary miscalculation, had handed effective power in Egypt to the British by refusing to join in the suppression of Arabi's rebellion.[2] However, French

[2] Perhaps the French Prime Minister in 1956, M. Guy Mollet, had this in mind when he decided to join Britain in the invasion of Suez. Unfortunately for both parties, the outcome was rather different to that of 1882.

politicians and engineers were aware that control over the upper reaches of the Nile waters, upon which Egypt was ultimately dependent, would go far to mitigate the blunder. Furthermore, they argued, in the absence of any proper legal authority in the area, the former Khedivial provinces were "up for grabs"; so, early in 1896, one Commandant Jean-Baptiste Marchand received instructions from his government to lead a small military expedition to the Upper Nile and to raise the Tricolor at Fashoda.[3]

Within days of receiving this alarming intelligence, British ministers were astonished to learn that an Italian army under General Baratieri had been comprehensively defeated by the Emperor Menelik at Adowa on 1 March. They were not unaware of the good relations which existed between Menelik and the French, who, despite their own interest in the area, were encouraging Abyssinian claims to all Sudanese territory to the east of the White Nile from Lake Victoria to Khartoum. Also, there were fears of an alliance between Menelik and Abdullahi, who could not fail to be impressed by the success of his erstwhile enemy against the Italians, even if it was only a case of Christian dog eating Christian dog. Thus Italian appeals to the British to act in the northern Sudan, in order to draw Mahdist forces away from Kassala and relieve the pressure on their colony of Eritrea, did not fall upon deaf ears.

So it was that during the first fortnight of March, 1896, Cromer became the instrument of an extraordinary metamorphosis in the attitude of Her Majesty's Government towards the Sudan and was instructed to set in motion a limited campaign for the reoccupation, in the name of the Khedive, of Dongola (now Northern) Province. Even Cromer, whose attitude towards the Khedive and his ministers was that of a rather impatient schoolmaster towards occasionally recalcitrant pupils, was surprised that his instructions did not seem to include any suggestion that he might inform at any early stage the Egyptian Government of what its army was about to do. This ommission was not entirely due to carelessness or insensitivity on the part of HMG, for as soon as the cat was out of the British bag the French attempted various manoeuvres by which the campaign might be prevented, or at least delayed, until Marchand had sweated his way through the jungles and swamps of central Africa and reached the Upper Nile.

First the French commissioner of "*la Caisse de la Dette*"[4] voted against the grant of money for the campaign and persuaded his Russian colleague to do likewise. However, the objectors were outvoted by the other four commissioners, British, Austrian, German and Italian. Next the French alerted the Sultan of Turkey that

---

[3] In fact he did not start from Brazzaville until nearly a year later.
[4] To cope with Egypt's huge foreign debt an international commission know as *La Caisse de la Dette* had been set up in 1876 and continued to adminster Egypt's General Reserve Fund.

his prerogative to order into action troops of the Ottoman Empire, of which Egypt was theoretically part, was being usurped, in name by the Khedive, in practice by the British. The Sultan cabled the Khedive quite politely requesting an explanation. Abbas II, whose hearty dislike of the British in general and of Cromer and Kitchener[5] in particular had been exacerbated by London's high-handed treatment of him over this issue, was himself opposed to the Dongola expedition and could only reply to the Sultan to the effect that it was a British idea which he was powerless to resist. The Sultan, himself bereft of any real power to influence events, had been through the diplomatic motions and bowed to the inevitable.

Cromer, having for many years wrestled manfully and with some success to put Egypt's financial affairs in order, was anxious that his handiwork should not be undone by military extravagance; thus he was glad to support the claims of the Sirdar, Sir Herbert Kitchener,[6] a proven economizer, to the leadership of the expedition. There was little personal liking between the two men but their working relationship was good and they seemed to understand one another. Kitchener needed Cromer's total support to fight off the challenge for command of the operation. If any British troops were to be used, Kitchener, who was only a substantive major in the British Army, was likely to be superseded by a more senior officer, for example the former Sirdar General Grenfell, or even the old warhorse Sir Redvers Buller. Cromer was to have full political control, as the British Government, although by now a Conservative administration, wished to maintain for the time being the fiction of the Sudan being a purely Egyptian problem. On the question of the use of British troops all parties were in a dilemma. The British Government was anxious lest their presence dilute the "Egyptian-ness" of the venture. Cromer feared the expense and Kitchener loss of command. On the other hand without them the whole plan might go terribly wrong. The Soudanese battalions of the Egyptian Army were brave enough but wild and rather thin on the ground and nobody was quite sure that the Egyptian fellahin conscripts, despite their much improved performance over the last decade or so on the frontier, would stand firm against a really determined dervish attack. However, the Intelligence Department under Wingate had built up a sufficiently accurate picture of the Khalifa's forces to know that they presented no great military problem, at least in the early stages, and for the Dongola campaign it was decided to bring only one British infantry battalion, the North Staffordshires, to

[5] This ill-feeling had increased in 1894 after the new Khedive, Abbas II, had criticized the British officers of the Egyptian Army during an inspection on the Frontier. Kitchener had threatened to resign and the incident, which had been engineered by the Egyptian Deputy War Minister, was smoothed over but continued to rankle.

[6] It was largely thanks to Cromer's support that Kitchener had been appointed Sirdar when Grenfell resigned in 1892. His main rival was Wodehouse, a much more popular officer.

Major-General Sir Archibald Hunter, "Second-in-Command" of the Egyptian Army 1896–98.

the front and, in the event, it was hardly used. The preponderance of Egyptian forces, and therefore Kitchener's command, was preserved.

This was to be a war of logistics and Kitchener's memories of the Gordon Relief Expedition warned him that unless transport and supply arrangements were meticulously coordinated the whole operation would collapse with or without the intervention of the Khalifa. Furthermore, it went without saying that the deeper the penetration into the Sudan the more formidable the logistical problems would become. This time he did not want to be dependent on thousands of flimsy camels or upon a river which ran the wrong way and, in places, quite fast. Therefore railways must be built and must be built quickly and cheaply.

Kitchener's methods of dealing with the salient problems which confronted him are object lessons in the skilful selection and use of personnel and the judgement of priorities. He was confident that the actual fighting in the Sudan would be of lesser importance than the administration of the campaign and could be left with safety to Hunter, the current commander of the Frontier Field Force. Colonel Archibald Hunter, a Scot with long experience in the Sudan, was described at the time as "a real live Cromwellian, brutal, cruel, licentious, religious, brave, able, blunt and cunning".[7] He was much admired by the native troops, particularly the Soudanese who would follow him anywhere. Kitchener would concentrate on getting the administrative work done, mainly by doing it himself. Delegation would be minimal. In the Dongola campaign there were only fourteen officers on his staff.

As for the railway, Kitchener was a sapper and did not want anyone near his own rank telling him how it should be built. He found a bright young sapper subaltern, the French-Canadian Lieutenant Edouard Percy Girouard, and put him in charge. Girouard was to be directly responsible to Kitchener and was to report to no one else.

Next in importance came the animal and river transport. Kitchener's memories of a desert littered with dead and dying camels during the 1884/5 campaign were vivid. Such waste was costly and inefficient and must be kept to a minimum so he summoned from India his youngest brother Walter, a major in the West Yorkshires, who had had some experience of animal transport duties in Afghanistan and who, as a model of fraternal devotion, could be relied upon to carry out his brother's wishes without question.

River transport was provided by a variety of vessels which will be dealt with later.

As much as he distrusted politicians, Kitchener was never one to ignore them and he ensured direct access to the Prime Minister, the Marquess of Salisbury, by inviting one of the great man's younger sons, Lord Edward Cecil, a subaltern in the Grenadier Guards, to join him as his second ADC. Whether this appointment was as clever as it sounds is open to doubt in view of Lord Edward's admitted dislike of the Sirdar. However, this judgement may be tempered by the fact that Lord Edward does not seem to have liked anyone else either and no one else seems to have liked the Sirdar.[8]

With Wingate, aided by the recently escaped Slatin and his two able Syrian assistants, Milhem Shakoor and Na'um Shuqair, in charge of intelligence and another Egyptian Army colleague of long-standing, Leslie Rundle (Wingate's brother-in-law) as Chief of Staff, Kitchener's team was more or less complete. However, his position was by no means secure and he had yet to prove himself. He

---

[7] Lord Edward Cecil's 1896 diary.

[8] Later Cecil's opinion of Kitchener changed. His satirical portrait of life in Egypt before the First World War, *The Leisure of an Egyptian Official*, contains an interesting and balanced assessment of his former chief.

Major Lord Edward Cecil, Grenadier Guards. ADC to the Sirdar 1896–8.

was an unpopular man and jealous rivals within both the British and Egyptian Armies would seek to exploit his slightest mistake or misjudgement. He knew that Cromer's support would evaporate at the first sign of extravagance and that the Director of Accounts to the Egyptian Government, Sir Elwin Palmer, (effectively Minister of Finance) was not his friend. For these reasons the campaign was to be run on a shoestring and all extraneous luxuries, or what seemed to Kitchener to be luxuries, were to be eliminated. Cecil's diary records that heads of departments were afraid to ask for anything, for if they did it might draw attention to what they already had and even that might be cut or removed. The doctors in particular were terrified of Kitchener with the result that the troops were denied all but the barest medical necessities. As for wounded enemies, in many instances the most merciful treatment they could expect would be a bullet or a swift thrust of the bayonet.

The character of the Sirdar has been examined in several contradictory biographies and the present writer does not intend to venture into this minefield. Suffice it to say that at least some of the shortcomings of which he has been accused, such as the lack of humanity in his treatment of a beaten enemy and his disregard for the comfort and well-being of his own men, were induced by the stringent financial circumstances which were imposed upon him.

It would be absurd to pretend that he was an attractive character at this stage of his career, but his efforts to hide his sensitivity and lack of self-confidence made him appear harsh and unforgiving. If there was a romantic side to him it was well concealed. He is said to have loved but once, Valentine Baker's beautiful and tragic daughter who died in Cairo in the 1880s. He was shy and uneasy in the company of women but in the furtherance of his career cultivated the friendship of the great ladies of society. If he preferred young men to his contemporaries it may have been because they were less inclined to argue with him. He was no great master of the battlefield, but how many of these have there been? His strongest quality was his ability to get things done and in the Sudan at the end of the nineteenth century he was the right man in the right place at the right time.

They were known as the "Band of Boys", none of them was over thirty years of age or above the rank of lieutenant but their contribution to the conquest of the Sudan was immeasurably greater than that of any other single group involved in the campaign. They were the young Royal Engineer officers, never more than nine in number at any one time, who built and ran the Sudan Military Railway. Their chief, Girouard, himself only twenty-nine,[9] had been trained in the "rough but

[9] Major-General Sir E. Percy Girouard's (1867–1932) remarkable career included running both the Egyptian and South African state railways, a colonial governorship and the post of managing director of Armstrong Whitworth.

A patrol of Major Tudway's Camel Corps.

splendid" school of the roaring Canadian Pacific Railway. Labour was provided by an army of Egyptian and Sudanese navvies, many of them convicts or prisoners of war, supervised by foremen, overseers and technicians of many nations, and guarded by an Egyptian Infantry battalion under El Kaimakam (Lieutenant-Colonel) Ibrahim Fathi Bey, the only Egyptian officer to be awarded the DSO in the campaign.[10]

Girouard's relationship with the Sirdar was unique. Unhindered by that deference to higher authority inherent in the British officer class and aware of his indispensability to his commander, he sometimes treated the awewsome Kitchener with scant respect and got away with it. His ability to build and run a railway in double quick time under impossible conditions and with strictly limited finances entitled him to privileges denied to others.

The Canadian was on his way to an appointment in Mauritius when Kitchener

[10] Later Fathi Bey became Minister of War in the Egyptian Government and died in 1925.

waylaid him in London and whisked him off to the Sudan. Arriving at Wadi Halfa at the end of March, 1896, a few weeks after the start of the invasion, Girouard found that the railway line was in working order as far as Sarras, but from there on to Akasha it had been destroyed by the dervishes following the withdrawal of Butler's Frontier Force in 1886. Two other sapper officers, Lieutenants Stevenson and Polwhele, had been working for the past six months on preparations for a line from Korosko to the Murrat Oasis but with Dongola as the objective of the campaign, it was decided to discontinue this work and concentrate on the "River" line to which end the two officers and their workforce were transferred to Wadi Halfa.

The line had been repaired up to Ambigol Wells by the third week of May but progress beyond there was delayed until the Mahdists had been defeated at their stronghold of Firket on 7 June. Thereafter it crept steadily and inexorably southwards and had reached Kosheh, over 100 miles from Wadi Halfa, by early August. But the immense pressure of work through a blazing summer was taking its toll. Polwhele died in July as did the civilian superintendent of workshops at Wadi Halfa and Girouard himself collapsed from heat exhaustion and was out of action for a month. Then in August disaster struck when freak storms of wind and rain in one of the world's driest areas carried away part of the embankment between Wadi Halfa and Akasha. Fearing for the success of the whole campaign the Sirdar took personal charge of the repair work to which he assigned three thousand five hundred labourers, completing the job by 6 September.

During this difficult period much of the transport burden was loaded upon Walter Kitchener's camels of which there were about two thousand, some apparently fitted with sun-bonnets. Gruelling marches were commonplace and even Walter's most seasoned and experienced assistant, 2nd Lieutenant (formerly Sergeant) T. H. Healey DCM and two bars, the Glaswegian slayer of Nur el Kanzi at Sarras in 1887, fainted with sunstroke. Language was a problem for Walter, as it was for many of the "Special Service" officers[11] who had not served in an Arabic-speaking country before, but Healey and another member of the transport staff, Captain L. C. Sherer of the Leicesters, who had been in the Egyptian Police, had a good working knowledge of the language, albeit of the "Bimbashi" variety. His Egyptian officers strove enthusiastically, if not always successfully, with the English as she is spoke. From one such budding linguist Walter received a telegram, which, if it did not edify, clearly amused as it is preserved amongst his papers.

It runs thus: "Commanding of the 1st battalion took 53 camels remains with me from Convoy No. 1 40 camels I hope from Your Excellency to help me to make this under command the officer with me from Convoy No. 4 to wait 15th battn.

---

[11] Officers seconded to the Egyptian Army for the duration of the campaign only.

which now at Abkeh Cataract the order of Hanter Pasha to me not forfeiture to enter the battle of Dongola.
Your obedient servant El Sag[12] Ibrahim Zaki".

The style if not the content may be familiar to many expatriates who seek their livelihoods in the Middle East today!

Meanwhile the Sirdar and Girouard had turned their attention away from the River railway, as to continue it further would mean eventually bridging the Nile somewhere between Dongola and Merowe in order to take the line on across the Bayuda Desert, roughly along the route taken by the Desert Column in 1885. The bridging work would be time-consuming and expensive and, once into the Bayuda, the track-laying gangs would have to be constantly and heavily protected from marauding dervishes operating from Metemma and Berber. Also, psychologically, this route and its associations with humiliation and retreat, would not have been a happy choice. Therefore the decision was taken to construct a line across the Nubian Desert from Wadi Halfa to Abu Hamed, at the apex of the Nile's great loop, whence it could be laid down the east bank of the river to the junction with the Atbara.

A major problem was the waterlessness, confirmed by the local Ababdeh and Bisharin tribesmen, of the Nubian Desert. A diversion through the Murrat Oasis, equidistant from Wadi Halfa and Abu Hamed, was considered but discarded as was the re-starting of the Korosko – Abu Hamed line which would pass through the oasis. Kitchener even considered switching his base to Suakin and reviving the often discussed Suakin – Berber railway scheme. However, speed was of the essence as the longer the campaign took the more money it would cost. If a few hundred convicts and prisoners died of thirst they would not be missed and the British and Egyptian officers with them would have to take their chances. It would be quicker to build the line direct from Wadi Halfa to Abu Hamed and for the railway itself to carry every drop of water with it as it went. Reconnaisances, in one case as far as Abu Hamed itself, were carried out by Royal Engineer officers but much of the topographical information required was obtained from the Ababdeh tribesmen of the northern deserts, anti-Mahdist to a man, and naturally steeped in the lore and techniques of desert navigation and survival.

The first spike was driven on New Year's Day, 1897, and Abu Hamed reached exactly ten months later with only 17 miles worth of track material in hand. As Colonel Sandes has put it in his book *The Royal Engineers in Egypt and the Sudan*, "Kitchener's Band of Boys ... had accomplished what may justly be classed as one of the most remarkable engineering feats of modern times". It had entailed surprisingly few casualties and water supplies had always reached the gangs in

---

[12] Abreviation of Saghkolaghasi or Adjutant-Major.

Construction of the Desert Railway.

time, but sadly the officer who had carried out the most daring and exacting reconnaisance of the route, Lieutenant E. Cator, RE, died of typhoid in February, 1897.

On the river both transport and an invaluable strike force were provided by the gunboats. Four, the *Tamai, El Teb, Abu Klea* and *Metemma*, had been in service for many years and for the later stages of the Dongola campaign were reinforced by three more stern-wheelers, *Zafir, Nasr* and *Fateh*. Later, in 1898, three new twin-screw vessels, *Melik*,[13] *Sultan* and *Sheikh* were introduced. Each gunboat was armed with five or six artillery pieces, including Maxim-Nordenfelt $12\frac{1}{2}$ pounders, Krupp 12 pounders and 4 inch howitzers, and four Maxim

[13] Today the *Melik* provides the headquarters of the Khartoum Sailing Club.

machine-guns. They were commanded, for the most part, by naval officers and the crews were made up of naval and civilian engineers, artificers and stokers, and Royal Marine Artillery gunnery NCOs, as well as native soldiers and crewmen. There were famous names amongst the officers: Beatty, Hood, Keppel, and for a time the *Melik* was commanded by Major W. S. "Monkey" Gordon, RE, a nephew of the Hero. *Zafir* boasted Major His Serene Highness Prince Christian Victor of Schleswig-Holstein as one of her officers and it may go almost without saying that our old friend Wortles (Stuart-Wortley) was summoned from his humdrum existence as a brigade major in Malta to lend his experience as well as his *sang-froid* to the Nile flotilla. Support was provided by a number of river-steamers, native sailing boats (gyassas) and barges (nuggars), some of the former Egyptian Government owned and others provided by Messrs Thomas Cook. The native craft were hired locally, pressed into service or sometimes captured from the enemy.

# 19 Dongola

On 14 March, 1896, the British garrison in Cairo – the Queen's Bays, the North Staffordshires and the Connaught Rangers – was on exercises outside the city when the commanding officer of the North Staffordshires, Lieutenant-Colonel T. A. Beale, received his marching orders to proceed to Wadi Halfa with all despatch. Simultaneously the Maxim sections of his battalion and the Connaught Rangers were temporarily amalgamated and detached for service with the Egyptian Army. Ironically, one of the officers included in this four-gun battery was Lieutenant O. D. Blunt of the Connaught Rangers, a nephew of Wilfred Blunt, the leading critic of British policy in Egypt and the Sudan.

All Egyptian Army reservists were recalled to the Colours and a number of Special Service officers were seconded from the British Army to the Egyptian for the duration of the campaign. When the War Office dragged its feet on this, the Sirdar's specially appointed "political" ADC, the lugubrious Lord Edward Cecil, was brought into play, writing to his father, the Prime Minister, begging him "to sit on the War Office heavily".

A week later the North Staffordshires enjoyed marching past Shepheard's Hotel on their way to the railway station while the pretty girls out from England for the season, collectively known as the Fishing Fleet, crowded the verandah waving and clapping. Full of excited anticipation the men swaggered along, band playing and colours flying, their moment of glory before a hot, dreary, disease-stricken campaign in which, through no fault of theirs, they were to be denied virtually any active role.

Wadi Halfa, today deep beneath the waters of Lake Nubia, was a dump both literally and metaphorically. Stores, workshops, barracks, tents, Greek shops, cafés and doubtless at least one House (or mud hut) of Joy sweltered together beside the busy river. British troops had not been seen there for some years and Lieutenant Farley of E Company North Staffordshires, was shocked when one of his men was seized and stripped by the inquisitive wives of the resident Soudanese soldiers. Farley's somewhat stilted account of the event does not reveal whether they were satisfied or disappointed by what they found, but in view of their husbands' undoubted qualifications, almost certainly the latter.

Whatever temptations there may have been for the Staffordshire men in Bloody Hell-Fire as they called the place, their spiritual welfare was more than adequately safeguarded by the presence of two padres, one of whom was the redoubtable Father Brindle who assured Lord Edward Cecil that "the men will do anything if they are going to have a good fight later on". Father Brindle was a comforting sort of man to have on hand in more than the religious sense. Farley had heard that during the Gordon Relief Expedition he had quelled a mutiny in the "Royal Blankshires" (presumably the Royal Irish Regiment) single-handed.

But Lord Edward found that the social as well as the meteorological climate of Wadi Halfa left much to be desired. Not only was he lumbered with Count Trambi, the Italian Military Attaché, "a sore trial" and "foreign, a fault most Italians have" to boot, but he was obliged to rub shoulders with the officers of the North Staffords, worthy fellows no doubt but not all of them out of the top drawer. However, on one occasion when he called and left his card at their mess everyone was "mercifully out". Sadly his troubles did not end there as he was constantly irritated by the presence of his *bête noire* Slatin who liked to allude mysteriously to secret sources of information (quite possibly genuine) and asked "incessant questions" in an unbecomingly "perky" manner. On top of all this he had to cope with the manners of the Great White Czar, as he christened the Sirdar, which were hardly those of the drawing-room at Hatfield. The day when his master insulted him not more than six times was "the dawn of peace". Only Walter Kitchener, he discovered, was impervious to his brother's behaviour. All in all an unhappy time for the Prime Minister's son.

At this point the Khalifa's reaction – or lack of one – to the invasion of his territory requires some examination. Abdullahi had his sympathizers in Cairo and even in England, so he was probably advised of British intentions almost as soon as they were known in Egyptian official and business circles, allowing for the time it took to get a message to Omdurman. Yet he seems to have taken few immediate steps to counter the threat. As far back as 1891 intelligence reports had indicated to Wingate that the Khalifa regarded Kereri, an open plain a few miles north of Omdurman, as the natural killing-ground on which to destroy an invading army. The reasons why he should have favoured such a battlefield, so eminently suited to the deployment and use of the modern weapons which his enemy possessed and he did not, must be sought in the light of his character, experience and background. First, all his military experience had been in the guerrilla-style slaving operations and tribal warfare of his youth and in the annihilation of the old Turko-Egyptian army during the rise of the Mahdi. He had no conception of the destructive power of well-trained, well-officered troops equipped with sophisticated weapons. Nor, with the exception of Osman Digna, had any of his surviving emirs. Thus it was natural for him to adopt the strategy which had been so successful in destroying Hicks, for example. The "Turk" must be lured further and deeper into the Sudan where, with ever lengthening lines of communication, exhausted, thirsty and afraid, he would at last be given the *coup de grâce*.

Next, it should be remembered that men and women age prematurely in the harsh climate of the Sudan and by 1896 Abdullahi was certainly over fifty, although his precise date of birth is not known. He had not left Omdurman and its environs for the past eleven years. He was a hard-working man but his work was largely sedentary; exercise is regarded with disfavour in the East and his way of life was hardly conducive to great physical fitness. The prospect therefore of leading his army personally over great distances was not an inviting one and he had no intention of letting the bulk of it out of his sight. Who knew what it might get up to?

Finally, the northern part of his domain was very far away. To the best of our knowledge he had never been there; most of the tribes in the area were unfriendly to him and his Baggara and, indeed, it was to him almost a foreign country. After all, if the "Turks" reconquered Dongola Province, what difference did it make? If they were foolish and insolent enough to come any further they would get their just deserts.

Probably the only leading figure in the Sudan who had any idea how this invader should be handled was Osman Digna. He knew that any form of direct confrontation, either in attack or defence, at any time or place, would be disastrous. The only wise tactics would be those of harassment and delay, swift raids and getaways, attacks on camel convoys, on railway gangs, on the telegraph line and isolated posts. But, we are told, he was always reticent and self-effacing in the Khalifa's presence and it is unlikely that he would have argued this case with much force, assuming that he put it forward at all.

However, Osman, perhaps on his own initiative, decided to renew his activities on the Red Sea littoral. Reacting to clashes between his partisans and local Friendlies, two Egyptian columns from Suakin and Tokar respectively set out to trap him at a place called Khor Wintri. But, on 16 April, Osman managed to draw the Suakin column, under the Governor, Colonel Lloyd, into close country and a cavalry patrol under an infantry officer, Captain M. A. Fenwick,[1] failing to take proper precautions, was attacked and put to flight by about two hundred dervish horsemen. A few of the troopers kept going all the way back to Suakin but sixteen were speared to death when their horses, careering madly over rough and uneven

---

[1] Fenwick died in the cholera epidemic a few months later.

ground, fell. Some of the men, under an Egyptian officer who claimed his horse had bolted, found their way to the main body which had camped at Teroi Wells. Meanwhile, Fenwick, described by Churchill as "twice a VC without a gazette", managed to rally about forty men and held on to some higher ground throughout the night. By daylight the dervishes had withdrawn and Fenwick and his men were able to rejoin the column at Teroi Wells. There they found some disarray as enemy attacks during the night had failed to bring out the best in the Egyptian reservists, who made up part of Lloyd's force, and wild firing in the dark had endangered everyone but the attackers. Pulling themselves together they marched towards Khor Wintri and joined up with the Tokar column, consisting of two hundred and fifty men of the 10th Soudanese under Major Sidney. These troops had also clashed with some of Osman's men but the 10th were experienced and reliable and had driven the enemy off inflicting a number of casualties with little loss to themselves. Lloyd was now faced with the problem of finding Osman's main force and bringing it to battle, but in this he was no more successful than many of his predecessors. One is inclined to think that in this he may have been fortunate in view of the performance of the Suakin column over the past twenty-four hours. In any case, and for whatever reason, the expedition was abandoned and the force returned to Suakin on 18 April. However, its arrival there had been preceded by the Egyptian troopers who had fled from the Khor Wintri ambush and rumours of disaster had spread through the town. The townspeople, eager to be on the winning side, were preparing to slay the infidels, mostly Greeks, and place their goods and money in protective custody. The expedition had denuded the town of troops but fortunately HMS *Scout* was lying in the harbour and the appearance of her sailors in the streets dampened the enthusiasm of the population for the religious and financial reforms which they had been contemplating.

So yet another attempt to bring the elusive Osman to book had ended inconclusively. Soon both he and the Egyptian garrison were required elsewhere and by the end of May the majority of the Egyptian and Soudanese troops had been transferred to the Nile theatre and replaced at Suakin with an Indian contingent of four thousand men. Osman, after conferring with the Khalifa, transferred his headquarters to Adarama on the Atbara River to await developments.

The story, such as it is, of the Indian contingent at Suakin is a dismal one. The cavalry regiment, two battalions of infantry with a mountain battery and a section of sappers under General Egerton, arrived full of enthusiasm for the coming adventure, convinced they were to take part in the campaign, if only in a diversionary role, but in the event they languished at Suakin and Tokar for seven months throughout the worst season of the year with nothing to do and nowhere to go. Their chief medical officer, Lieutenant-Colonel Carr-Calthorp, recorded in his report that out of seventy-nine British officers, only nineteen escaped a spell in

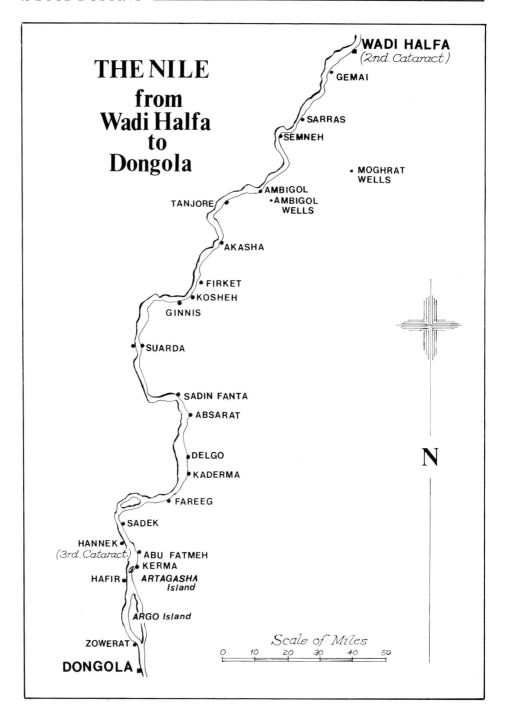

**THE NILE**
**from**
**Wadi Halfa**
**to**
**Dongola**

WADI HALFA
*(2nd. Cataract)*

GEMAI

SARRAS
SEMNEH

MOGHRAT
WELLS

AMBIGOL
AMBIGOL
WELLS

TANJORE

AKASHA

FIRKET
KOSHEH
GINNIS

SUARDA

SADIN FANTA
ABSARAT

DELGO
KADERMA

FAREEG

SADEK

HANNEK
*(3rd. Cataract)*   ABU FATMEH
KERMA
HAFIR   ARTAGASHA
*Island*

ARGO Island

ZOWERAT

**DONGOLA**

*Scale of Miles*
0   10   20   30   40   50

N

hospital and sixteen were invalided back to India, Egypt or the United Kingdom. The fact that throughout July and August the temperature at night never fell below 90° coupled with a relative humidity of 100% led Carr-Calthorp, a man with many years service in India, to refer to some nights as "the worst I have ever lived through". A reduction in the salt ration may not seem to us to have been a wise move and nor was the men's accommodation of the best. During the rare rainstorms, tents had to be pitched in the barrack rooms as water poured through the ceilings. However, the Indian troops, accustomed as they were to hardships of all kinds, coped remarkably well and only ten men died.

Meanwhile the bulk of the Egyptian Army had transited through Wadi Halfa[2] en route to Sarras and Akasha, and Ababdeh Friendlies patrolled the surrounding desert with little interference from the enemy. Despite the urgings of Mohamed wad Bishara, the Governor of Dongola, the Mahdist commander in the north of the province, Hammuda Idris, showed little inclination to take effective action of any kind and was replaced, not without argument, by a veteran of many a frontier skirmish, Osman Azrak.

Shortly before his dismissal, some of Hammuda's mounted men clashed with an Egyptian cavalry patrol under Major Burn-Murdoch[3] near Akasha on 1 May. Burn-Murdoch's experience on this occasion was not entirely dissimilar to Fenwick's a fortnight before. Coming unexpectedly upon a superior force, he sought to retire on his supporting infantry (11th Soudanese) but his three squadrons were cut off from behind in a ravine. There followed a confused fight in clouds of dust from which two of the three squadrons departed with unseemly haste, preferring to observe the outcome from afar. Burn-Murdoch and his officers managed to rally the third squadron and with a spirited charge drove the dervishes from the ravine. Thus encouraged, the two cautious squadrons returned to the fray and the dervish horse, seeking to renew the attack, were held at bay with dismounted carbine fire. By this time the 11th Soudanese had arrived and the dervishes broke off the engagement. Only two Egyptians were killed but so intense was the heat that one Soudanese infantryman actually died of sunstroke.

It may have been Hammuda's failure to follow up his initial advantage on this occasion which cost him his command but he did not long survive his humiliation.

The Sirdar's progress and that of the railway was held up by the presence of the Mahdist forces under the disputed command of Hammuda and Osman Azrak at Firket some forty miles south of the railhead which by the end of May had reached

---

[2] But not the North Staffords who were not brought to the front until the end of August.
[3] Major (later Major-General Sir) J. F. Burn-Murdoch of the Royals commanded the Egyptian cavalry in the Dongola campaign but left the Egyptian Army soon afterwards and was replaced by Lieutenant-Colonel R. G. Broadwood (killed in action 1917) of the 12th Lancers.

Major J. F. Burn-Murdoch, Royal Dragoons, served with the Heavy Camel Regiment 1884/5, commanded the Egyptian Cavalry 1896.

Ambigol Wells. Thus the first major offensive of the campaign was to be the battle of Firket on 7 June, 1896.

This battle gave the first clear indication of the absolute superiority of the Anglo-Egyptians over their opponents in virtually every respect. The approach march was well planned and well co-ordinated and the attack itself carried out with dash and determination. The defence, on the other hand, was slack, ill-prepared and half-hearted. Firket confirmed the view that the main obstacles to the reconquest of the Sudan were financial and climatic rather than human.

For the assault on Firket Kitchener divided his army into two columns, and, borrowing Wolseley's old nomenclatures, christened them River and Desert respectively. The River Column, under Hunter, consisted of the 1st (Lewis's),[4] 2nd (MacDonald's)[5] and 3rd (Maxwell's)[6] Infantry Brigades of the Egyptian

[4] Colonel D. F. (Taffy) Lewis, CB, Cheshire Regt. (1855–1927).
[5] Major-General Sir Hector MacDonald, KCB, DSO, Gordon Highlanders and Royal Fusiliers, (1853–1903). The son of a crofter, MacDonald had been commissioned from the ranks.
[6] General the Rt Hon Sir John Maxwell, PC, GCB, KCMG, CVO, DSO, Black Watch (1850–1929).

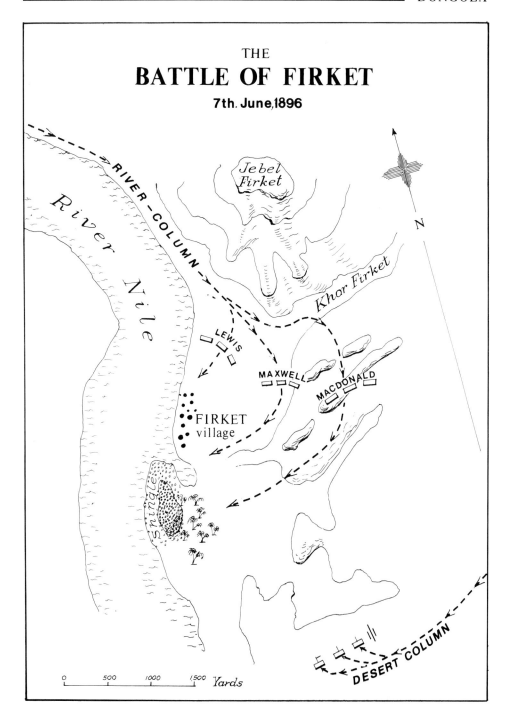

THE
# BATTLE OF FIRKET
### 7th. June,1896

Colonel Hector MacDonald, a former sergeant in the Gordon Highlanders, celebrated for his leadership of Soudanese troops.

Colonel John Maxwell of the Black Watch, an Egyptian Brigade commander during the campaign of re-conquest.

Army and two field artillery batteries, a total of about seven thousand men. The Sirdar himself would accompany this column. The Desert Column, under the cavalry commander Major Burn-Murdoch, some two thousand strong, included seven squadrons of cavalry, eight Camel Corps companies, a Horse Artillery battery and the Maxim machine-guns of the North Staffords and Connaughts, the only British troops involved. One battalion of Soudanese infantry, the 12th, was attached to the Desert Column from MacDonald's brigade and mounted on camels. The plan, simple but calling for skill and timing, required both columns to set out from Akasha on the afternoon of 6 June. The Desert Column would march east away from the river, swinging south to outflank the Mahdist positions at Firket village and the rocky hills to its east, then west to come up in rear of these positions. The River Column, meanwhile, would march more or less due south along the river bank and launch a frontal attack.

Throughout the night the men and animals of both columns stumbled and floundered over some fifteen miles of rough tracks in the sweltering darkness but, with an accuracy which gives the lie to the amateurish image of the Victorian officer, by dawn both had reached their attacking positions. Astonishingly, complete surprise had been achieved, indicating an almost incredible lack of intelligence, in both senses of the word, and preparedness on the part of Hammuda and Azrak. Proud and quarrelsome, these two men exemplified the military ineptitude of the Mahdist hierarchy. True, their three thousand Baggara, Jaalin and *jehadiya* were heavily outnumbered but only the Baggara had any stomach for the fight. The Jaalin, long disillusioned with the Khalifa's version of Mahdism, were later to break into open rebellion and there can be little doubt that Wingate's department had been working assiduously since the beginning of the campaign, and before, to undermine the morale of the black *jehadiya*, many of whose fellow tribesmen, Dinka, Shilluk, Nuer, Nuba and so on, were already serving in the Egyptian Army, better paid, better fed and with decent weapons. An added incentive to desertion was the bounty of £E1 paid to each *jehadi* deserter, the equivalent of ten months' pay at Mahdist rates.

One of the sapper officers with the River Column, Lieutenant (later Major-General) Bowman-Manifold,[7] describes how at 4.30 am on the morning of 7 June the column reached the start line. With Firket Mountain on their left and the river on their right, the infantry brigades deployed. A neighing horse caused Hunter to mutter, "That's given the show away", but it had not and the beating of drums, thought at first to be an alarm signal turned out to be a call to dawn prayers. More patrolling and less praying on the part of his opponents would have made

[7] In keeping with Kitchener's policy of giving great responsibility to very junior officers, Manifold was in complete command of the laying and maintenance of the telegraph throughout the campaign of re-conquest.

Slatin (the picture bears no resemblance to him whatsoever) finding the body of Hammuda Idris after the Battle of Firket.

Hunter's job a good deal more difficult. As it was, disgorging through a narrow gap between the hills and the river on to a broader scrub-covered plain, he was able to deploy his battalions unhindered with Lewis on the right, aiming for the village and river, and MacDonald on the left driving for the hills. As these two brigades diverged, so Maxwell came through in the centre. Simultaneously Burn-Murdoch opened up with his artillery and Maxims. Bearing in mind the darkness and complete lack of communication between the two columns this was a remarkable feat of co-ordination.

MacDonald's Soudanese soon rolled the *jehadiya* off the hills and Lewis's Egyptians had little trouble with the Jaalin in the village, although the C.O. of the 4th Egyptians, Captain Sparkes, had his horse shot in four places. A sharp counterattack by Baggara horsemen on MacDonald's left flank battalion was ruthlessly and decisively mown down. Dervish resistance crumbled quickly and Hammuda was killed, but, unsighted by the lie of the land, the Desert Column failed to cut off many of the retreating Mahdists and a number, including Osman Azrak, made good their escape southwards. Some bolder spirits, mostly Baggara, held out for a while but soon after 7 am the Sirdar's first important victory in the campaign of re-conquest was complete.

Although insignificant in an historical context, Firket represented a morale-boosting achievement to the Egyptian Army and its British officers. Cheap in lives, Firket had laid to rest the nagging fear of the inadequacy of the fellahin soldiers for their task, and after the battle Lord Edward Cecil was astonished to notice that they showed no signs of fatigue. Their casualties amounted to about one hundred of whom only twenty were fatal.[8] On the other side, however, well over half the total force had become casualties, including 800 dead.

But the good fortune of the invaders did not hold and nature, if not the Mahdists, had a trick or two up her sleeve. During June cholera, sweeping down from Egypt, struck the army. In a vain effort to escape its effects, the North Staffords were removed from Wadi Halfa a few miles south to Gemai and the Egyptian Army camp at Firket was abandoned. In those days there was no prophylactic defence against this deadly intruder and its victims usually died a swift but beastly death. The summer heat was devastating, the hospital facilities primitive and a majority of the afflicted perished; nineteen out of twenty-four

---

[8] One of these was El Saghkolaghasi Suleiman Abdullah, one of two Kurdish brothers who were Adjutant-Majors of the Camel Corps under Major Tudway. They were experienced and highly respected officers, both having served in the Turkish Army in the Balkans as well as in the Sudan against the Mahdi in the 1880s. Suleiman died following the amputation (a frequent cause of death) of his wounded leg. Later the other brother Mustafa lost part of a hand in a shooting accident before Omdurman.

(*Right*)    Lewis's Brigade assaulting Firket Village.

British and nine hundred out of twelve hundred native troops and camp followers. Although there was much talk at the time of the heroic efforts of the medical staff, Cecil's diary records the opinion of his colleague Captain Watson[9] that the medical arrangements for the British troops were very bad and that all the patients were packed, uncared for, in one tent. Lord Edward was a stern critic of everybody and everything but, bearing in mind the disgusting manifestations of this disease, a hellish picture of men suffering and dying uncomforted in crushing heat and overpowering stench assails the imagination.

Throughout the period of the epidemic, which fizzled out in August, typhoid, dysentery and other illnesses induced by heat, bad water and poor sanitation, continued to take their usual toll. Father Brindle and others saw the amount of beer consumed by the North Staffords as an exacerbation of the problem and the ever-critical Cecil has sharp words in his diary for his brother Grenadier, Count Gleichen, for his intake of alcoholic beverages. However, these practices were undoubtedly much less harmful than the water which his lordship had himself drunk from a pool containing three dead dervishes after the Battle of Firket. Be that as it may, the final stage of the campaign of re-conquest, which involved a far greater number of British troops, was firmly decreed "dry" – at least for Other Ranks – by the Sirdar.

In the previous chapter the other natural phenomena which conspired to impede the conquerors have been mentioned. Southerly winds hampered the flow of supplies by sailing boat and barge, freakishly severe "haboubs" and rainstorms undid months of excavation and track-laying. But, with the Nile at its highest in August,[10] the gunboats *Tamai*, *El Teb*, *Metemma* and *Abu Klea* and the transport steamers *Kaibar*, *Dal* and *Akasha* had negotiated the Second Cataract with the aid of "tug-of-war" teams of soldiers, convicts and local "volunteers" (the khourbash both aided recruitment and encouraged enthusiasm for the work) and had reached the "front" and railhead at Kosheh by the 23rd. At the same time the latest addition to the flotilla, the *Zafir*, of which much was expected, arrived by rail in sections. However, this heavily armed 135-footer proved a severe disappointment when her low-pressure cylinder blew almost as soon as she had been assembled. Nevertheless, Kitchener was ready to resume the advance and MacDonald's brigade was pushed forward to Absarat on 23 August, a desert march accomplished without serious incident. But Lewis, who followed, was not so fortunate. Tempestuous weather set in on 25 August without much reducing the searing heat. Marching from Kosheh across the desert to Sadin Fanti on the 27th, a tramp of thirty-seven miles, Lewis's Egyptians and Soudanese were overtaken and overcome by a tremendous storm of dust, then rain, before they

[9] Lieutenant-Colonel J. K. Watson, CMG, CVO, CBE, DSO, 60th Rifles (1865–1942), ADC to Kitchener 1894–1901 and to the Khedive Abbas Hilmi, 1905–14.
[10] During the "Big Rains" in Ethiopia.

could reach one of the water depots specially provided for them by Walter Kitchener's camel transport. Over half the brigade collapsed and some struggled back to Kosheh. Nine men died, the episode becoming known, perhaps over-dramatically, as the Death March, a journalistic rather than military label.

This may be an appropriate moment to dwell briefly upon Kitchener's extraordinary relationship with the Fourth Estate. He hated journalists, although he had the occasional favourite, and they hated him. He grudged them every facility, side-tracked them whenever possible and insulted them on sight. His idea of a Press conference was to shoulder his way through the assembled hacks growling, "Out of my way, you drunken swabs!" And yet, with few exceptions, the war correspondents reported on both the man and his doings with gushing enthusiasm. There are a number of explanations for this. The reporters them-selves, in common with nearly everybody else serving with or attached to the Egyptian Army, were terrified of the Sirdar. Also they feared his power to send them packing if he did not like the cut of their jibs. Back at home their editors did not want bad or critical news of the campaign which was nationally popular and seen as a crusade to avenge Gordon. Furthermore, Victorian society was deferential to authority, at least in public, in sharp contrast to ours today. Even Churchill, though many of his private letters were scathing, forebore to criticize Kitchener in his classic *The River War*, hinting only that Hunter rather than the Sirdar was the true hero of the re-conquest and describing the former as "the darling of the Egyptian Army", a sobriquet which infuriated loyal Walter Kitchener. Finally, it may be argued, apart from the Sirdar's personal boorish-ness, that there was little to criticize. Such disasters as struck his army were mostly of natural origin and unavoidable. Campaigning troops expected and received no luxuries, in which category in those days was included proper medical care, thus accompanying journalists were not surprised by what they found. Such criticism as there was came later and we will deal with it in its proper place.

Now at last the poor North Staffords, the Cinderellas of the campaign, were ordered south from Gemai. Colonel Beale had been invalided home and Major T. Currie ("a good old thing but stupid and frightened" – Cecil) had assumed command. On 10 September, after many delays caused by the August storms, the battalion reached Kosheh by rail. On the 12th and 13th it was "steamered" up to the Egyptian Army's latest forward position at Kaderma in preparation for the action known as the Battle of Hafir.

Meanwhile, learning of the difficulties which the Egyptian Army was facing and which appeared to have delayed its advance after Firket, the Governor of Dongola, Mohamed Wad Bishara, sought the Khalifa's permission to attack but was ordered to await reinforcements. A realist and a much wilier commander than most of his colleagues, Bishara took the promise of reinforcements which, when they did arrive, consisted of a few hundred men, with a pinch of salt and prepared two alternative defensive positions to the north of his provincial capital, Dongola. These were the villages of Kerma on the east bank, along which the Anglo-Egyptians were advancing, and Hafir about half a mile upstream on the west bank. Unlike his incompetent lieutenants at Firket, Bishara was determined not to be taken by surprise and when on 18 September patrol reports reached him confirming the advancing enemy's overwhelming numerical superiority, that night he transferred his entire force to the prepared positions at Hafir on the west bank – one of the few shrewd tactical moves made by a Mahdist commander in the campaign. Thus, as the Sirdar's infantry had no means of crossing the river in any large numbers, an operation which anyway would have led to the severe casualties inherent in opposed river crossings, the battle developed into a dual between Bishara's six small Egyptian-manned cannon supported by his *jehadiya* riflemen on the one side and the Anglo-Egyptian steamers and artillery on the other. Bishara also possessed one old Nordenfeldt machine-gun, probably captured from Hicks, which was no match for the Maxims mounted on the steamers.

The first intimation of unusual activity on the part of the hitherto lethargic dervishes was given when the telegraph-wire, which kept pace with the army, was cut on 6 September. Then, on the 15th, there was a brief clash between Egyptian and dervish cavalry patrols. By the 18th, the day on which Bishara slipped across the river, Kitchener was ready to attack Kerma and all was prepared for an assault at dawn the following morning. Accompanied by the three gun-boats *Tamai, Abu Klea* and *Metemma* – *El Teb* was stranded on a rock in the Third Cataract – puffing upstream, virtually the entire Egyptian Army, now reinforced by the three battalions of Major David's[11] 4th Brigade as well as the North Staffords, approached the village as the sun rose, only to find it deserted. But the gunboats, churning on ahead, quickly spotting the dervish fleet of gyassas moored to the opposite bank and the entrenchments and gunpits concealed in the palm groves of Hafir, opened the engagement with salvos from their Krupps and Maxim-Nordenfeldts, accompanied by long bursts from the Maxim machine-guns. Simultaneously the Egyptian artillery came into action from the comparative safety of the east bank, almost out of range of their unwilling compatriots manning the dervish cannon. However, the gunboats, reaching the narrows opposite the village, came under fierce and unusually accurate fire.

On the flotilla leader's vessel, the *Tamai*, the "admiral" himself, Commander the Hon S C G. Colville, was hit in the wrist and Armourer-Sergeant Richardson,[12] blazing away with a Maxim, was killed. Rather ignominiously, the

[11] Lieutenant-Colonel E. F. David, Royal Marine Light Infantry (1862–1898).

[12] Richardson was probably the only machine-gunner to be killed in action during the campaigns of 1896–98. His regiment is nowhere recorded but it is most likely that he was a Royal Marine artilleryman (most of the Egyptian Army Maxims were handled by NCOs of that regiment), but he may have been in the Ordnance Department.

this is the Village of Saverda. amongst hate tukkus & s ome
of the houses are on the plain

C. HENTSCHEL S?

HQ 5S ephines RIGHT
SQUARDA

yptian Cavalry
under BURN MURDCH.
CHASING THE DERVISHS

uld I hold my chaps in EVERY-WHERE THE enemy were scene G
cavalry who went for them in small groups.

Some of the Enemy, burn the Rifle when
fired at close quarters. & in the great heat
bettering fire to their cotton clothes

this draining Cloth lasts but it smells. dust & saved the heat is
Mr Frementons

Egyptian cavalry operations under Major Burn-Murdoch. He is quoted as saying (bottom
left) "I couldn't hold my chaps in. Everywhere the enemy were seen, my cavalry went for
them in small groups".

*Tamai* turned and scurried away downstream "to report to the Sirdar", as
Churchill puts it. The Sirdar's reaction to this report is not recorded, but his
instructions must have been brief and to the point as the *Tamai* steamed back into
the thick of the fight with remarkable rapidity. Soon the *Metemma* (Captain
Oldfield, Royal Marine Artillery) found things too hot for her as well and, turning
about, ran downstream. Dervish snipers perched in the tops of the palm-trees
seem to have presented a particular problem to the gunners on the steamers' decks
as the snipers' angle of fire enabled them to shoot downwards over the tops of the
gunshields. For two and a half hours this inconclusive duel continued until the

Sirdar, fearing for his indispensable gunboats, ordered them to steam on past Hafir to Dongola. At the same time he pushed his artillery and three battalions along a sandbank on to Artagasha Island. Covered by eighteen guns and long-range rifle fire, the steamers ran the gauntlet of the narrows and chugged on towards Dongola. With most of his infantry squatting uselessly on the riverbank, reduced to the role of goggle-eyed spectators by Bishara's clever move of the night before, the Sirdar was forced to accept a stalemate for the time being. Nevertheless, the tremendous pounding to which the Mahdists had been subjected had taken its toll. Both Bishara and Osman Asrak had been wounded and about two hundred of their men killed. Unable to reach their food supplies which lay in gyassas within range of the Sirdar's guns and fearing for their line of retreat, the dervishes slipped away from Hafir, which they had so courageously defended throughout the day against overwhelming odds, during the night.

Finding Hafir deserted, Kitchener, who had lost only two men (Sergeant Richardson and an Egyptian officer) killed and eleven wounded, on the morning of the 20th made use of Bishara's gyassas to start transferring his army to the west bank, on which lay Dongola some 35 miles upstream. This operation took two days and was completed by the afternoon of the 21st when the army set forth on the last stage of the re-occupation of Dongola Province in the name of His Highness the Khedive Abbas Hilmi the Second. Meanwhile the gunboats were bombarding Dongola for the defence of which metropolis (a collection of mud-huts) Bishara was preparing – an intention frustrated by a group of emirs led by his second in command, Musad Qaydum.

Halting at Argo Island and, for a full day's rest, at Zowarat, Kitchener arranged his army for the final approach march and, it was assumed, battle for the provincial capital. Starting in the late afternoon of the 22nd and marching through the night the Anglo-Egyptians choked in each other's dust beneath a full moon and bright stars. For some reason unrecorded, the Connaughts and North Staffords of the composite Maxim battery wore their red tunics, perhaps the last British troops to do so on active service. As dawn approached and the troops deployed for action, the North Staffords, convinced that their patience and frustration was about to be rewarded, were placed in the centre of the front line. At about seven o'clock Mahdist cavalry was sighted on the right flank but withdrew as the Anglo-Egyptians advanced. The writers of the day, including Churchill, assumed that this was a planned withdrawal by Bishara in the face of overwhelming odds. It was not until three-quarters of a century later that the researches of Major Ismat Zulfo revealed that the wounded dervish commander was seized and bound by his own emirs moments before he could launch a suicidal attack on the invaders.

So there was no battle of Dongola and the campaign ended in anticlimax. Bishara, still under arrest, and the remnants of his army crossed the Bayuda

Desert and eventually reached Metemma, suffering great hardship on the way. This brave man, cast in the mould of Wad Nejumi, refused to denounce his subordinates to the Khalifa or to defend himself. Suspected of cowardice, his reputation suffered and his exoneration came only with his death on the field of Kereri.

# 20 Abu Hamed and Berber – a contrast

Two white stone crosses side by side
  Mark where the true blood flowed,
Where Sidney and Fitzclarence died
  To win the desert road.
And ringed about them close at hand
  In trenches not too deep,
Unnamed, unnumbered in the sand,
  Their dead black troopers sleep.
SIR RENNELL RODD.

By the end of September, 1896, Kitchener had occupied Debba and Merowe thus consolidating the Anglo-Egyptian presence in Dongola Province. In terms of combat casualties, 47 killed and 122 wounded, the campaign had been inexpensive but at least a thousand lives had been lost in the cholera epidemic and by other diseases. On the Mahdist side, relatively small forces had been used, all actions had been fought defensively and casualties, by Mahdist standards, had been light. The Khalifa had ventured little and the bulk of his army was still intact but his opponent had gained a strong psychological and strategic advantage.

However, Kitchener's mandate from Cromer and the British Government had been the re-occupation of Dongola, not of the whole of the Sudan. Further he could not go without their reappraisal of the political, military and, in particular, the financial implications of forward movement. Therefore, for the time being, British troops were not required at the front and the North Staffords returned to Cairo in early October. For them the campaign had been a cruel and costly disappointment. Only their small Maxim detachment had seen any real action and the battalion as a whole, barely having fired a shot in anger, lost through disease and accident 64 dead (ironically the North Staffords had been the 64th Regiment) including one officer, the sergeant-major and the band sergeant. By the time Dongola was reached the effective strength of the battalion had been reduced by sickness from nine hundred and ten to five hundred and twenty, or by 43%.

Meanwhile, France and her ally Russia had not been inactive. Although, as we have seen, a majority of the Commissioners of the Debt[1] had approved the use of reserve funds for the campaign, the representatives of France and Russia had brought an action against the Egyptian Government in the Mixed Courts[2] on the grounds of the illegality of this decision. The plaintiffs won the case, a victory which was upheld on appeal. The Egyptian Government was obliged to repay the £E500,000 in question to the Commissioners but Lord Cromer had foreseen the judgement and had arranged for a British Treasury loan to Egypt of £800,000 at 2 3/4%. It is unlikely that the French expected the British to be thwarted by legalities, but whatever tactics could be deployed to delay British occupation of the whole of the Sudan were worth using in the hope that some form of *de facto* French claim to the Upper Nile could be established by Marchand before the final collapse of the Mahdiya.

Emboldened by Kitchener's success and with majority public opinion behind them, for once Her Majesty's Ministers did not dither for long; indeed, as Cromer has pointed out in *Modern Egypt*, the initative had slipped from the grasp of the politicians into the hands of the soldiers. Whatever first intentions may have been, it was impossible now to regard the occupation of Dongola as anything other than the first step in the re-conquest of the entire Sudan. For the Egyptian Army to stay where it was indefinitely would not only have been expensive and pointless but extremely dangerous. Despite his low opinion of the Khalifa's strategic abilities, Cromer later admitted his concern at the possibility of "some European adventurer of the type familiar in India a century or more ago" arriving in Omdurman and advising the Khalifa to concentrate on attacking Kitchener's lines of communication and cutting him off from Egypt. Withdrawal was out of the question, so the only way was forward. Nevertheless, the Egyptian Army was faced with many months of operational inactivity, while "*el sikka el hadid*" (the iron road) crept across the Nubian desert from Wadi Halfa to Abu Hamed, as yet still in Mahdist hands.

This railway, the construction of which started in January, 1897, had made little progress during the first few months of the year. Hampered by a shortage of material, some of which was delayed by an engineering strike in England, and of skilled personnel, it was not until midsummer that work started in earnest, and, writing to the Adjutant-General, Sir Evelyn Wood, on 5 June Kitchener proudly reported that 1,900 yards of track had been laid in four hours and ten minutes. The problem of water supplies for the workforce was eased when wells were successfully sunk at two points along the line, seventy-seven miles and one

[1] *La Caisse de la Dette* (See Chapter 18).
[2] The Mixed Courts were set up in 1875 to adjudicate in civil cases between foreigners and Egyptians (including the Egyptian Government) and between foreigners of different nationalities. They were finally abolished in 1949.

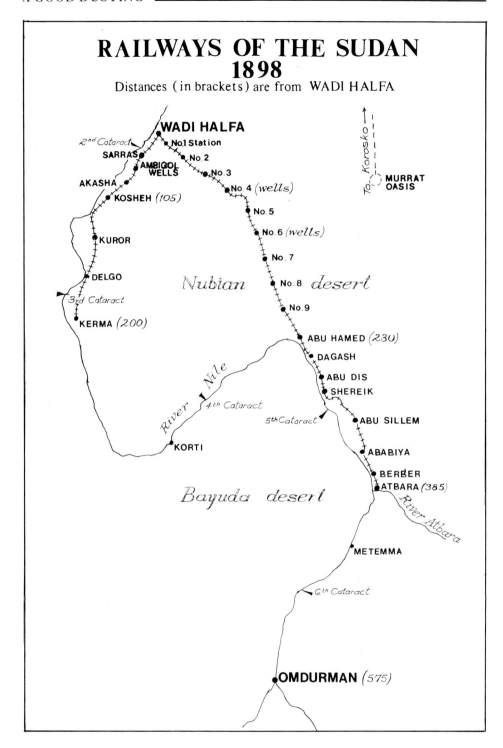

RAILWAYS OF THE SUDAN
1898
Distances (in brackets) are from WADI HALFA

hundred and twenty-six miles respectively from Wadi Halfa, yielding several thousand gallons of water per day, thus considerably reducing the turn-round times of the supply trains.

The British Government had virtually committed itself to crushing "the baleful power of the Khalifa" in a speech to the House of Commons by the Chancellor of the Exchequer, Sir Michael Hicks Beach, in February, 1897, but it was not until the end of July that the next operational step in the process was executed. By the middle of that month the Desert Railway had reached a point about one hundred miles out from Wadi Halfa. Beyond there it was considered imprudent to risk the safety of the workforce, and indeed the success of the whole project, without first seizing Abu Hamed, which, so long as it remained in Mahdist hands, might be used as their launching-pad for raids on the line as well as an obstacle to further advances up-river. Now, with the Nile rising, it would soon be possible for the steamers and gunboats to be hauled over the Fourth Cataract above Merowe in support of a general advance.

In May a strong cavalry patrol had established the absence of effective Mahdist forces along the route from Merowe to Abu Hamed. This patrol, under Captain Le Gallais of the 8th Hussars, clashed only once with dervish cavalry in a sharp skirmish in which it lost eight men killed and six wounded (including Captain W. E. Peyton, 15th Hussars)[3] to the dervishes' fifteen killed. Reporting on this to Sir Evelyn Wood, one of his few allies at the War Office, the Sirdar mentioned his need for "a good young cavalry leader", adding that he had asked Broadwood, on home leave, to look out for one. Broadwood's efforts seem to have been rewarded by the recruitment to the Egyptian Cavalry of a certain Captain Douglas Haig of the 7th Hussars.

But let us turn our attention for a moment from the invader to the invaded. The progress of the Desert Railway seems to have held little meaning for the Khalifa. He was strong in the belief, one so far as we know shared by most of his inner circle, that Kitchener, like his forerunner Wolseley, would use the Korti-Metemma route across the Bayuda Desert as the main axis of his advance. Now Metemma was the capital of the Jaalin tribe and this tribe, long disenchanted with the Mahdiya, could not be trusted to resist the advance, indeed would undoubtedly collaborate with it. Certainly the Khalifa would have been aware that the Jaali chieftain, Abdullah Wad Saad, had attempted to obtain the backing of the Anglo-Egyptians for a proposed rising against him in 1894. So, summoning Wad Saad to Omdurman in June, 1897, the Khalifa ordered the unhappy chief to evacuate his tribesmen from Metemma and its environs so that they could be replaced by a Baggara army from the west, recently arrived at Omdurman and

[3] Described by a brother officer as "a splendid speciman of a man", Peyton had three spear wounds, including one in the back which touched his lung. However, he seems to have recovered as he was Mentioned in Despatches after the Battle of Omdurman over a year later.

preparing to move north under its emir, Mahmud Ahmed, a ferocious young relative of the Khalifa. When Wad Saad, understandably fearful for the safety of the lives and property of his tribe at the hands of Mahmud's rapacious and unruly horde, tried to protest he was brusquely warned that no argument would be tolerated and was ordered from the presence. Returning home he immediately sent an appeal for aid to the Egyptian Army, which was received at Merowe by Major-General Rundle, the Chief of Staff, and acted upon with all speed. A convoy of rifles and ammunition was despatched under escort across the Bayuda to Metemma, but, with astonishing stupidity, Wad Saad had sent another message, this one to the Khalifa, containing a defiant challenge to his authority. Mahmud's army was already on the move and the Khalifa acted with as much speed as had Rundle, sending a messenger to Mahmud by fast camel ordering him to dispense with the niceties and reduce the Jaalin, their capital and their recalcitant leader with fire and sword. Mahmud reached Metemma in the last days of June and, to give him his due, seems to have made an unsuccessful attempt to negotiate with Wad Saad. Rundle's convoy had not arrived and in any case probably would have fallen into Mahmud's hands. Not without some initial reverses, the fierce Baggara stormed Metemma on 1 July, overwhelmed its defences and massacred its inhabitants. A few escaped to Jakdul where they met the convoy from Korti, which returned, disconsolate, to its base.

The appearance at Metemma of Mahmud's army of 10,000 to 12,000 men, the first potentially aggressive move by the Khalifa since the Egyptian Army had crossed the frontier over a year earlier, and its possible use in due course to reinforce the weak garrisons at Abu Hamed and Berber, encouraged the Sirdar to lose no more time in striking against these two important riverside towns. During the last week of July, 1897, the formidable Scots duo of Hunter (now a Major-General) and MacDonald (a Lieutenant-Colonel) were secretly briefed by the Sirdar and the Intelligence Department[4] for the coming operation. The plan was to cover 140 miles from an assembly area at Kassinger above Merowe in a series of forced marches along the north bank of the Nile and swoop upon Abu Hamed before reinforcements from Berber could arrive (Mahmud was still at Metemma some 240 miles to the south). Once again, as at Firket, surprise was of the essence. But it was a tall order and almost inevitable was it that at some stage of the long approach march the column would be detected by enemy patrols.

---

[4] It is unlikely that Wingate himself took much part in the planning of this operation as he had only recently returned to the Sudan from a mission to the Emperor Menelik of Abyssinia led by Mr Rennell Rodd of the Foreign Office. Ostensibly the purpose of this mission was to discuss boundaries but its main objective was to ensure Menelik's neutrality in the campaign against the Mahdiya. That wily monarch gave no specific undertakings but did not intervene in the war despite efforts on the part of the Khalifa to enlist his aid. Lord Edward Cecil and Count Gleichen also took part in the Rodd Mission. See Gleichen's *Mission to Menelik.*

The troops earmarked for the operation, but kept in ignorance of it until the last minute, were the cream of the Egyptian Army; MacDonald's brigade of four battalions, the 9th, 10th and 11th Soudanese and 3rd Egyptians; an artillery battery consisting of six Krupp 12-pdrs., two Maxims and, surprisingly still in use, a couple of old multi-barrelled disasters of infamous memory, a Gardner and a Nordenfeldt,[5] and one troop of cavalry. The fighting troops were accompanied by a transport echelon of one thousand three hundred camels under Lieutenant Healey. These animals carried eighteen days' supply of food and ammunition for the three thousand, six hundred men. Lieutenant Manifold, RE, would unwind a telegraph wire as they went, hopefully keeping the column in constant touch with the Sirdar at Merowe.

Setting out from Kassinger in the early evening of 29 July, Hunter hoped to avoid the worst effects of the crushing heat by marching mostly at night. The lack of paths or tracks made the going very difficult and the absence of shade meant that during the daytime the men sweltered sleepless under their blanket tents. Passing the site of the Battle of Kirbekan and the wreckage of Stewart's steamer *Abbas* with scarcely a sideways glance, Hunter and MacDonald drove their men ruthlessly and a rapid rate of progress was achieved. On 4 August the village of El Kab was reached, well over halfway to their target. Here a shot was fired at the column, warning Hunter that the cat was out of the bag. He pressed on even harder, despite the death from exhaustion of three Egyptian soldiers, normally men of almost limitless endurance, and the collapse of fifty more. Perhaps we should spare a thought for the British NCOs who marched with their battalions. The officers rode horses or camels but the NCOs were not provided with mounts. Tramping along beside the hardy Egyptians and long-legged Soudanese, these rough diamonds were as much the reinforcing steel of the Egyptian Army as they were (and are) of the British. Whether fighting, marching or hauling boats over rapids, with crude jests and a flood of English, Arabic and Hindustani obscenities they urged, threatened and cajoled their "oulad" (boys) to greater feats of courage and endurance. "'Eave, yer buggers, 'eave till I can cut weddin' rings off yer arseholes," one was heard bellowing as the fellahin soldiers strained at the tow-ropes of a steamer plunging and snorting over a cataract.

At Kuli on 5 August the column was joined by 150 Ababdeh Friendlies with the report that reinforcements were en route to Abu Hamed from Berber. A final effort brought the bulk of Hunter's 3,600 men to Ginnifab, within striking distance of Abu Hamed, by the dawn of the 7th, having averaged nearly sixteen miles per day since leaving Kassinger. Detailing half the 3rd Egyptians under Lieutenant J. F. Wolseley (the great man's nephew) to guard the transport,

---

[5] Probably these obsolescent weapons were still in use with the Egyptian Army as their .45 calibre ammunition was interchangeable with that of the Martini-Henry rifles with which the Egyptian troops were equipped.

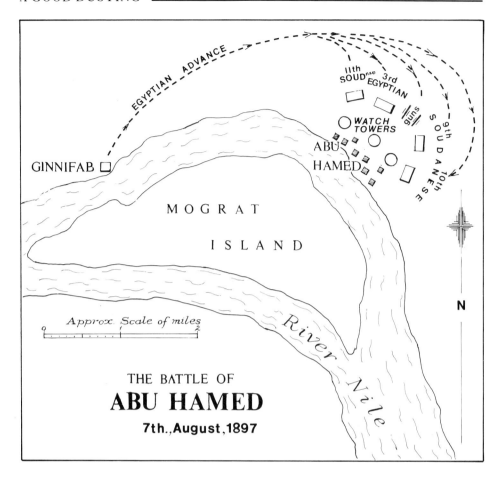

THE BATTLE OF
# ABU HAMED
### 7th., August, 1897

Hunter circled the village to the north and then wheeled his battalions to face west towards the river along which Abu Hamed straggled for about 500 yards. The usual collection of mud-huts and narrow alleys, the village itself was guarded by three watchtowers erected in the days of Gordon. Forewarned of the Egyptian advance, the dervish commander, the Emir Mohamed El Zayn, had caused trenches to be dug and houses fortified. His garrison of seven hundred, roughly three hundred *jehadiya* and four hundred ansar, were said to be made of sterner stuff than most of the opposition so far encountered by the invaders, and so it proved.

For the attack, Hunter deployed his infantry and artillery in a curved line; 11th Soudanese (Major V. T. Bunbury, Leics Regt) on the right, the artillery (Major N. E. Young, RA) with the remaining half-battalion of the 3rd Egyptians (Lieutenant-Colonel J. Sillem, Welsh Regt) next, then the 9th Soudanese (Captain H. V. Ravenscroft, Manchester Regt) and the 10th Soudanese (Major H. M. Sidney, DCLI) on the left.

The *jehadiya* riflemen showed both discipline and courage, holding their fire until MacDonald's brigade, led by its commander, was within 100 yards of the trenches and then letting fly with a co-ordinated hail of bullets. Despite covering fire from the Krupps and machine-guns, the 10th, who found themselves slightly out of formation and were obliged to halt to avoid coming under fire from the 11th on the opposite flank, suffered severely. Two out of their four British officers, the C.O. Major Sidney and Lieutenant Edward Fitzclarence[6] of the Dorsets, were killed, as were twelve Other Ranks and a further fifty were wounded. Nevertheless, the brigade swept through the trenches into the village and fierce street and house-to-house fighting ensued, the Soudanese working gleefully with the bayonet. Hopelessly outnumbered, only a few dervish cavalry escaped. Mohamed el Zayn was taken prisoner but most of his ansar and riflemen, scorning surrender, died fighting. This determined resistance inflicted unusually heavy casualties on the Anglo-Egyptians amounting to over eighty killed and wounded, mostly from the 10th Soudanese.

After the battle there was a moving incident of a kind usually associated with the romantic novels of that period when a mortally wounded veteran of the 10th, Nafar (Private) Hassan Ahmed, asked that his medals, probably his most treasured possessions, should be given to Hunter Pasha, a comrade-in-arms through the long years of frontier patrols and skirmishes.

Touched though he must have been, Hunter had other things on his mind. The satisfactory outcome of his gruelling march and testing fight had been telegraphed to headquarters, but his force was dangerously isolated and he was not overburdened with supplies. However, in the event he had little to fear. The relief force from Berber turned back when it learnt of the fall of Abu Hamed and Mahmud dithered at Metemma. Meanwhile, the Sirdar had started to move the gunboats up the rising river on 4 August, simultaneously sending instructions to railhead for work to resume. *El Teb* was wrecked on the Fourth Cataract, its crew, including Beatty, miraculously escaping almost certain death in the raging torrent. When the Royal Marine Officer in charge of negotiating the boats over the cataract, Major David, was relieved by Commander Keppel better progress was made, despite much confusion and disarray among the locally recruited Shaigia and regular Egyptian Army "tug-of-war" teams, and by 29 August five gunboats, *Tamai, Metemma, Fateh, Nasr* and the repaired *Zafir*, had reached Abu Hamed.

At about the same time the Camel Corps under Major Tudway had pushed across the Bayuda to Jakdul and joined up with the remnants of the Jaalin from Metemma. Tudway had passed this way twelve years before as a subaltern in

---

[6] Fitzclarence was a reputed great-grandson of King William the Fourth. Remarkably Sidney and he were the only British officers of the Egyptian Army to be killed in action during the campaign of re-conquest (1896/8), although a number were seriously wounded and several died of disease.

Wolseley's Mounted Infantry Camel Regiment. Hunter, consolidating his position at Abu Hamed, had despatched the Ababdeh Friendlies to check on the situation at Berber and was astonished to learn that this vital town had been evacuated. The garrison commander there, the Emir Zaki Osman, despairing of aid from Mahmud who was taking his time ferrying his semi-mutinous Baggara across from Metemma to the east bank while carrying on a rambling correspondence with the Khalifa, had no wish to share the fate of his colleague at Abu Hamed and had decided to clear out while the going was good.

Hunter's telegram reporting this unexpected turn of events faced the Sirdar with a difficult decision and marked the beginning of a period of uncertainty for him which festered into a boil of self-doubt and fear of betrayal by his superiors. On the one hand he was eager to take advantage of Zaki Osman's precipitate withdrawal. The immediate occupation of Berber by the Egyptian Army would not only bring Omdurman 130 miles nearer but would prevent its re-occupation by the Mahdists and open the shortest route from Suakin to the Nile along which both reinforcements and supplies could travel. Furthermore, this great and sudden leap forward would impress those Red Sea and riverain tribes still perched on the fence between Anglo-Egypt and the Mahdiya. On the other hand, Kitchener was short of men and money. His "front" which was already stretched from Dongola to Abu Hamed would be extended by a further 130 miles. The uncompleted Desert Railway had to be constantly supplied and protected (although the capture of Abu Hamed had considerably lessened the danger of raids on the line and workforce) and the Korti-Metemma route patrolled. Alarmingly, the Italians were talking of withdrawal from Kassala which had proved an unproductive liability for them, and their departure and the town's possible re-occupation by the Mahdists would expose the Sirdar's left flank to danger.

However, a rapid and positive decision was reached and on 3 September, 1897, with Cromer's somewhat reluctant acquiescence, Hunter was ordered to occupy Berber, where he arrived on the 5th with an advance party of half a battalion of Soudanese (9th) in four gunboats. The Sirdar himself lost no time inspecting his latest acquisition, riding across the desert from Merowe to Berber in a few days. On 22 September he informed Wood at the War Office that he had five battalions at Berber and three more pulling boats over the cataracts. A few days later he wrote again to Wood expressing his concern that his Egyptian and Soudanese troops had been away from their homes and families for too long. But in those days home leave for Other Ranks in the course of a long campaign was almost unheard of and in any case he had no men to spare for leave. Mahdist morale, he told Wood, had not yet cracked and Kassala must be garrisoned.

The question of Kassala weighed heavily on the Sirdar's mind. The detested Palmer at the Ministry of Finance in Cairo held the purse-strings and, being

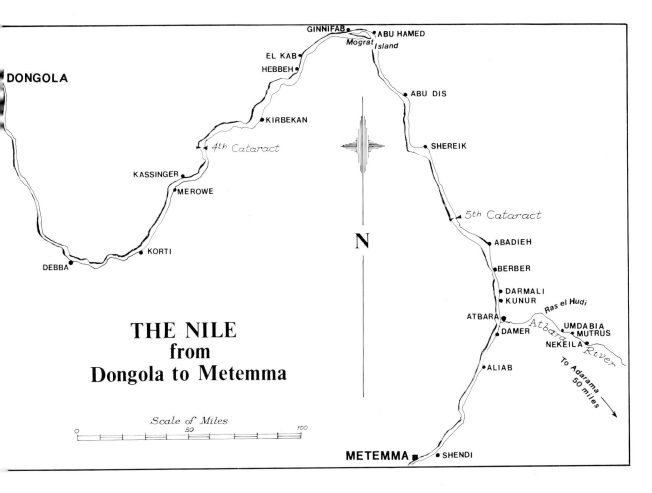

THE NILE
from
Dongola to Metemma

Scale of Miles

entirely without military understanding, opposed the allocation of special funds for an expedition from Suakin to occupy Kassala. Several other factors, including the fear of being superseded by the previous Sirdar, Sir Francis Grenfell, who had recently been appointed to command the British Army of Occupation in Egypt (the Army of No Occupation, Kitchener called it) and sheer physical exhaustion and strain after eighteen months campaigning in an atrocious climate, combined to bring Kitchener to the verge of a nervous breakdown. On 18 October, 1897, he cabled his resignation to Lord Cromer.

This rather theatrical gesture was not, however, intended to be taken seriously, at least not too seriously, and Cromer who, despite occasional doubts, had confidence in Kitchener, apparently handled the tantrum by simply not referring to it. In November the two men met in Cairo where Kitchener was reassured that there was no thought of replacing him with Grenfell, even if and when British troops were sent to the Sudan. Nevertheless, financial wrangling continued and in a letter to Wood of 17 November Kitchener complained, "I have to fight for money" but denied rumours that he did not get on with Cromer, which, he said, "were traceable to foreign sources". In truth, these sources were probably about as foreign as Kitchener's jealous rivals in the British Army and his enemies among the British officials in Cairo. That Cromer was playing something of a double game there is little doubt. He had never been very keen on the reconquest of the Sudan, in his view a frivolous and expensive adventure which Egypt could ill afford. However, if it had to be done, he wanted Kitchener, an "Egyptian" officer and therefore responsible to him, to do it, not Grenfell or some general from home answering to the War Office. So he poured hot and cold; through Palmer he kept the financial squeeze on Kitchener but, through Salisbury, protected him against his enemies and rivals in London.

Thus, in due course, funds were made available for the occupation of Kassala which took place formally on Christmas Day, 1897, when Lieutenant-Colonel C. S. B. Parsons, RA, with an Egyptian reserve battalion from Suakin, received the town from the Italians and ran up the Khedivial flag.

Meanwhile, operations on the ground and river continued. The flotilla of gunboats having been dragged over the 5th Cataract was playing havoc along the dervish-held riverbanks upstream from Berber. In mid-October, the *Zafir*, *Fateh* and *Nasr* under Commander Keppel reached Shendi (opposite Metemma) and for a couple of days and for the loss of only one man rained shot and shell on Mahmud's fortifications and blazed away with their Maxims at everything that moved. At the same time reports reached Berber that Osman Digna was on the move again after a long absence from the stage. A battalion group (11th Soudanese and Camel Corps) marched the eighty miles to Adarama on the Atbara River where the desert fox had been twiddling his thumbs for many months. His deserted camp confirmed his departure but his precise itinerary is uncertain. Some accounts have him withdrawing as far as Shabluka, others marching directly to join Mahmud at Shendi, where, indeed he was to be found with four or five thousand men early in the following year.

The Desert Railway reached Abu Hamed on 31 October, exactly ten months after the first spike had been driven. Only seventeen miles of tracklaying material remained unused so the line could only be pushed forward as far as Dagash until fresh supplies of material arrived in the New Year. During the last weeks of 1897 the Intelligence Department was insisting that the Khalifa was preparing substantial reinforcements for Mahmud and Osman Digna and even that he was determined to march north himself at the head of his Omdurman army to confront the insolent Turk. There may or may not have been substance to these rumours, which came to nothing. They may even have been invented, or at least embellished, by Wingate and his staff but they were enough for the call to go out for British troops and on New Year's Day, 1898, they were summoned.

The work-horse of the campaign of re-conquest.

(*Overleaf*)   " 'Eave, yer buggers, 'eave!" A gunboat being hauled over a cataract.

The assault on Abu Hamed. Major Bunbury leading the 11th Sudanese into the attack.

# 21 An Old-Fashioned Battle

Then Tommy, Tommy Atkins,
Do your duty like a man!
Let your chest stop lots of bullets
For this life is but a span.
Far better to be planted
On some sunny southern shore
Than come back where you're not wanted
When your fighting days are o'er!
            Lance-Sergeant Colin Grieve, Seaforth Highlanders. c. 1898

A British Infantry Brigade under Major-General William Gatacre,[1] a wiry fifty-five year old martinet, reached Berber from Egypt by the end of February, 1898. This brigade consisted of the 1st Battalions of the Warwicks, Lincolns and Cameron Highlanders, all part of the British Army of Occupation in Egypt. Supporting troops included a Royal Artillery detachment equipped with two 40-pounders, six 5 in. howitzers and six Maxim machine-guns, and a company of Royal Engineers. A little later the 1st Battalion Seaforth Highlanders arrived from Malta and was held in reserve for a while in Egypt.

The British soldier of the day was a brave, hardy and good-hearted soul but his intellectual horizons were limited and there was some confusion among the men as to whose side they were on. Was it the Khedive they were after or the Khalifa, or was he one and the same? No matter, there would be fighting, loot, booze and women, albeit black but probably cleaner than the whores of Cairo and Alex or even Aldershot. They were to be disappointed on the last two counts. Corporal George Skinner, a 30-year-old former teacher serving with the Medical Staff Corps,[2] recorded his horror and consternation when he heard that "this was to be

---

[1] Major-General Sir William Gatacre, KCB, DSO (1843–1906). Although Gatacre was almost universally unpopular, Kitchener seems to have got on with him well enough. "Gatacre," he wrote to Wood, "appears to me to be just the right man for the post."
[2] During the campaign members of the Medical Staff Corps were amalgamated with the Army Medical Service to become the Royal Army Medical Corps.

Major-General W. Gatacre, commanding British Division 1898.

a tee-total expedition" and "of course the troops began to moan when it was known that the officers were getting as much as they wanted". This blow was confirmed by Kitchener in a letter to Wood: "am refusing to allow beer to be sent on. I had some experience of it in '96". And, as for girls, "I am sure," he continued to Wood, "it will be better for the Seaforths to be with the Brigade here (Berber) rather than at Assouan where there are 3,000 Sudanese ladies of the soldiers."

Few remembered the journey to the front with pleasure. Skinner travelled with the Lincolns, who, even on the first leg by rail from Cairo to Upper Egypt "were packed like sardines . . . the dust making everyone look more like nigars (sic)". For some it was all too much. Sergeant Haines of the Lincolns cut his own throat "from ear to ear", Skinner's diary records without elaboration. The worst part was the 230-mile trip in open trucks from Wadi Halfa to Abu Hamed (Skinner increases the distance by some 120 miles), frequent "campseines", Skinner's version of the Arabic word *khamseen*, covering the men with choking dust once again.

But the Medical Staff Corps section of nine men under a staff-sergeant had supplied itself with whisky before leaving Cairo and convivial evenings were "whiled away with pipe and song". Also the food en route was an improvement on that provided by the cookhouse at Kasr el Nil Barracks in Cairo. The ration per man per day was 1 lb of bread, 1 lb of fresh meat (mostly goat), ½ lb onions, 1 lb potatoes, ½ oz. tea, 2 oz. sugar, ½ oz. salt and ⅓ oz. pepper. So long as they were travelling through the populated areas of Egypt this could be supplemented by local purchase at prices within reach of the most impecunious Tommy – 14 eggs for a piastre (1p) and 6 chickens for 20 piastres, for example.

Skinner, with his background as a teacher, was rather more appreciative of the marvels of ancient Egypt, glimpsed from train or steamer, than some of his colleagues or even officers. Once into the Sudan there was little to be seen, but at Abu Hamed the troops were shown the more recent and less elaborate tombs of Sidney and Fitzclarence.

At this time the railhead had reached Shereik, about seventy miles short of Berber, and after a series of marches the British arrived at the Egyptian Army encampment, where they were served with coffee, the traditional cup of welcome. The 9th Soudanese, nicknamed the 2nd Battalion Cameron Highlanders, greeted their namesakes with particular enthusiasm, even cooking their teas for them, we are told. The Camerons had been brigaded with the 9th at the battle of Ginnis in 1885 and had afterwards presented them with a set of bagpipes.

But for the moment we must leave this scene of good fellowship to follow the fortunes of the opposition whose leaders' relationships with each other were not quite so harmonious.

Mahmud and his army had remained in and around Shendi and among the unburied dead at Metemma for months. Once the surviving local population had been plundered of all it had, food for the Baggara ran short, disease raged and desertions increased. Mahmud's problems grew when he was joined by another four or five thousand men, mostly Beja, under Osman Digna. They mixed like oil and water. The cunning old fox and the fierce young tiger did not see things in the same light. Mahmud had no experience of fighting the British, whereas Osman had clashed with them many times and knew that direct confrontation spelt defeat. The Baggari warlord, however, was scornful of the veteran's advice. Long experience may have taught the Beja how to avoid destruction, he mocked, but not how to achieve victory. The Khalifa, although he had drawn Mahmud's attention to Osman's seniority, does not seem to have appointed one or the other as overall commander, perhaps because the loose and ill-defined tribal, religious, civil and military hierarchies of the Mahdist state did not lend themselves readily to such clear-cut appointments. Therefore the strategic disputes between the two captains was referred to the Khalifa, causing further delay and confusion.

Mahmud wanted to march downstream and attack Kitchener at the junction of the Nile and the Atbara. Osman knew that this would be suicidal and appealed to the Khalifa to order Mahmud to leave the Nile and march eastwards to the Atbara. By the time the Khalifa's decision was received they had reached the village of Aliab on the east bank of the Nile and had suffered considerably from the Sirdar's marauding gunboats. The Khalifa agreed with Osman and even Mahmud may have been relieved to march away from the constant shelling and machine-gunning. Reaching the Atbara after a thirsty trek, the two emirs again disagreed on the next step. Osman advised that they should move away from the Anglo-Egyptians, down the semi-dry bed of the river in a south-easterly direction, arguing that the Sirdar would not continue his advance south while his eastern flank was threatened. Mahmud, on the other hand, regarded this as nothing but an excuse to avoid battle. The Anglo-Egyptian army drew him like a magnet, so, without consulting the Khalifa and ignoring Osman's advice, he marched north-west towards the junction of the two rivers. However, upon reaching a place called Nakheila he decided that discretion might be the better part of valour and constructed a large zariba in which he built huts, dug trenches and waited for the invaders to appear.

Now, in mid-March, 1898, the Sirdar was moving his 14,000 men from their latest encampment at Kunur on the Nile to Ras el Hudi on the Atbara, only a few miles from Mahmud's zariba. But he was torn with doubt and indecision and during the first week of April underwent another of his crises of self-confidence. He wished to avoid assaulting the zariba as he feared a heavy "butcher's bill" and consequent displeasure at home and in Cairo. His aim was to tempt or bait Mahmud into a furious headlong attack upon the deadly ranks of Lee-Metford .303s, with which the British infantry were now equipped, and the scything Maxims. On the other hand Mahmud might at last listen to wiser and more cautious voices and slip away, and the chance to destroy him would then be lost.

In the British Brigade rumours of the imminence of a dervish attack and/or the impregnability of the Nakheila zariba were encouraged by Gatacre's barely articulate and alarmist speeches to the troops. So jittery did they become that one night a stray donkey wandered into camp and was shot at by a Lincoln sentry. This sparked off a brisk bayonet fight between Lincolns and Seaforths in which several men were wounded. From then on bayonets were not to be fixed without specific instructions from an officer.

A reconnaissance in strength by Hunter on 30 March failed to lure Mahmud from his stronghold and served only to increase Kitchener's doubts. Hunter reported that the zariba was formidably defended with barriers of thorn, a stockade, rifle-pits and trenches. Uncharacteristically he counselled caution while Gatacre urged attack. To the consternation of that worthy civilian, Kitchener sought the advice of Cromer,[3] who in turn consulted Grenfell and the War Office. There followed a flurry of inconclusive telegrams. Of course it was a decision that only Kitchener could take and Wolseley, now Commander-in-Chief of the British Army, was disappointed and indignant that the Sirdar, the man on the spot, was apparently incapable of making up his own mind. In these circumstances it is especially odd that Kitchener did not go himself to inspect the zariba. Instead, on 5 April, he sent Hunter out again. This time Hunter's patrol was attacked by dervish horse and had to withdraw under some pressure. Several Egyptian cavalry troopers were killed and Captain Persse of the Scots Greys wounded.[4] But still the enemy would not emerge in full strength and on the following day Kitchener made up his mind to attack.

In the event, as will be seen, all three senior officers, Kitchener, Hunter and Gatacre, had greatly overestimated the strength of Mahmud's position[5] and the defensive capabilities of his ansar. Nor were they aware that Osman Digna had no intention of taking part in any forthcoming hostilities and would remove himself and most of his men from the scene in the early stages of the battle.

Earlier, on 25 March, the Sirdar had despatched the 15th Egyptians under Major T. E. Hickman of the Worcesters, two guns and some Jaalin Friendlies in three gunboats to Mahmud's rear headquarters at Shendi, the object being not only to destroy the place and its small garrison but to hamper Mahmud's line of retreat and further demoralise his army by capturing their women and other belongings. There was little resistance and the fleeing defenders were pursued

---

[3] Cromer had once been an artillery officer but had no experience of active service.

[4] The recently arrived Douglas Haig took part in this action as Broadwood's staff officer. According to his own account he extricated the cavalry from a dangerous situation by checking the precipitate withdrawal of two squadrons, redeploying others and bringing the Maxims into play.

[5] For example, the much vaunted stockade seems to have been low and full of gaps.

The ill-fated gunboat *Zafir* in action at Shendi.

by the Jaalin who wrought some vengeance for the massacre of their fellow tribesmen. The flotilla returned to base loaded with women and loot; the former, Churchill's *River War* records perkily, "contracted new family ties with the Soudanese soldiery and, as far as can be ascertained, lived happily ever afterwards".

The troops had been ready for action for weeks and were eager to get on with the job. Kitchener decided upon Good Friday, 8 April, as the day on which Mahmud would be least likely to expect an attack from a partly Christian force. Either he was crediting his opponent with a knowledge of the Christian calendar which he was unlikely to possess or Wingate had arranged for his agents to leak the information that Good Friday was the one day on which the Anglo-Egyptians would *not* attack. Be that as it may, as the holy day dawned, the army was deployed for the assault about 800 yards to the north of the zariba.

Mahmud's zariba was roughly circular. To its east and west the approaches to it were covered in scrub and to the south there was a fringe of vegetation between its outer defences and the semi-dry riverbed of the Atbara.[6] Only to the north was the ground open and it was from this direction that the Sirdar intended to attack. Why attack across open country when the objective could be approached under cover from any other direction? We can only guess at the reasons for this decision. Probably Kitchener and his brigadiers feared that the troops would become confused and tangled in the scrub, that the companies, battalions and brigades would lose contact with each other and with their commanders. The Victorian infantryman was not trained as an individual as his equivalent is today. Barrack-square drill and battlefield formations were directly related. Dressing and instant obedience to a word of command or bugle all were vital to the success of an attack or the steadiness of a withdrawal. Perhaps also it was thought the effect of a lengthy and concentrated artillery bombardment would so stun and shell-shock the defenders that it would make no difference from which direction the infantry came. But whatever the Sirdar's thinking, the simplistic tactics he adopted risked the heavy casualties he feared so much. At the time there was no public criticism of this aspect of the battle; indeed so fulsome and exaggerated was the praise heaped upon all concerned, from the Sirdar downwards, in the British Press that those who took part were rather embarrassed. Nevertheless, the senior men could not resist the temptation to criticize each other in private. "Gatacre's formation for attack," wrote Hunter to his former colonel after the battle, "was as bad as bad could be, ours (the Egyptian Army's) was the correct one." In fact there was little to choose between them and Walter Kitchener, jealous of any credit which might be diverted from his brother, laid into both generals indiscriminately. Gatacre was "a red-hot madman," he wrote to his wife, and if Hunter had been in charge there would have been "a butcher's bill of a thousand".

At the start-line the Anglo-Egyptian infantry was deployed along a curved front of approximately 1,500 yards. Way out to the left (east) of this line were the eight squadrons of Egyptian cavalry under Broadwood, accompanied by Haig who observed the infantry battle from this position and later commented unfavourably but unofficially to the Adjutant-General, Wood, on the tactics employed. The enemy's trenches, he said, should have been enfiladed by the Maxims and the retreat cut off, but he believed that the Black (Soudanese) battalions could not be relied upon to shoot and manoeuvre efficiently, thus limiting the Sirdar's options. From left to right were poised the British Brigade under Gatacre, 2nd Egyptian Brigade (9th, 10th and 11th Soudanese and 2nd Egyptians) under MacDonald and 1st Egyptian Brigade (12th, 13th and 14th Soudanese and 8th Egyptians) under Maxwell. In reserve under Lewis was 3rd Egyptian Brigade (3rd, 4th and 7th Egyptians). Two batteries of artillery were positioned to the right of Maxwell's

---

[6] The River Atbara flows only during the rainy season in the Ethiopian highlands where it rises. During the rest of the year its bed contains a few stagnant pools.

Major F. J. Pink leading his battalion, the 2nd Egyptians, in the attack. Turkish caption reads "Second Battalion – Advance!" Artist believed to be Lieutenant Felix Ready, one of Pink's officers.

brigade and two between and just forward of MacDonald's and Gatacre's. Also present was a Rocket Battery under Lieutenant David Beatty, RN. This was placed first on the left and then on the right of the line. The Maxims were with the cavalry.

The proceedings opened at 6.15 am with an artillery barrage which brought the Mahdist cavalry thundering out of the zariba in the direction of their Egyptian counterparts but a few bursts from the Maxims sent them galloping off to the

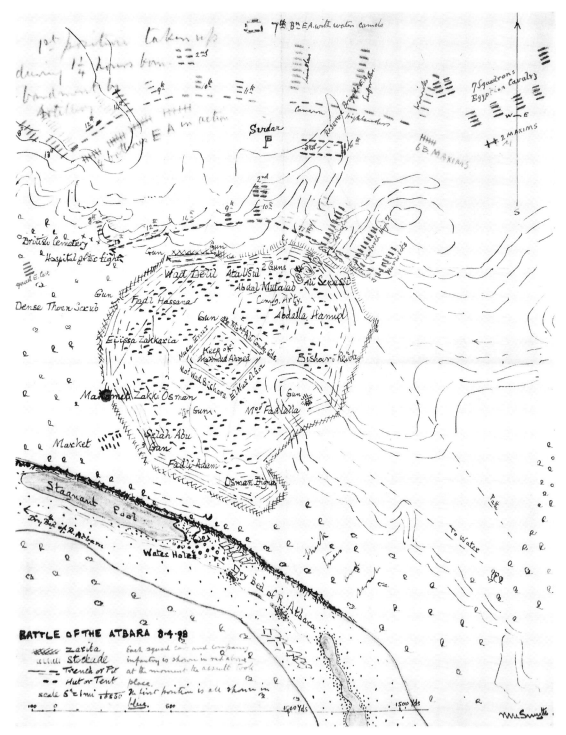

Original map by Captain N. M. Smyth, VC, Egyptian Army Intelligence Department.

south whence they did not return to the fray. The rockets set fire to many of the straw huts but the effects of the bombardment are uncertain. Haig in his letter to Wood, and quoting Captain Fitton of the Intelligence staff, says that Mahmud and other prisoners under interrogation shrugged it off saying that it killed only donkeys and camels. However, it is most unlikely that a sustained barrage lasting an hour and a half would have had no effect on the morale of those at the receiving end, particularly as they were unaccustomed to that type of warfare, and all the accounts by eye-witnesses record the physical and material devastation it caused.

For perhaps the last time in British military history, a brigade commander placed himself at the head of his brigade and led it into battle on foot with drawn sword – a kind of infantry Cardigan but with less disastrous results. Beside Gatacre were his ADC, Captain Ronald Brooke of the 7th Hussars, his chief clerk, Lance-Sergeant Wyeth of the Army Service Corps carrying a large and conspicuous Union Jack, and his orderly, Private Cross of the Camerons. Behind this little group were the Camerons in line abreast and behind them the Lincolns ("first rate in every way" – Kitchener to Wood), the Warwicks and the Seaforths, drawn up in column of companies.

At 7.45 am the barrage lifted and the thin note of a bugle, taken up by others, sounded the Advance. With beating drums, skirling pipes and flashing bayonets, the long curved mass of troops, black, white and brown, surged forward. No gun spoke from the zariba and the *jehadiya* riflemen held their fire, aware of the limitations of their decrepit Remingtons (some were without sights) and their own marksmanship.

The British infantry marched forward with parade-ground precision, "as slow as a funeral" in Hunter's opinion, officers assuming an air of nonchalance, NCOs checking the dressing of the ranks and barking orders of adjustment. Occasionally they halted to allow the Camerons to aim and fire but the rest of the brigade remained at the slope. By adopting this formation Gatacre had effectively reduced the fire-power of his brigade to a fraction of its potential.

On his right, Hunter's two forward brigades were moving into the attack at the double with all six Soudanese battalions massed at the front. Unlike Gatacre, the Egyptian commanders Hunter, MacDonald and Maxwell rode into battle on their chargers; to dismount would have meant an undignified scamper for the three relatively stumpy Scotsmen trying to keep up with their stork-legged warriors.

The *jehadiya* opened up at about 300 yards. Young Neville Cameron, a subaltern in Captain Findlay's C Company, afterwards posed his father, a Crimean veteran, a rhetorical question, "How many out of a regiment," he wrote, "will survive encountering such fire from other European troops?" Cameron lived to witness the answer both in South Africa and France but, despite the *jehadiya*'s inaccuracy, a number of his company, including its commander, did not.

The zariba presented a much less daunting obstacle than had been reported

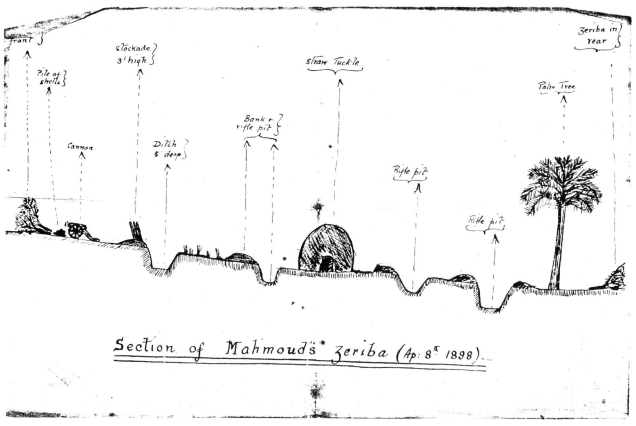

Front
Pile of shells
Stockade 3' high
Straw Tuckle
Zeriba in rear
Cannon
Ditch 5 deep
Bank + rifle pit
Rifle pit
Rifle pit
Palm Tree

Section of Mahmoud's Zeriba (Ap. 8ᵗ 1898).

Original drawing by Lieutenant R. Meiklejohn, Royal Warwickshire Regiment.

following Hunter's reconnaissances. Lieutenant Moir, RE, had devised various explosive and grappling contraptions with which to blow up and rip away the thorn bushes and palisade. In the event the men simply used their blankets to protect their hands from the thorns and Gatacre, first to reach the zariba, was attacked by a whirling dervish with a huge spear as he tugged at the loose branches. "Give him the bayonet, lad!" he growled at Cross and strode on into the blazing inferno to which Mahmud's fortress had been reduced. Meanwhile, the flag-bearing Wyeth had been seriously wounded by a bullet in the leg and died a few days later when it was amputated. This incident led to criticism from Brooke, who's brother Reginald in a letter to a friend, accused Gatacre of causing the death of a fine soldier by exposing him as an obvious target under his unnecessary Union Jack.

"The Blacks went through the zariba like paper," wrote Walter Kitchener, and, as a result, suffered fewer casualties at this stage than did their British comrades, whose stately progress up to the defences had cost them the majority of their one hundred and twenty-five killed and wounded. The mayhem and carnage within the zariba was a nightmare of horror. Men, women, children and animals, shattered and disembowelled by shell-fire, littered the ground and filled the entrenchments. Both British and Egyptian Army officers temporarily lost control of their men who rampaged through the Mahdist camp venting their blood-lust indiscriminately. Even dervishes holding out the traditional mimosa sprig of submission were ruthlessly shot, bayoneted or clubbed. "Tommy was as bad as the Blacks," observed Walter Kitchener, and remembered Brooke remonstrating furiously with a British private: "Hey, you, what did you shoot that man for?" and getting the indignant reply, "Well, sir, I didn't think he was quite dead!" Cameron, reaching the river bed on the far side, found that only three of his men were still with him, the rest were either dead, wounded or going about some grisly business of their own. The planned role of his and F and H Companies had been to tear away the zariba and defend the gap, thus allowing the rest of the brigade to pour through it. However, in the event, enthusiasm overcame discipline and all charged on together. Despite the inhibiting formation adopted by Gatacre, the four British battalions managed to loose off some 56,000 rounds of ammunition, probably about half during the advance and the remainder inside the zariba.

Mahmud himself, found crouching wounded in a dugout, was seized by men of the 10th Soudanese and rescued from their bayonets by a staff officer, Captain Franks. Dragged bleeding before the Sirdar, he glared unwaveringly at his conqueror, responded defiantly to a few brief questions and was removed for interrogation, humiliation at a "Roman Carnival" parade through Berber a few days later, harsh imprisonment at Rosetta and premature death.[7] Osman Digna, whose men had taken little part in the action, escaped capture yet again.

The poetic Ulsterman, Lance-Sergeant Colin Grieve, arriving to join his regiment, the Seaforths, shortly after the battle, wrote home to say that the English battalions had had very few casualties as the Jocks had done all the work "in one of the greatest bayonet fights since the Crimea". Of course his own regiment "was not what it used to be (as) that lot that joined us in Malta played the mischief with it". But Neville Cameron was more restrained and admitted to his father that "we fully recognise the mass of exaggeration and twaddle in the papers about the job".

Inadequate medical facilities, shelter and transport for the wounded were another subject of complaint against Gatacre. Left to swelter in the unshaded first-aid post outside the zariba for some twelve hours after the battle, the wounded suffered the torments of the damned. Eventually borne away to the field hospital at Umdabia about eight miles distant by Egyptian stretcher-bearers, many succumbed to their untreated wounds before proper attention could be

[7] He died in 1906, still under forty years of age.

The Emir Mahmud is brought before the Sirdar by men of the 10th Soudanese. The three officers immediately behind the Sirdar are (l to r) Lord Edward Cecil, Colonel Wingate and General Hunter.

provided. Doubtless Gatacre, as well as the Sirdar himself and other senior officers, bore some responsibility for this but the ultimate blame must lie with Cromer and Palmer whose constant nagging over money forced Kitchener to economize on essentials. However, one of Kitchener's staff officers, Captain Sir Henry Rawlinson,[8] contrasted the British medical services unfavourably with the Egyptian and placed the blame squarely on the SMO of the British Brigade, Lieutenant-Colonel MacNamara, a "weak, theoretical, silly old man". Later the trembling MacNamara was given a "real good dressing down" by the Sirdar.

Burial arrangements, too, seem to have been skimped. Three padres, including the ubiquitous Father Brindle, officiated at the interment of the British fallen, but when Lieutenant Meiklejohn of the Warwicks returned to inspect the cemetery a couple of months later he found to his horror that poor Findlay's feet were sticking out of the ground (whether or not booted like Herbert's before him, Meiklejohn does not relate). Meiklejohn felt that the dead should be buried in coffins not just wrapped in blankets as apparently "kangaroo rats burrowed down and ate the bodies". "However," he mused philosophically, "it doesn't matter I suppose and it may happen to a good many of us before long."

[8] General Lord Rawlinson (1864–1925) the successful commander of the 4th British Army in 1918. After the Great War he was Commander-in-Chief India, where he died.

Anglo-Egyptian losses were officially recorded as eighty-one killed and four hundred and seventy-eight wounded. In the British Brigade, as suggested by Grieve, the majority of the casualties were in the two Highland regiments. Of the Camerons, as well as Captain Findlay, Major Urquhart, Piper Stewart and a dozen others were killed in action. Major Napier and four or five private soldiers later died of their wounds and about forty men were less seriously wounded. The Seaforths too suffered considerably. Their commanding officer, Colonel Murray, was shot in the arm and Second-Lieutenant Gore, one of the youngest officers in the battalion with only nine months service, was killed outright coming through the zariba. Captain Baillie died after having his wounded leg amputated and five rank and file were killed in action. Captain Maclachlan, Lieutenants Vandeleur (accidentally shot by a Soudanese soldier) and Thomson and about twenty men were wounded. The two English county regiments suffered less seriously although Colonel Verner of the Lincolns was badly wounded in the face, invalided home and placed on half-pay. Two other officers of the battalion, Lieutenants Boxer and Rennie, and thirteen other ranks, were wounded and Sergeant Malone and Private Taylor were killed. The Warwicks lost Privates Hale, Howling, Lee and Powers killed in action and Lieutenant Greer and a dozen men wounded, Private Tuckey dying later of his wounds.

Of the Soudanese battalions, the 11th was particularly severely mauled, taking over one hundred casualties in killed and wounded. Half a dozen British officers and NCOs were wounded, Captain Walsh of the 12th Soudanese losing a leg, but none killed. Several of the British sergeants with the Egyptian Army received the DCM as did Gatacre's orderly Cross who died of typhoid a few weeks later.

The Mahdist dead were not officially counted. Contemporary reports indicated a figure of between two and three thousand but it has been suggested that Kitchener concealed the true and much larger number in order to avoid an international outcry against such slaughter. It is difficult to find any grounds for such an assertion, particularly as a far greater number of dead were meticulously counted and reported after the Battle of Omdurman five months later.

The infantry tactics adopted at the Battle of the Atbara were unimaginative and as old as war itself, reflecting little credit upon the Sirdar, although he received much. Given the discipline and steadiness of the British troops in the advance, the elan of the Soudanese and the destructive power of the artillery, any reasonably competent officer could have fought and won this battle, perhaps with lighter casualties. Kitchener's real achievement was to have brought a force of this size to such a remote and inhospitable spot, feed it, water it and maintain its fighting condition. The Good Friday battle opened the road to conclusions with the Khalifa whose only major force outside Omdurman was now broken and scattered. But much sweat was to drip from many bodies before the final goal was reached.

# 22  A Long Hot Summer

Scene.  *The office of the commander of A Company, 1st Btn. Royal Irish Fusiliers, Mustafa Pasha Barracks, Alexandria, in the early summer of 1898. The* COMPANY COMMANDER *sits at his desk lighting a small cigar. By the door stands the* COLOUR SERGEANT *at attention, his sun helmet squarely on his head, his pace-stick under his left arm.*

*Company Commanders Orders are over and a few men have been sentenced to light punishments for drunkenness and fighting with the men of other regiments in the town.* (Beggin' yer honour's pardon, sor, dey insolted the rig'ment, sor!).

COMPANY COMMANDER:    Wish I had a guinea for every time I've heard that one, Colour Sarnt!

COLOUR SERGEANT (*wintry smile flickering across granite features*):    Sor!

COMPANY COMMANDER (*thinking of a glass of madeira in the mess*):    Anything else?

COLOUR SERGEANT:    Yessor, there's Corp'l Mullin to see yer, sor.

COMPANY COMMANDER:    What's he want?

COLOUR SERGEANT:    Transfer to the machine-gun batt'ry, sor.

COMPANY COMMANDER:    Transfer, eh? Don't know about that, Colour Sarnt, good steady feller Mullin. Don't want to lose him, do we?

COLOUR SERGEANT:    Nosor, steady man, Sor.

COMPANY COMMANDER:    Well, get him in anyway.

*The* COLOUR SERGEANT *flings open the door and roars* Corp'l Mullin! *With a crash and stamp of heavy boots,* MULLIN *marches in, halts, throws up a quivering salute and stands rigidly to attention in front of the* COMPANY COMMANDERS' *desk. He is a short, broad man, sweating slightly in the humid heat,*

*but impeccably turned out. He is in his mid-thirties, sporting a heavy "Kitchener"*
*moustache, concealing his long upper lip and a few tobacco-stained teeth.*

COMPANY COMMANDER:    What's this about a transfer to the Maxims then,
Corp'l Mullin?

MULLIN:    Yessor, its not that I'm after leaving the comp'ny, sor, its just
that I done the course and I really fancy them gons, sor.

COMPANY COMMANDER:    And the extra thruppence a day, eh?

MULLIN:    Well, with the new nipper and all sor . . .

*(Mullin has over ten years service and is married "on the strength".)*

COMPANY COMMANDER:    Ah, yes – how is the little blighter?

MULLIN:    Now theres a right little varmint for yer, sor. Why, my Molly was
doin' a bit of sewin' for yer honour's lady and he was a-bellowin' for her ti. . . .

*(a strangled grunt from the Colour Sergeant stems the flow)*

COMPANY COMMANDER:    Well, I tell you what, Mullin, I'll have a word with
Captain Churcher. He did say something the other day about needing another
corporal in the battery and you passed the course well enough. Sorry to lose you
though. All right then, fallout!

*The* COMPANY COMMANDER, *who had dined with the Gordon Highlanders the*
*previous evening, winces slightly as, in response to another roar from the* COLOUR
SERGEANT, *Mullin crashes back one pace, salutes, turns about with a thunderous*
*blow of his boot and stamps out into his little niche in history – the extra thruppence*
*a day already burning a hole in his pocket.*

. . .

On returning to Egypt after the Battle of Omdurman Corporal M. Mullin was
awarded the Distinguished Conduct Medal and promoted to Lance-Sergeant.

When Hiram Maxim perfected his 600-round-per-minute water-cooled .303
calibre 40lb machine-gun in the early 1890s he ushered in a new and terrible era
in the history of war. Until the appearance of the tank, a generation later, Corporal
Mullin and his successors dominated the battlefield. Field-Marshal Montgomery
has written that this weapon, and its descendant the Vickers, probably killed more
soldiers than any other in history.

As we have seen, the Nordenfeldt, the Gatling and the Gardner were heavy and
unreliable, doing little to prevent the Hicks massacre or the breaking of the
squares at Tamai and Abu Klea, but a decade after these disasters fifty Rhodesian
policemen armed with four Maxims withstood an onslaught by five thousand
Matebele tribesmen, killing or wounding some three thousand of them. In the
Dongola campaign the Maxim proved its worth, but at Omdurman, operating
under ideal conditions, it came into its own. However, one estimate crediting the
forty-four Maxims present at the battle with three-quarters of the Mahdist
casualties is in fact an impossible statistic, in view of the known ammunition

"Whatever happens we have got
The Maxim Gun and they have not."

expenditure figures. Although we may be aghast at the folly and stupidity of the Khalifa in ordering his ansar to charge head-on in broad daylight on a clear day straight into this hail of death, we should remember that throughout the Great War, only sixteen years away, far more sophisticated commanders on both sides (including two, Haig and Rawlinson, who were at Omdurman) continued to do the same thing, with some modifications, for four years because they could not think of anything else to do.

. . .

For the summer of 1898 the Anglo-Egyptian army in the Sudan was distributed in various camps along the Nile between Berber and the recently created Fort Atbara, the terminus of the Desert Railway which reached that place in early July.

The British Brigade was concentrated at Darmali and Selim. As usual, heat, disease and boredom were the principal enemies which faced the troops. Some of the officers managed to wangle home leave (the Sirdar was no more open-handed with leave than he was with money), or at least a few weeks in Egypt, but there were no such privileges for the men. Skinner, however, was an exception. His medical duties took him to Egypt with a party of sick and wounded and on 8 May he is to be found at Shellal where "we all went to the Greeks and a very enjoyable evening in the shape of a sing-song washed down with a little pilsner and whisky". Arriving in Cairo on 13 May, he had his first taste of English beer since leaving there in January with the Lincolns. But all good things come to an end and by the 20th he was on his way back up river.

Meanwhile, Sergeant Grieve, who had thought little of Cairo ("a den of iniquity") and even less of Kasr el Nil Barracks ("never went into a dirtier barracks in my life . . . more like stables") was not enjoying the Sudan any better. A born "ticker" in the great tradition of the British Army, he found the all-important tea made with muddy Nile water undrinkable and the food "not fit for pigs to eat, the men have lived on their own money all summer[1] and it has been the death of a lot and the ruination of hundreds of mens' constitutions". Unfortunately, in his own case this was all too true. Bursting a blood vessel in his lung he was invalided to Netley, the main military hospital of the day near Southampton, and discharged from the army. He had missed the Atbara and would miss Omdurman. He had had all the grind and none of the glory. Would he get the Sudan medal, he wondered, would he get a pension?[2] We do not know, but it was disease which riddled his chest not bullets and he was not "planted on some sunny southern shore" but in the damp earth of his native Belfast in the mist and drizzle of a November afternoon in 1900, as much as casualty of the Sudan as "poor young Gore of ours", as Grieve himself had put it, or the handful of other Seaforth Highlanders who died in battle.

Many at Darmali and Selim shared his eventual fate. Fifty British deaths were recorded there but many more died after evacuation to Egypt or England. Kitchener, despite his long experience in the Sudan, was bewildered; where did the men get enteric (typhoid) from, he asked in one of his letters to Wood. Presumably the doctors could have told him but he was much feared by the medical profession, who, like journalists, were seldom allowed to approach him and even had they given him the answer, there was nothing he or they could do about it. However, the majority were reasonably fit and by no means overweight. Skinner, at 5ft 4 ins, a portly 11st 12lbs on leaving Egypt, was a streamlined 9st 2lbs on his final return there ten months later. Early morning route marches, bayonet drill and musketry as well as swimming, football and trips on the river kept the men busy and time does not stand still. The officers occupied themselves with polo, duck-shooting and writing memos to each other. Towards the end of July, as

---

[1] Wherever the Anglo-Egyptian army was encamped Greek and Syrian traders immediately set up shop supplying both officers and men with goods of every kind brought from Egypt.
[2] A fellow invalid at Netley was awarded the princely sum of 9d per day for a year.

the campaigning season approached, fresh troops and equipment requested by the Sirdar, authorized by Cromer and approved by the Cabinet began to move up river from Egypt.

Three new gunboats, the *Sultan*, the *Melik* and the *Sheikh*, bristling with deadly weaponry, arrived in sections in June for on-the-spot assembly. A new force of Friendlies, some two thousand five hundred strong, was recruited, principally from the Ababdeh and Jaalin but including elements of the Gimaab, Batahin,[3] Bisharin, Shaigia and Shukria. The most effective group, the Jaalin, were commanded by Sheikh Ibrahim Farah, who had charged the British squares at Abu Klea and Abu Kru in his Mahdist days, and the Gimaab by Misara, a son of the old slaver Zubeir. There was no great rush of volunteers to lead these turbulent and unpredictable tribesmen but the Sirdar, as usual, knew the right man for the job and summoned Stuart-Wortley from Bad Nauheim where he had been taking the waters after a heart attack. On arrival Wortles was provided with one other British officer, Lieutenant Charles Wood, the son of his former chief Sir Evelyn, two liason officers from the Intelligence Department, Effendis Tanos Shehata and Hassan Sherif, and a warning from Wingate that he would be dealing with tribes "whose respective interests are somewhat conflicting". Firearms were issued sparingly and only to the least unreliable. Thus equipped, this exotic host was ferried over to the east bank, the clearance of which would be its responsibility, and left pretty well to its own devices.

Meanwhile Hunter's Egyptian Division had been reinforced by Collinson's[4] (formerly David's) 4th Egyptian Brigade. Tudway's Camel Corps had been expanded from six to eight companies and Broadwood's cavalry from eight to nine squadrons. But the most significant reinforcement was a fresh Brigade contingent consisting of 2nd British (Infantry) Brigade (1st Bns Grenadier Guards and Northumberland Fusiliers, 2nd Bns Rifle Brigade and Lancashire Fusiliers) under Brigadier-General the Hon Neville Lyttelton,[5] the 21st Lancers, 32nd and 37th Field Batteries, RA (5 inch howitzers and 9-pounder Maxim-Nordenfeldts) and the Royal Irish Fusiliers Maxim Battery with four mule-drawn Maxim machine-guns under Captain D. W. Churcher[6] with Lieutenant M. Wilson, thirty-four NCOs and men and fourteen civilian (local) mule drivers. The exclusion of the Royal Irish Fusiliers as a whole from the campaign was a matter of speculation and resentment, especially when it became known that the Grenadiers

---

[3] This tribe had a special reason for animosity against the Khalifa who had maimed and butchered sixty-seven of its number with particular cruelty.

[4] Lieutenant-Colonel John Collinson, CB, Northamptonshire Regiment (1859–1901). Died while Governor of Kassala.

[5] General the Rt Hon Sir Neville Lyttelton, PC, GCB etc., Rifle Brigade (1845–1931). He was the first officer to hold the appointment of Chief of the General Staff (1904–8).

[6] Colonel Douglas Churcher (1866–1926). Commanded 1st Bn Royal Irish Fusiliers 1911–14.

Brigadier-General the Hon. N. Lyttelton commanded 2nd British Brigade at the Battle of Omdurman.

and Rifle Brigade were to be brought from other Mediterranean stations to take part. Whatever the reasons for this decision, the celebrated war correspondent W. H. Steevens of the *Daily Mail* was impressed by the physical appearance of these machine-gunners. "Set faces, heavy moustaches, necks like bulls," he wrote, "the score or so men were the admiration of the whole camp". Additionally, the battalion had provided two officers and sixty-six men to staff a Remount Depot for the Sirdar's army. So great had been the demand for inclusion in one or other of these contingents that as the Editor of the regimental gazette, *Faugh-a-Ballagh*, informed his readers "the Commanding Officer decided in favour of the oldest and fittest soldiers, some of whom are wearing the Egyptian Medal and Star of 1882. With 15 years' Indian experience, many are in possession of the Indian Frontier Medal".

The 21st Lancers were luckier. The only British cavalry regiment serving in Egypt at the time, it had been converted from Hussars to Lancers in the previous year. Of battle honours it had none and was eager for blood and to throw off the satirical regimental motto "Thou shalt not kill" with which it had been dubbed by other cavalrymen. However, two of its officers, the second-in-command Major W. G. Crole-Wyndham (the only officer in the regiment to have passed Staff College) and Major J. Fowle, commanding B Squadron, had served in Wolseley's Light Camel Regiment and thus had Sudan experience. Another, Major Harry Finn, commanding A Squadron, had been commissioned from the ranks of another cavalry regiment after winning the DCM for gallantry in Afghanistan. But the regiment was short of subalterns and eight vacancies for troop leaders existed. As may be imagined there was stiff competition among young cavalry officers for these appointments and each applicant had to be approved by the Sirdar personally. As all the world knows, one of these eager beavers was a short, slight young man with an intolerably good opinion of himself, Winston Spencer Churchill of the 4th Hussars. Kitchener did not care for this bumptious youth who, in his opinion, was nothing but a damned scribbler, whatever his connections. But these connections were too powerful and combined pressure from the Prince of Wales (doubtless dazzled by Winston's mother, the beautiful Lady Randolph), the Prime Minister and the Adjutant-General could not be resisted and the Sirdar's objections were overwhelmed. However, he extracted an undertaking that there would be no writing for newspapers, a stipulation which the 20th century's most astute politician easily circumvented simply by writing personal letters to the Editor of the *Morning Post* who published them.

The Grenadiers arriving from Gibraltar were not lacking officers but other potential shortages gave rise to concern. Apprehensive at the prospect of warm "fizz", the officers' mess president of the battalion telegraphed his opposite number in the Warwicks as to the availability of ice in the Sudan. Cruelly, the reply advised him to direct his enquiries to the Khalifa.

The Northumberlands too had an inauspicious start. When marching through Cairo's stifling August streets to the railway station, the PT sergeant-instructor, the fittest man in the battalion, fainted. Packed 42 to a truck, the men were no less uncomfortable than the Lincolns had been the previous January and a good deal hotter. The officers, at only eight to a compartment, were rather more spaciously accommodated, so Lieutenant William Lonsdale Hale could afford to be philosophical when he observed that "4th class accommodation is better than 1st class marching".

Brigadier "Andy" Wauchope,[7] a Black Watch veteran of the River Column, was appointed to command 1st British Brigade (still Camerons, Seaforths, Lincolns and Warwicks) and Gatacre was promoted to overall command of the British Division of two brigades. Old "Backacher"[8] (Gatacre's "official"

[7] Major-General A. G. Wauchope (1846–99). Killed in action in South Africa.
[8] Doubtless a Victorian euphemism for a more soldierly version.

Brigadier-General A. G. Wauchope commanded 1st British Brigade at the Battle of Omdurman.

nickname), although he seems to have had little aptitude for public speaking, was wont to address his command on every possible occasion, drawing forceful attention to the shortcomings of his officers and men. This was not well received, young Hale for example writing home that Gatacre "was a gasbag . . . who talked drivel . . . and would make a splendid corporal", and after another such harangue that "he talked more rot than man has ever talked before . . . the general opinion is that he ought to be locked up". But there is no indication that Kitchener was anything but satisfied with his irascible satellite. He thrived on the tension, insecurity and rivalry of his subordinates. Himself deeply unpopular and the object of much jealousy in both the British and Egyptian Armies, especially so at this stage of his career, he never sought popularity and regarded those who attracted it with suspicion. It would be safe to assume that he was personally indifferent to his senior commanders and departmental heads. A man was either useful to him or he was not and, in their various ways, Gatacre, Hunter and Wingate were useful.

By mid-August the build-up of reinforcements was almost complete and as these arrived in the concentration area around Fort Atbar so the Sirdar began to push Egyptian units further up river. Now he had at his disposal 8,200 British and 17,600 Egyptian and Soudanese troops, 44 guns and 20 machine-guns on land, 36 guns and 24 machine-guns on the gunboats, 2,469 horses, 896 mules, 3,524 camels and, not to be forgotten, 229 donkeys. This was a workman-like force with no spare flesh or embellishments, but a little decoration was added by the presence in the Sirdar's entourage of Majors Calderari and Baron von Tiedmann, respectively the Military Attachés of Italy and Germany. Sadly, we lack comment on these gentry from that astringent observer of military observers, Lord Edward Cecil. However, we do know from other sources that von Tiedmann's sartorial elegance under the most unfavourable conditions was a credit to his batman and his Prussian sense of occasion.

In Omdurman the target of all this manpower and hardware dithered and pondered. In retrospect it is plain that the Khalifa's position there was hopeless. His army was a contradiction in terms, a courageous rabble; its small-arms obsolete and unmaintained; its ammunition defective; its artillery, such as it was, manned by unwilling Egyptians awaiting the first opportunity to desert to the enemy; his most able emirs and advisers dead, several done to death at Abdullahi's own command; tens of thousands of his bravest warriors frittered away in Abyssinia. Advice he received in plenty, little of it sound, much inspired by inane prophesies and fantastic dreams and some urged upon him, indirectly, by Wingate's agents. The best, needless to say, caused the giver to be cast into prison. Abandon Omdurman, begged the Baggara emir Zaki Osman, withdraw south-west to Kordofan and Darfur whence you came. There we can roam and fight on our own terms and in our own land, luring the Turk away from his life-lines, the river and the railway, into the desert which he fears and where he will thirst and perish.

But to Abdullahi such talk was defeatist heresy. It is, at least on the face of it, odd that this son of generations of nomadic herdsmen and slave-traders should have become so completely urbanized. Nothing but total defeat would wrench him from his festering slum of a capital, which to one who had never seen a civilized town or city was a shining jewel of his own creation, and his greatest strategic handicap was the mental chain which shackled him to it.

More acceptable advice came from Osman Digna. Send men north to the Shabluka Gorge (the sixth cataract) about fifty miles downstream and there build forts and emplace guns. Block the passage of the gunboats with great boulders and even mines. Then, added Osman, aware of the unpopularity of counsellors who advocated purely defensive measures, the Turk, once halted may be outflanked and attacked at will.

At first this policy was adopted and working parties under the Egyptian artilleryman Yusef Mansur were despatched to Shabluka to construct seven forts and install guns. This work was screened by a mounted force under the emir Abdel Bagi with the dual role of protecting Mansur's men (and making sure the Egyptian himself did not desert) and collecting as much information as possible about the advancing host. But early in July with the construction work well under way, this strategy was abandoned and all but Abdel Bagi's patrols ordered back to Omdurman. The reasons for this change of plan are uncertain but sure it is that the Battle of Shabluka would not have been one which the Sirdar would have wished to fight. The surrounding terrain is hilly and rugged and it would have been difficult to bring the artillery, Maxims and cavalry into action. The progress of the gunboats might indeed have been impeded, some might even have been lost[9] and the infantry denied their tremendous supporting firepower. Probably Wingate's Fifth Column in Omdurman worked hard to discredit the plan, perhaps arguing that the defenders could themselves be easily outflanked and cut off from base. In their endeavours the agents would have been assisted by the extreme difficulty the Khalifa was experiencing in supplying the men at Shabluka. The disaffection and decimation of the camel-breeding tribes and their herds had brought about a grave shortage of transport animals. Nor was food itself plentiful. The working population of the Gezira and other grain producing areas had been drastically reduced by famine, particularly that of 1889, the ravages of the Baggara settlers and conscription. An army of some 50,000 in and around Omdurman had to be fed, not to speak of the civilian population.

[9]It was in this vicinity that the *Talahawiyeh* struck and sank in 1885.

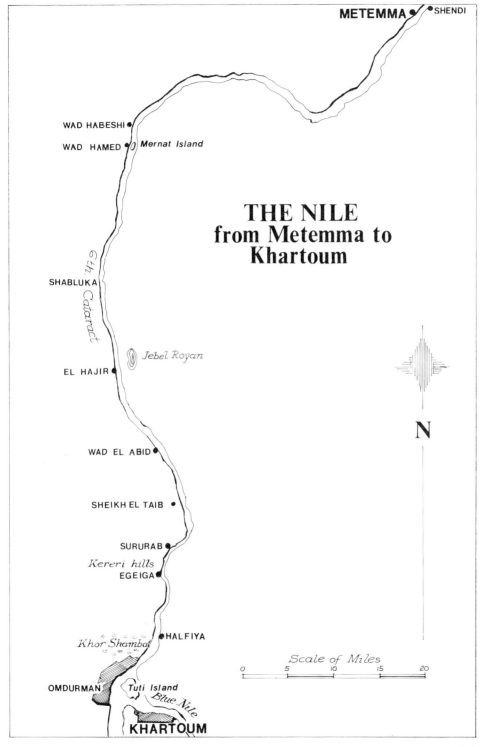

METEMMA ● ●SHENDI

WAD HABESHI ●

WAD HAMED ● *Mernat Island*

# THE NILE
## from Metemma to
## Khartoum

SHABLUKA

*6th Cataract*

*Jebel Royan*

EL HAJIR ●

N

WAD EL ABID ●

SHEIKH EL TAIB ●

SURURAB ●

*Kereri hills*
EGEIGA ●

● HALFIYA

*Khor Shambat*

*Scale of Miles*

0    5    10    15    20

OMDURMAN    *Tuti Island*
*Blue Nile*

KHARTOUM

So Shabluka was abandoned and with it another chance, however slim, of inflicting a serious reverse, or at least heavy casualties, upon the invaders.

In mid-August these invaders, with Lewis's Brigade in the van, renewed their advance upstream and by the third week of the month camps and depots had been established at Wad Habeshi and Wad Hamed, only a few miles north of Shabluka. Throughout the summer a variety of rumours had swept the army. The Khalifa was retreating and the men were "cribbing . . . under the impression they will be done out of another scrap," Corporal Skinner had recorded in early July. But three weeks later he had better news – the Khalifa, he had heard, was forming an armed reserve of twenty thousand women. However, Skinner was unimpressed by the British reinforcements which had arrived to cope with these fictitious Amazons. "2nd Brigade . . . were about 6 to 1 worse than 1st Brigade", wrote the 1st Brigade veteran. Among these reinforcements, of course, was Lieutenant Hale who found himself on the same steamer as his divisional commander and *bête noir*, Gatacre, whose presence was not "hailed with joy" as he and his staff "took up too much room". When the steamer struck a sandbank eight hundred and sixty Fusiliers (could they all have been on one boat?) had to wade ashore stark naked. We do not know if Gatacre was forced to share this indignity as the photos which Hale took of the evacuation, which today would be eagerly snapped up by the media, were in 1898 considered unfit for publication. The Medical Officer of the battalion, Lieutenant R. D. Jephson, wandered off to do a little shooting, presumably in his birthday suit, failed to return in time for re-embarkation and was left behind, a misdemeanor which in due course earned the unfortunate doctor a severe roasting from an irate and unforgiving divisional commander.

At 6 a.m. on Wednesday 24 August, 1898, the Sirdar reviewed his army at Wad Hamed for the last time before the final advance. There were some twenty thousand troops on parade, extending, we learn from Alford and Sword, over two miles. On the same day the cavalry and Hunter's Egyptian Division moved off southwards followed at dawn on the 25th by the British.

The countdown had begun.

# 23 Armageddon

The last days of August, 1898, were trying in the extreme for the Anglo-Egyptian invaders. Whether packed shoulder to shoulder in steamers or barges, stumbling through clouds of dust or crouched shivering under soaking blankets, the men were permanently wet with sweat, rain or spray. Arriving at their destinations for the night, units would be chivvied from pillar to post by staff officers who could not make up their minds where each regiment, battalion or battery was to bivouac. No sooner had the men settled when they would be moved, which often meant the laborious and lengthy business of re-loading transport animals for a move of a few hundred yards. Then thorny zaribas had to be constructed, a task especially unpopular with the kilted Highlanders, meals cooked and rough shelters (this was the rainy season in the central Sudan) erected. For the exhausted infantrymen there were guards to be mounted and pickets to be found while those off-duty lay down to sleep dressed and equipped in "full war-paint", as Lieutenant Hale described it – for officers this meant sword, revolver, cartridge pouch, clasp-knife and field glasses, uncomfortable bed-fellows. Men were short on sleep and temper and there was much mutual recrimination, particularly between staff and regimental officers.

Back in Cairo, Kitchener's Deputy Assistant Adjutant-General, Captain Sir Henry Rawlinson, Bart, Coldstream Guards, had found Colonel R. H. Martin, commanding officer of the 21st Lancers, "sharp, active and keen", but on the line of march Rawlinson felt that Martin was wearing out his men and horses with unnecessary patrolling in the heat of the day. Martin, on the other hand, complained to the Sirdar that the Egyptian cavalry was being given greater opportunities to patrol and skirmish than was his own regiment. However, this does not seem to have prevented one of his subalterns from charging into an

"Packed like sardines". Lancashire Fusiliers on board the transport steamer *Ambigole*.

enemy camp, slaying a dervish and charging out again, perhaps not exactly the kind of intelligence-gathering work which the Sirdar and Wingate had in mind. On another occasion recorded by Rawlinson, when the 21st came upon a force of some 450 enemy horse, Martin broke off contact without waiting for Egyptian cavalry reinforcements and thus "gave his men a long tiring day and achieved nothing". Nevertheless, the Lancers made a brave sight as, festooned with accoutrements of every kind, they jogged along on their Syrian ponies exciting admiring cries of "Khalifa mafeesh!" ("There is no Khalifa") from the sparse local population. This was no time for neutrality.

As a strategist Corporal Skinner was amazed to find Shabluka Gorge undefended, but those who ascended its rapids by steamer found its natural hazards hair-raising enough. On the 28th the ill-fated gunboat *Zafir*, which, it will be recalled, had blown a cylinder two years before, sprang a leak and sank even before entering the gorge. Its crew, including the flotilla commander, Keppel, and Prince Christian Victor, were lucky to escape with their lives.

Prince Francis of Teck, who served with the Egyptian Cavalry and was twice mentioned in despatches.

With the main army advancing along the west bank, Stuart-Wortley and his Friendlies cleared what little resistance they found along the east bank, keeping a sharp eye on that flank of the advance.

On 26 August the final concentration area from which the last stages of the approach march to Omdurman would be launched was established at El Hajir opposite Jebel Royan above the Sixth Cataract. At this point, despite the debilitated state of 1st British Brigade, which by now had spent eight months sweltering in the Sudan, and the unacclimatized condition of 2nd British Brigade, only 327 men, or less than 4% of strength, were listed as unfit for active duty. Of these some 250 were well enough to be used as extra fire-power or landing parties on the gunboats. Now only about forty miles lay between the army and its objective. Rawlinson's journal records the bare facts of the last four days before the battle.

| 29 August | Halted at Wad el Abid to get up boats and steamers. Cavalry reconnaissance only met four odds and ends dervish horsemen. |
| 30 August[1] | Left el Abid at 5.30 a.m. after a wet rainy night and marched about 11½ miles to Sheikh el Taib – cool cloudy day. |
| 31 August | Left Sheikh el Taib 6 a.m. and marched to Sururab about 10 miles – good camp – hot day – no shade. |
| 1 September | Marched 5.45 a.m. over Kereri ridge which was not occupied to Egeiga (el Ijaija) about seven miles distant from the Mahdi's tomb. |

As the advance progressed the commanders on both sides were receiving regular reports on each other's movements, morale and apparent intentions. Abdel Bagi handled his screen of scouts skilfully, keeping in almost constant contact with the British and Egyptian cavalry but staying out of trouble. A steady trickle of deserters[2] from both camps added to the two-way flow of information and Wingate's spies and agents were "coming in from the cold" of Omdurman as the army approached. The most notable of these was one Taib el Hussein, a former secretary in the Khalifa's treasury (el Beit el Mal). This man was apparently able to produce a complete parade-state of the Mahdist army and a reasonably accurate version of the Khalifa's current battle plan.

[1] On this day, more for the sake of form than in expectation of any result, the Sirdar sent a final warning to the Khalifa. See Appendix I.
[2] According to Skinner thirteen Soudanese soldiers, probably ex-*jehadiya* taken prisoner and enlisted in the army earlier in the campaign, deserted to the Mahdists and one was shot in the attempt.

Stuart-Wortley (left foreground) in consultation with Slatin. The two men in tarbooshes are probably the Intelligence Dept. officers Tanos Shehata and Hassan Sherif. Note informality of dress.

But the first major clash of this final phase of the campaign took place not between the main armies on the west bank of the Nile but on the east bank when, on 1 September, supported by gunboats, Stuart-Wortley's Friendlies attacked a number of Mahdist positions. These operations, spearheaded by the Jaalin contingent under Sheikh Ibrahim Farah, were successful in capturing several villages and forts. The Mahdist commander on the east bank, the Emir Isa Zakariya, was killed, officially in the fighting, but according to one account he was taken prisoner and stabbed to death by a Friendly. The story goes that this so infuriated Stuart-Wortley that he shot the offending Friendly himself. Perhaps not surprisingly, and assuming that it actually took place, the incident is not recorded in Stuart-Wortley's reminiscences or his official report.

That afternoon the 37th Field Battery Royal Artillery (Major F. B. Elmslie) with six 5-inch howitzers firing 50 lb lyddite shells was landed from barges on the east bank with instructions to bombard the Mahdi's tomb and the gun positions in Omdurman. Churchill, watching from Jebel Surgham (or Surkab), observed the shelling of the Mahdi's tomb probably with mixed feelings as there could have been little pleasure in witnessing the destruction of the only building of any architectural merit in the city. By the evening not only had the tomb been severely damaged, and with it the morale of the Khalifa and his ansar to whom it was a symbol of all for which they stood, but most of the Mahdist artillery had been silenced by the concentrated fire of the howitzers and the gunboats *Melik*, *Sultan* and *Sheikh*.

It may be interesting to dwell for a moment on the extraordinary diversity of the crews of Keppel's flotilla. The *Melik*, for example, was commanded by the late General Gordon's nephew, Major "Monkey" Gordon, a sapper like his uncle. His crew would have included a Royal Marine Artillery NCO, a few Royal Naval ratings both on deck and in the engine-room, a civilian (probably Greek) chief engineer and a number of Egyptian and Sudanese deckhands and stokers. The infantry landing-party on board the *Melik* consisted of a score or so of "light duties" Grenadier Guardsmen under Second-Lieutenant E. Seymour. The ships' companies of the other gunboats were similarly constituted with landing parties of Northumberland Fusiliers under Captain S. C. Ferguson in the *Sultan*, Lancashire Fusiliers under Lieutenant A. J. Allardyce in the *Sheikh* and so on. Several of these parties were used as infantry protection for 37th Battery on the east bank.

While the Friendlies, howitzers and gunboats were thus busily and damagingly occupied, patrols of Lancers, Egyptian cavalry and Camel Corps from the main army on the west bank were pushed forward, with the British to the left nearest the river. Churchill and his fellow cavalrymen, having had their first sight of the Mahdi's tomb and the city of Omdurman from Jebel Surgham, descended cautiously into the plain beyond. Some three miles on, as they breasted a low ridge, what appeared at first to be a zariba came into view, from the shelter of which a few horsemen rode to observe the advancing cavalry. Some troopers dismounted and, opening fire at extreme range with their Lee-Metford carbines, toppled two of the enemy scouts from their horses, causing the others to withdraw unhurriedly, taking with them one of their casualties. Then, suddenly, the zariba seemed to ripple and stir. It was made not of thorn bushes but of men, thousands upon thousands of men.[3]

Perhaps it is fitting that the greatest warrior-statesman of our time should have been among the last witnesses of a sight which will never again be seen: a medieval host in full battle array with beating drums, blaring horns, armoured knights on prancing horses, a multitude of foot-soldiers in their coats of many colours brandishing the traditional weapons with which man had done battle for

[3] The true strength of the Khalifa's army at the Battle of Omdurman has never been precisely established. Estimates vary from 35,000 to 60,000 and the Intelligence Department report puts the number at about 52,000.

The Anglo-Egyptian army and fleet of gunboats advancing upriver.

centuries. Away over to Churchill's right, Lieutenant Henry Hopkinson[4] of the Egyptian Camel Corps heard "a dull roar like surf beating on a sea-shore". The ansar were advancing at a steady jog which ate up the few miles separating them from the Anglo-Egyptian patrols with alarming rapidity. Discretion being the better part of valour, the cavalry commanders Martin and Broadwood ordered withdrawal.

In the course of their advance the Egyptian mounted troops had crossed the boggy western extremity of the Khor Shambat, soaked by the heavy rain of the night before (31 August/1 September). Now, returning by the same route, the camels found the going sticky and the swifter ansar, both on foot and horseback, began to gain on them as they floundered through the mud. Hopkinson, with some

[4] Colonel H. C. B. Hopkinson, CMG, CBE, Seaforth Highlanders (1867–1946). Later Commandant of the Alexandria City Police (1902–17) and Director of the Municipality (1917–23).

The gun-boat *Sultan* in action against Omdurman's defences and the Mahdi's tomb on the day before the battle.

understatement, describes this as an "exciting moment", but reaching firmer ground the Camel Corps managed to outstrip their pursuers. Meanwhile, Captain Douglas Haig, covering the Egyptian withdrawal with his squadron, felt that the order to retire had come none too soon. Some of the dervish horsemen were "uncomfortably near" and had to be held off with dismounted carbine fire, Haig himself joining in. By mid-afternoon the dervish advance had halted and the mounted patrols had regained the shelter of the main army, now encamping itself in and around the village of Egeiga where it was to pass the night.

Five of the six British and Egyptian infantry brigades were arranged in an arc some 2,000 yards from end to end, with their backs to the river, facing west. The reserve brigade, Collinson's 4th Egyptian, cavalry, Camel Corps, auxiliary services and baggage were bivouacked between the five "perimeter" brigades and the river. The gunboats, after their return from the bombardment of Omdurman, were moored to the bank behind the army and the artillery and Maxims were forward with the infantry. 37th Field Battery and the Friendlies remained on the east bank. The three forward brigades of Hunter's Egyptian Division were protected to some extent by a shallow trench and low parapet but the British took no such precaution, contenting themselves with the construction of the usual flimsy zariba, an omission on Gatacre's part which does not seem to have given rise to any comment from the Sirdar and, in the event, made little difference to the safety of the troops.

Now the principal danger to the invaders was a night attack which would neutralize their immensely superior fire-power. Greater in numbers and more skilled in hand-to-hand fighting, the dervishes' only hope of victory lay in getting close enough to use their swords and spears and this could only be achieved in the dark. This possibility caused considerable anxiety among all ranks of the Anglo-Egyptian army and every precaution was taken to safeguard against it. In addition to strong patrols and pickets, the ground in front of the zariba was swept throughout the night by the searchlights on the gunboats, a phenomenon which is said to have bewildered and dismayed the Khalifa and his emirs. But no such attack took place and there are a number of points to be taken into account when discussing what would seem to have been a ruinous decision on the Khalifa's part.

Except for a few "smash and grab" raids by Osman Digna's Fuzzy-Wuzzys around Suakin in the 1880s, night attacks by Mahdist forces had rarely been mounted since the fall of Khartoum over thirteen years before. With few exceptions the emirs doubted their ability to control their *rubs* at night; they would not be able to see their men and their men would not be able to see the all-important standards of their leaders. Many would desert and others would wander off in the wrong direction or in search of loot. Furthermore, it is by no means certain that the Khalifa knew the precise position of the Anglo-Egyptian army. He may have thought that at least part of it was still behind the Kereri Hills and that Egeiga was an advance outpost. In any case, Mahdist military decisions were not taken on purely military grounds. Tradition, dreams, omens, the verbal and written instructions of the late Mahdi, tribal conflicts and loyalties, jealousy and rivalry between emirs, all played more important roles in decision-taking than logic and reality. Some years later Lord Cromer wrote, "The dervishes were themselves devoid of all military qualities with the exception of undaunted courage". It is difficult to disagree.

So the Khalifa waited, fatally, for the dawn of 2 September, the last which many thousands of his warriors would ever see. Of the various options which had presented themselves to him including a night attack, the defence of the city of Omdurman itself or retreat into Kordofan, he chose the only one which spelt certain and total defeat and which denied him any chance of inflicting significant casualties upon the invaders, namely a mass frontal attack in daylight over open ground. Thus the Battle of Omdurman, from the Anglo-Egyptian point of view and in Walter Kitchener's words, was "picturesque and safe, which is my idea of what a battle should be".

From Corporal Skinner we have some very precise, if not necessarily accurate, timings. At 5.50 a.m. on 2 September, 1898, he says, the advancing Mahdist army was sighted from the zariba. At 5.57 the Sirdar's artillery opened up and at 6.15 the infantry and the Maxims joined in. Of course there are variations in the times recorded by other eye-witnesses, but, according to Churchill, it was the Mahdist gunners who fired the first shots of the battle, bringing two guns into action at 3,000 yards and firing two shots which fell about fifty yards short of the Anglo-Egyptian lines. This is almost certainly incorrect as the Mahdists had no guns with such a range.

To the student of tactics Omdurman is an uninteresting battle, although, understandably, the participants did not find it so. On the Mahdist side no generalship was displayed and on the other little required. Reduced to basics the battle simply involved large numbers of tribal warriors attempting, with great courage and total lack of success, to fling themselves upon serried ranks of disciplined professional soldiers equipped with modern firearms. Naturally the attackers were mown down and blown up in their thousands, while the defenders recorded casualties in killed and wounded of less than 2% of their strength.

The progress of the battle is usually divided into three phases; Phase One being Osman Azrak's dawn attack on the Egeiga zariba with his six *rubs*, totalling about 8,000 men, supported by Ibrahmin el Khalil's Kara[5] army of 4,000 coming in on his right; Phase Two, the Anglo-Egyptian advance out of the zariba at about 9.00 a.m., threatened on its right by the rubs of the Khalifa Ali Wad Helu and Sheikh el Din's *mulazamin* totalling about 14,000 men (which we shall call collectively Green Standard), and to its front by the Khalifa Abdullahi's own Black Standard, about 12,000 strong; Phase Three, the final rout of the Mahdist forces and the occupation, with little resistance, of the city of Omdurman.

The appearance of the Mahdist army from behind Jebel Surgham brought the Anglo-Egyptian gunners on land and on the gunboats into action at about 2,900 yards, causing immediate and serious casualties. The Mahdist advance was angled across the Anglo-Egyptian front from left to right. Lieutenant Hale was astounded by this folly. "They haven't read that moving to the flank in fours and within range is dangerous," was his dry understatement. But the Mahdist objective may well have been an imagined Anglo-Egyptian position a mile or two north of Egeiga behind the Kereri Hills. Perhaps only Ibrahim el Khalil was intended to deal with the Egeiga zariba, assumed to be much weaker than it was, but Osman Azrak was forced to deviate from the plan and swing due east in an

---

[5] A region to the West of the Sudan, now in Chad.

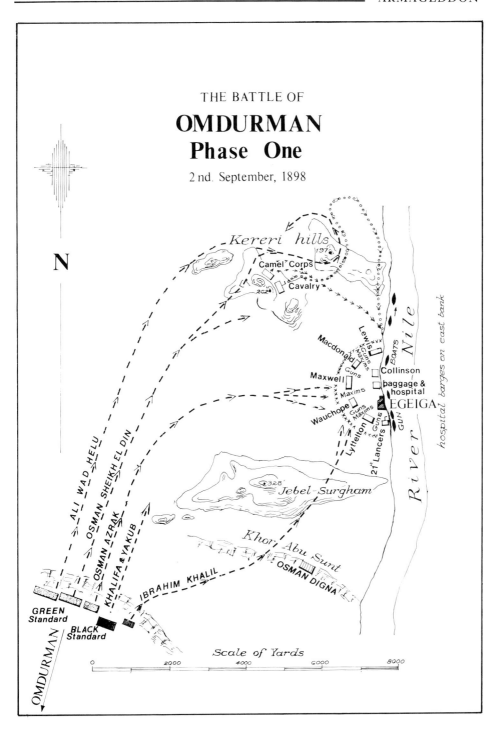

THE BATTLE OF
# OMDURMAN
## Phase One
2 nd. September, 1898

N

*Kereri hills*

Camel Corps
Cavalry

Lewis
Macdonald

Maxwell

Wauchope

Lyttelton

Collinson
baggage & hospital
EGEIGA

21st Lancers

*River Nile*

BOATS

GUN

*hospital barges on east bank*

ALI WAD HELU
OSMAN SHEIKH EL DIN
OSMAN AZRAK
KHALIFA & YAKUB

IBRAHIM KHALIL

*Jebel Surgham*

*Khor Abu Sunt*

OSMAN DIGNA

GREEN Standard
BLACK Standard

OMDURMAN

*Scale of Yards*

0    2000    4000    6000    8000

attempt to deal with the devastating broadside from that quarter, while Green Standard continued on its original course towards the Kereri Hills. If the Khalifa and his emirs had so misplaced the Anglo-Egyptians in their own minds it might explain the ease with which Broadwood was able to draw Green Standard away to the north in a manoeuvre with which we will deal shortly. This theory is supported to some extent in a statement made by one of the Khalifa's servants, an Abyssinian youth called Abdullah, to Colonel H. W. Jackson,[6] at Berber in April, 1899. According to Abdullah, who was with the Khalifa throughout the night before the battle, his master believed that the English were "on the river" and the Egyptians "moving behind Jebel Kereri".

At nearly 2,000 yards the Grenadiers, right-hand battalion of Lyttelton's 2nd Brigade, followed by all four battalions of 1st Brigade and the Royal Artillery Maxims, opened fire. Douglas Churcher's Royal Irish Fusilier Maxims, positioned at the junction of the two British brigades, opened up at 1,700 yards ("I have never heard such a fiendish row in my life") and Hale says the Northumberlands waited until the enemy were within 1,200 yards. Soon it was clear that the two left-hand battalions of the British Division, Lancashire Fusiliers and Rifle Brigade, were serving no useful purpose in their original positions and were moved across behind 1st Brigade as this seemed to be the sector at which the main thrust of the Mahdist assault was directed. Of the Egyptian Division, only Maxwell's Brigade in the centre was actively involved in Phase One as the attack had been obliterated before coming within range of MacDonald and Lewis on the right of the line.

Based on the known ammunition expenditure for the battle as a whole, we can arrive at a guesstimate of some 200,000 rounds of small-arms fire being directed at the Standards of Osman Azrak and Ibrahim el Khalil during Phase One. Add to this at least a thousand rounds of shell-fire and it is not surprising that by about 7.45 a.m. these two formations had virtually ceased to exist. Major F. I. Maxse,[7] brigade major to Colonel Maxwell, wrote afterwards of the high standard of marksmanship in Wauchope's Brigade, but Walter Kitchener was not so impressed. The Mahdist standard-bearers got nearest to the zariba, he wrote, "probably because they were aimed at!". To an extent his criticism is corroborated by Major H. M. Adamson, the M.O. of the Lincolns, who saw one standard-bearer staggering on after all his comrades had fallen "with the fire of

---

[6] Sir Herbert Jackson, as he later became, was a well-known "Sudani" in his day. Distinguished as both soldier and administrator, he fought with the Gordon Highlanders against Arabi and at El Teb and Tamai and with the Egyptian Army in nearly all the main actions against the Mahdiya. After commanding the troops at Fashoda (see Chapter 26) he joined the Sudan administration and was Governor of Dongola for twenty years, eventually retiring to his farm at Merowe where he died in 1931.

[7] General Sir Ivor Maxse, KCB, CVO, DSO, Coldstream Guards (1862–1958).

half the brigade (Wauchope's) concentrated on him until he fell". During the lull between Phases One and Two a young war-correspondent (unnamed) rode out to inspect the "dead" warrior who rose to his feet and charged the inquisitive reporter with a spear. Missing his assailant with all six shots of his revolver this would-be Henty faced the choice of humiliating flight in full view of the entire army or death. But the decision was taken for him by an old Soudanese soldier who emerged, presumably from the ranks of Maxwell's Brigade, and ran the standard-bearer through with his bayonet. Adamson does not tell us the distance from the Anglo-Egyptian line at which this event took place but it sounds a good deal closer than the 350 yards which Neville Cameron (in the same brigade as Adamson) believed to be the nearest any dervish had reached and no doubt it was an exceptional case.

It was during Phase One of the battle that most of the few British infantry casualties were sustained, but the *jehadiya*, with the morning sun in their eyes, and at the extreme range of their decrepit firearms were even more than usually inaccurate. Nevertheless, Captain Caldecott of the Warwicks, Corporal Allan and Private Millar of the Camerons, Private Johnstone of the Seaforths and Private Smith of the Rifle Brigade were killed and about 90 others wounded. Most wounds, from spent bullets, were slight but Sergeant Sanderson of the Lincolns lost an eye and a medical orderly, Private Calthorp of the same regiment, the tips of his fingers while he was bandaging a casualty. Skinner, tending the wounded of 1st Brigade, got a bullet through his sun-helmet (doubtless a treasured memento for the rest of his life) and Major Adamson found himself under fire of another kind when caught in the act of cutting off a wounded man's equipment by the Principal Medical Officer, Surgeon-General Taylor. "As you get older," remarked Taylor pompously, "you'll feel constrained to unbuckle equipment instead of cutting it through." Whether this advice was intended to improve Adamson's professional skill or was simply the Pavlovian reaction of one of Kitchener's senior officers to anything which smacked of extravagance is an open question.

Several hours earlier, before dawn, British and Egyptian mounted patrols had again spread out over the plain of Kereri, the high ground of Jebel Surgham and the Kereri Hills. The 21st Lancers, covering the left front of the Anglo-Egyptian position, having sighted and reported on the forward movement of the Mahdist army, were withdrawn into the zariba. Broadwood's force (nine squadrons of cavalry, eight companies of Camel Corps and the Horse Artillery battery with Krupp 7-pounders) was ordered to take up defensive positions in the Kereri Hills as forward protection for the vulnerable right flank of the zariba which was held by Lewis's all-Egyptian brigade, containing at least one battalion of highly doubtful quality.

As the frontal attack on the zariba developed, the ansar of Green Standard

Lt.Colonel R. G. Broadwood, 12th Lancers, commanded the Egyptian Cavalry 1897–98.

traversed the plain and swarmed up the rocky slopes towards the thin line of dismounted Camel Corps holding the crest. Henry Hopkinson, who seems to have favoured maritime similies, remembered afterwards that "they came on like waves of the sea", impervious to the concentrated Martini-Henry[8] carbine fire of the six forward Camel Corps companies with Horse Artillery support. In danger of being swamped by the waves, the camelmen mounted their beasts and retired northwards "slowly and in good order" but a section of the Horse battery, bravely continuing its covering fire, was overwhelmed and two of its guns captured.

Now the Camel Corps was hotly pressed and under heavy but inaccurate rifle fire. Over rough country a dervish foot-soldier could run faster than a floundering camel and here at last was a chance to get to grips with the cowardly Turk.

[8] One of the less comprehensible Cromer/Kitchener economies was the failure to re-equip the Egyptian Army with the Lee-Metford .303. However, expense apart, it may have been felt that to arm the Soudanese, the "teeth" of the army, with a magazine-loaded weapon would vastly increase expenditure of ammunition without improving standards of accuracy.

Reaching another section of the Horse Battery, which was hurling shrapnel into the swiftly advancing ansar, the camelmen were preparing to dismount and take up a second defensive position when orders were received to retire on the zariba to the south. Dashing for the river, the Camel Corps sought and received the protective fire of the gunboats covering the right (or northern) flank of the Anglo-Egyptian line, thus enabling it to reach the shelter of the zariba by the skin of its teeth, having lost about twenty men and a number of camels killed and wounded.

Meanwhile Broadwood had prepared his squadrons for a desperate charge against those *rubs* of Green Standard which were sprinting and galloping at right-angles to the Camel Corps as they raced to cut it off from the zariba. But the intervention of the gunboats enabled Broadwood to concentrate instead on drawing large numbers of ansar, including many *mulazimin* armed with rifles, away to the north. Having led them on a wild goose chase of some three miles, he slipped back along the river bank to the zariba, protected by the gunboats and recovering en route the two captured Krupps.

The apparent ease with which Broadwood executed this manoeuvre is difficult to explain without resorting to the theory that Green Standard's commanders[9] believed they were following the cavalry to another Anglo-Egyptian position somewhere to the north or north-west of the Kereri Hills. If, as is generally accepted, they had been ordered to assault the right flank of the Egeiga zariba, why did they allow themselves to be lured away in the opposite direction by a quarry they were unlikely to catch? It may have been sheer indiscipline and the frustration of losing the Camel Corps, but it is more likely that they were trying to do precisely what they had been ordered to do, namely, to find and attack an enemy position which did not exist.

Whatever the explanation for yet another serious Mahdist blunder, by the time Broadwood and his squadrons had returned tired and thirsty to the zariba, the Standards of Osman Azrak and Ibrahim el Khalil had been smashed, both commanders had been killed, at least half their warriors were dead or wounded and Phase One was over.

The Charge of the 21st Lancers at the Battle of Omdurman is perhaps the best known single episode of the Sudan campaigns. The participation in it and description of it by the most dramatic figure of the twentieth century (so far), Winston Churchill, has tended to give it a military significance which it did not have. Nevertheless, a brief account of the charge and the events which led up to it provide a suitable opening for Phase Two.

---

[9] It is not clear if either Wad Helu or Sheikh el Din were personally in command. According to Major Zulfo in his book *Karari*, Wad Helu's troops were commanded by one Abdullah Abu Siwar and Sheikh el Din may have stayed far from the scene of action.

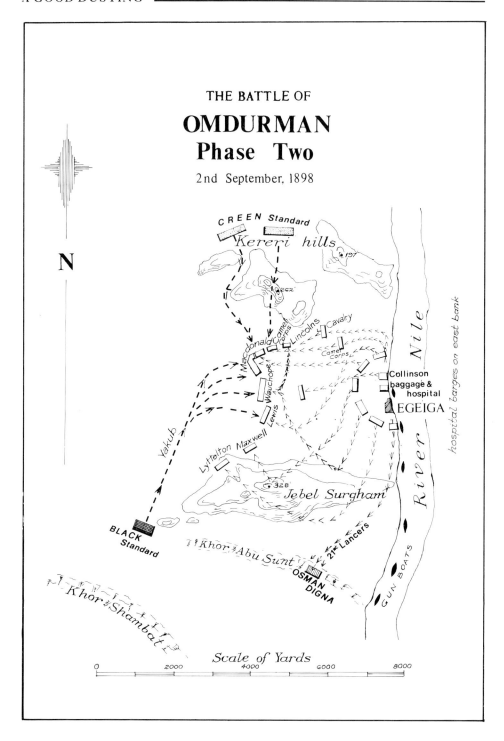

THE BATTLE OF

# OMDURMAN
## Phase Two

2nd September, 1898

The charge of the 21st Lancers.

At about 8 a.m. the 21st were ordered forward to their now familiar stamping ground of Jebel Surgham and its environs with instructions to harass the remnants of the recently shattered Standards and prevent them from reaching Omdurman. This was a tall order for a regiment of light cavalry less than four hundred strong, and at this stage the Sirdar was apparently unaware that the Khalifa's Black Standard consisting of twelve thousand of his finest and bravest troops lurked, unscathed, behind Jebel Surgham.[10] Kitchener's written instructions to Colonel Martin were kept by Major Crole Wyndham, second-in-command of the regiment, and are to be found among his papers at the National Army Museum. "Annoy them as far as possible on their flank," they read, "and head them off if possible from Omdurman." Above all Kitchener wished to avoid having to lay siege to a defended city which would not only delay victory but would involve his troops in costly street and house-to-house fighting.

Advancing to the east of Jebel Surgham, Martin was unfortunate that in his path was the only remaining Mahdist commander with any military wisdom or tactical

[10] Stuart-Wortley on the east bank of the Nile had been informed of this by a deserter but was unable to convey the message to the Sirdar on the west bank, although he attempted to do so by heliograph.

ability. Osman Digna's small residual force consisted of about seven hundred poorly armed Hadendowa, the last of the Fuzzy-Wuzzys, who had not only broken the square at Tamai but had specialized in chopping up British cavalry. Hoping for just such an opportunity, Osman had sought and obtained reinforcements from Black Standard. These he concealed, along with most of his own men, in the Khor Abu Sunt, a dry watercourse running approximately east-west to the south-east of Jebel Surgham. Over the years Osman had learnt all about the British. Their infantry were to be avoided but persuade their cavalry to charge over broken ground upon which your men were concealed and you could make mincemeat of them. So, exposing a thin line of men along the northern edge of the khor to full view, Osman lured Martin into a trap, one which an experienced Egyptian cavalry officer would have immediately recognized.

The rest has been vividly described by Churchill and others. The charge against an apparently thin ragged line, the shock of last-second realization of the trick, the brief ferocious hand-to-hand fighting in the knor, the frightful wounds inflicted on men and horses by sword and spear, the fierce courage of a brave people fighting their last battle, matched by the heroism of men like Kenna, de Montmorency and Byrne, who, having cut their way through the carnage, returned to it to save their stricken comrades. In these few moments, 40% of all the British casualties in the battle were sustained; one officer, Lieutenant Grenfell, a nephew of the former Sirdar, and twenty men were dead and fifty officers and men were wounded, some horribly. Over one hundred and twenty horses were killed, lost or had to be destroyed. When Martin returned to the Sirdar he had little to report save the partial destruction of his regiment. His mission was unfulfilled and he had failed even to detect Black Standard behind Jebel Surgham. But the charge was spectacular and, as Walter Kitchener mused, maybe it had been good for recruiting. The Press liked it and so would the Great British Public, so the Sirdar swallowed his irritation, at least outwardly, and, in due course, Martin, along with several other nonentities, was rewarded with a CB. The three VCs[11] were more deserving, as were the men who received the DCM, as well as many who did not.

Phase Two proper got under way at about 9 a.m. The handling of the advance to Omdurman was by no means exemplary. Kitchener had never commanded an army of this size on a battlefield before, nor, indeed ever conducted exercises on this scale. Nor had his staff officers any such experience. Only three members of his staff had passed Staff College and one of these was his Financial Secretary. He cared nothing for the chain of command and his "gallopers" and ADCs careered about the desert with orders for brigade and battalion commanders while Gatacre and Hunter were largely ignored. This system, or lack of one, may have saved

---

[11] See Appendix J for citations.

Captain P. A. Kenna, V.C., 21st Lancers.

Lt. the Hon. R. H. L. J. de Montmorency, V.C., 21st Lancers.

Private Thomas Byrne, V.C., 21st Lancers.

Lieut. N. M. Smyth, V.C., Queen's Bays, attached Egyptian Army.

time and worked in a rough and ready way but it risked the danger of junior commanders receiving contradictory orders from different sources.

Theoretically the "perimeter" brigades were supposed to march out of the zariba for the seven-mile advance to Omdurman in echelon from the left. Collinson was to (and did) follow with the transport. At the last minute either Kitchener or Hunter decided that Lewis's brigade was too unreliable to remain on the exposed right flank and was switched with MacDonald's veteran Soudanese reinforced by three artillery batteries and eight Maxims.[12] So the order of march from left to right was Lyttelton, Wauchope, Maxwell, Lewis, MacDonald, Camel Corps and Egyptian cavalry; but a certain disarray set in quite quickly. The two British brigades on the left, racing each other for Omdurman, outpaced Maxwell in the centre while MacDonald and Lewis, in the course of their switch, drew further and further apart so that by the time the Khalifa decided to unleash Black Standard from behind Jebel Surgham, at about 10 a.m., a gap a mile wide yawned between the two right-hand brigades. Fortunately for the Sirdar, Black Standard, under the Khalifa's brother Yakub, attacked on too broad a front and brought down upon itself the fire of five of the six Anglo-Egyptian brigades and most of its artillery and machine-guns. Nevertheless, MacDonald was dangerously isolated and Yakub's main thrust was directed against him. Lewis, under direct orders from the Sirdar to keep up with Maxwell on his left, ignored an appeal from MacDonald to come to his aid. Thus MacDonald was left to cope, not only with Black Standard's furious assault, but with a new threat from Green Standard, suddenly reappearing over the Kereri Hills from its fruitless wanderings to the north-west. Luckily for the resolute Scot the two attacks were unco-ordinated and that of Black Standard had been smashed by his tremendous fire-power before Green Standard's had been launched. In a text-book move, MacDonald realigned his battalions and batteries through 90 degrees to face the new assault, even finding time to scold one of his battalion commanders, Major Walter of the 9th Soudanese, for anticipating his orders. Henry Hopkinson, whose Camel Corps companies fought alongside MacDonald's brigade, was twice wounded in these fierce engagements. On the first occasion he was hit in the side "as though with a loaded stick" and found himself flat on his face only to be pulled to his feet by a Turkish brother officer with the unsympathetic injunction, "Malaish! Shid a hailak!" ("Never mind! Buck Up!"). A little later he was more seriously wounded and evacuated.

The sequence of orders and counter-orders during this stage of the battle is confused and contradictory, as, no doubt, were the orders themselves. It would seem that the Sirdar, riding with the British Division on the left of the line of

---

[12] It should be noted that the Maxim machine-guns in use with the Egyptian Army were of .45 calibre, heavier than the .303 version and with a slower rate of fire.

advance, at first ignored an attempted explanation of the situation on the extreme right offered by MacDonald's galloper, Lientenant Pritchard, RE, who had been sent to ask for help. However, later, when this request was repeated by Hunter, who could see more of what was happening in his sector of the battlefield, Kitchener relented and ordered Wauchope to swing right, come up behind Lewis and fill the gap between Lewis and MacDonald. But, Macdonald, by now preparing to cope with the threat from the north, required more direct reinforcement and sent Pritchard to Wauchope asking him to come up on his (MacDonald's) immediate right. Wauchope, under orders from the Sirdar to fill in on MacDonald's left, compromised by detaching the Lincolns and sending them on at the double to MacDonald's right, completing the gap-filling manoeuvre with the remainder of his brigade.

With eighteen guns and eight Maxims the fire-power at MacDonald's disposal was formidable and, despite the wild inaccuracy of his Soudanese riflemen, the second attack was pulverised as decisively as had been the first. Had the two attacks been co-ordinated MacDonald might have been in real difficulty but piecemeal they were easily dealt with and the arrival of the Lincolns, renowned for the high standard of their musketry, completed the destruction of Sheikh el Din's brave but badly led *mulazimin*. Nevertheless, the officers and senior NCOs of MacDonald's brigade were severely tested by their men's desire to rush forward and get to grips with their adversaries, which they managed with great difficulty to hold in check, and by the alarming rate at which ammunition was consumed.[13]

To suggest that the destruction of MacDonald's brigade (and with it the Camel Corps) might have resulted in the defeat of the Anglo-Egyptian army at Kereri stretches the imagination too far. Had MacDonald been overwhelmed, the right flank of the army would have been exposed to further assaults from both Black and Green Standards. Lewis's all-Egyptian brigade, the 7th Battalion of which, according to Churchill, showed signs of jitters at one point during the advance and had to have its "morale restored" by the 15th Battalion with fixed bayonets, would have come under severe pressure and might have broken. But Wauchope's stolid and experienced 1st British with its magazine rifles, six Maxims and artillery support would have proved an impossible nut for the poorly armed ansar to crack. With Maxwell, Lyttelton and Collinson still fully intact, the eventual outcome would, in so far as there are any certainties in war, have been unchanged. Nevertheless, the glitter of Kitchener's shining post-battle reputation would have been dulled and his careless handling of Phase Two exposed.

---

[13] The Egyptian Division (not including cavalry and Camel Corps), although only marginally engaged in Phase One, expended over 300,000 rounds of small-arms ammunition in the battle, over 100,000 more than the British. MacDonald's brigade alone loosed off an amazing 163,000 rounds.

In the centre of the battlefield, assisted by Lewis on his right and Lyttelton on his left, Maxwell cleared Jebel Surgham of some courageous resistance. The army of the Mahidya, wonderfully brave and disastrously led, was broken and in full flight. At about 11.30 a.m., the Sirdar, surveying the carnage around him, put away his binoculars and announced to his staff that he thought the enemy had been given "a good dusting". With that he rode forward to gather the fruits of his labours.

# 24 Triumph and Recrimination

Phase Three, the rout of the Mahidist army followed by the triumphal entry into Omdurman, was at once a relief and a disappointment to the victors; relief at the absence of any effective or organized resistance and disappointment at the unrewarding nature of the place which had cost so much in blood and sweat to conquer. Dire predictions of the frightful casualties likely to be incurred in the taking of the city had been bandied about but in the event fatalities amounted to one war-correspondent, the Hon Hubert Howard of *The Times* and *New York Herald*,[1] killed by a shell fired from the east bank by 37th Battery, still doggedly pounding away at the Mahdi's tomb, and a Soudanese corporal of the 13th Battalion speared by a Baggari horseman charging from the courtyard of the Khalifa's house.

As for the appearance and atmosphere of Omdurman, Slatin was the only European with the army who knew exactly what to expect, although Stuart-Wortley had glimpsed the now derelict Khartoum from the deck of the old *Talahawiya* thirteen years before when neighbouring Omdurman was only a fort. The memories most vividly recalled by those who entered the Khalifa's capital that afternoon were of squalor and stench. Skinner had a strong stomach and merely observed that the place consisted "of the same old mud-huts and walls everywhere" but the more fastidious Douglas Churcher was nearly sick on several occasions. The smell of death was everywhere, dead people, dead animals, some killed in the bombardment of the previous day, some of less recent demise.

[1] War-correspondents suffered quite severe casualties in the Sudan campaigns. Howard was the seventh to be killed and another, Cross of the *Manchester Guardian*, died of disease. Several were wounded, including the brother of Cecil Rhodes.

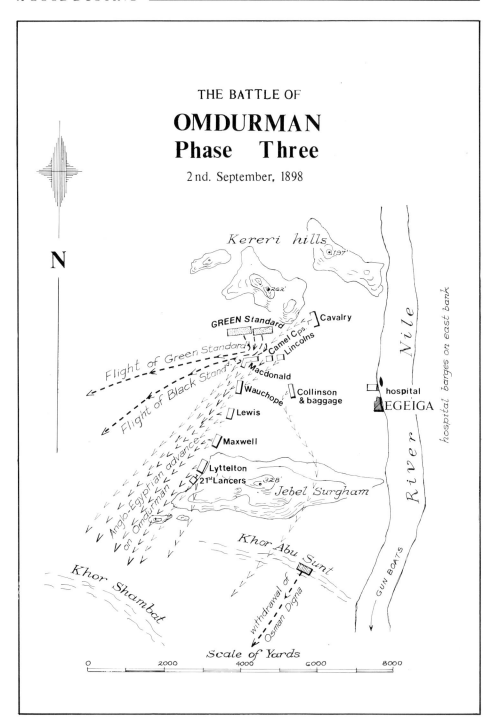

THE BATTLE OF

# OMDURMAN
# Phase Three

2 nd. September, 1898

The Sirdar's triumphal entry into Omdurman on the afternoon of 2 September, 1898.

After fighting and marching since dawn, water bottles long emptied, the men ignored the warnings of the medical staff and drank from any filthy puddle. Writing home a few days after the battle, Hale of the Northumberlands recounted how his battalion had come upon a ditch full of water. "Good, bad and indifferent, no one cared so we all quenched our thirst." He was writing his own post-mortem report and that of many of his comrades.

The 21st Lancers were more or less *hors de combat* but for the Egyptian cavalry the fall of the city did not mark the end of the day. After the rout of his army, the Khalifa, part of his entourage and a few surviving emirs, had fled the battlefield and returned to Omdurman, prayed, rested a while, collected a few of their women and headed off for El Obeid. Guided by Slatin and some of the Ababdeh Friendlies, Broadwood and his weary troopers gave chase but by the morning of

4 September their food had run out and utter exhaustion had set in. Leaving the desert-wise Ababdeh to follow the trail, Broadwood and Slatin returned, disappointed, to Omdurman. A few days later the Ababdeh followed suit, bringing with them the unwelcome news that Abdullahi had managed to reorganize a formidable force several thousand strong around him and was already a hundred miles from Omdurman en route to El Obeid. For the time being the hunt was over.

But the victory, acclaimed by the majority of the Press and public at home, was not without its critics. One focus of outrage to liberal opinion was the treatment, or lack of it, of the Mahdist wounded, a matter brought to its attention by the unpopular correspondent of the *Westminster Gazette*, Ernest Bennett. Although the Sirdar's conduct, and that of his men, was defended vigorously by most of the Press corps who had little enough cause to love him, and at least one of the chaplains with the army, the Rev Owen Watkins, a Methodist, it is difficult to escape the conclusion that Kitchener was indifferent to the fate of the wounded, and not only the enemy wounded.

We learn from Churchill that when the army marched out of the zariba at the beginning of Phase Two the Anglo-Egyptian wounded, the medical staff and camp-followers, were left behind virtually unprotected in the full knowledge that Green Standard, drawn away to the north by Broadwood earlier, was still in the vicinity. Indeed, some Baggara cavalry watered their horses within three hundred yards of the field hospital. The hospital barges (of which there were eight, although Churchill mentions only three) had been towed empty to the east bank for safety during Phase One but no provision had been made to tow them back again so no means existed for the evacuation of the wounded. Lieutenant-Colonel Arthur Sloggett, PMO of 1st British Brigade, who was himself later severely wounded during Phase Two, realizing that his patients and staff had been temporarily abandoned, galloped frantically after the departing Sirdar to ask for some troops to be sent back. So far as we know his request, if he ever had the chance to make it, was ignored. Perhaps in the sound and fury of battle this is not surprising, but surely a battalion or two from, say, Collinson's Brigade, could have been earmarked for this purpose before the advance started and a steamer provided to tow the hospital barges back to the west bank.

As for the Mahdist wounded, some, perhaps the luckier ones, were shot or bayonetted by the advancing troops applying what Churchill euphemistically described as "the customary Soudanese precautions". There was nothing unusual about that and it had indeed been customary on both sides since the earliest days of the Mahdist revolt. Nor was it convincingly discouraged by the British officers of the Egyptian Army. In their view, and that of their men, a wounded dervish was nearly as dangerous as a whole one, a belief not entirely without justification.

Several thousand were brought into Omdurman by their comrades or women-folk and these were treated by the British and Egyptian doctors as best they could be. The rest were left to shift for themselves. The Mahdist dead, counted on the day after the battle by, among others, Lieutenant Crispin of the Northumberlands (one wonders what he had done to so offend his Adjutant or Company Commander) with the aid of eucalyptus nose-pads and bottles of brandy, amounted to 10,800 so there may have been about double that number of wounded. However, six months later, in March, 1899, Captain Frank Burges of the Egyptian Army, who supervised the burial of the skeletons remaining on the battlefield, counted only 8,130 skulls, which seems to indicate that very large numbers of both dead and wounded had been removed by friends and relatives after the battle.

But many lay where they were on the sun-tortured battlefield until released by merciful death. Others, having dragged themselves agonizingly to the river bank, managed a few sips before they died. Years later, Major Adamson, the MO of the Lincolns, recalled his departure from Omdurman by nuggar (barge) several days after the battle in these words: "The voyage is a horrible memory, at least the first day of it, for all along the river edge were dead or wounded dervishes, great vultures tearing at the corpses or waiting patiently for the wounded to die. The Medical Staff of the Egyptian Army had struggled manfully but here was a task which they had not the personnel to tackle." Of course his last sentence is the nub of the matter. The expedition's budget had not allowed for any such contingency and to that extent the Sirdar did not bear the ultimate responsibility.

Historical events should not be taken out of their historical context but it is tempting to guess at what might be the consequences of such negligence today. Televised in all its gory detail and skilfully exploited by hostile Opposition politicians, the horror would surely overshadow the victory and lead to the dismissal of the military commander, the resignation of his civilian chief (in this case Cromer) and perhaps even the fall of the government. But as things were, Kitchener was elevated to the peerage and awarded £30,000.[2]

Anglo-Egyptian casualties in the battle were relatively insignificant. Two British and two Egyptian officers, twenty-nine British and eighteen Egyptian/Soudanese other ranks and a war-correspondent were killed. A total of three hundred and eighty-two of all ranks were wounded.

During the entire campaign of re-conquest less than sixty British officers and men had been killed in action but the number who died of wounds or sickness is very difficult to ascertain. Alford and Sword list one hundred and thirty-three

---

[2] Writing to Sir Evelyn Wood on 6 October 1898, Kitchener said he had wanted to refuse the peerage but the Queen had given him no opportunity to do so. Also brother Walter had told him, "You'd better accept as you won't get another chance".

"non-combat" deaths but their figure is incomplete. According to Neville Cameron one hundred and ten men of 1st British Brigade died in hospital in Cairo between the end of the campaign and 30 October, 1898, and none of these is listed by Alford and Sword. Moreover, we know that a number of men of 2nd British Brigade died on the way back to Egypt, in Alexandria and in Crete. Doubtless there were also many deaths among men of both brigades who had been invalided home (e.g. Lance-Sergeant Grieve). Total Egyptian Army losses are, if anything, even more difficult to arrive at. Approximately one hundred and fifty officers and men were killed in action or died of wounds during the campaign, two hundred and sixty died in the 1896 cholera epidemic and an unknown number from various other causes. But for the Soudanese and fellahin troops the war was not over and nor were the Sirdar's problems.

Mr Bennett and others, including no less a personage than Her Majesty Queen Victoria, were as dissatisfied with the treatment of the dead as they were with that of the wounded. The Mahdi's tomb, severely damaged by the bombardment of 1 September and the further shelling (which killed Howard) during the taking of the city, was blown up on Kitchener's orders by "Monkey" Gordon after several unsuccessful attempts, and the bones of the holy man, less his skull, were unceremoniously chucked into the Nile. The skull Kitchener decided to send to the Royal College of Surgeons. These decisions considerably upset the Queen but Kitchener claimed they had been taken in consultation with his native officers. There can be little doubt that if such consultations did take place his Egyptian and southern Soudanese officers would have recommended, or at least heartily approved of, such a course of action. However, after Her Majesty's intervention, Kitchener had the skull decently buried at Wadi Halfa. There was nothing to be done about the bones but a rebuilt tomb, its dome once again glittering in the sun, is a striking feature of modern Omdurman.

Two days after the battle, on Sunday 4 September, a memorial service for the Mahdi's most famous victim, Charles Gordon, was held among the ruins of the Governor-General's Palace in Khartoum. All units were represented at this ceremony but sartorially the show was stolen by the be-plumed magnificence of the German Military Attaché, resplendent in white by contrast with the drab khaki of the Anglo-Egyptians. Corporal Skinner, who is unlikely to have been present in person, maintained that the service was held over Gordon's grave, the site of which had been pointed out by two Greeks who claimed to have witnessed his death. That Gordon had (and has) no known resting place does not seem to have hindered identification of the spot and Skinner was not a man to allow an inconvenient fact to spoil a good story.

Unfortunately the ceremony, or at any rate its form, was not unmarked by inter-denominational controversy. The Church of England padre, the Rev A. W. B. Watson, objected to the participation of his colleagues (or rivals) representing the Roman Catholic, Presbyterian and Methodist churches, on the grounds that, as Gordon was a member of the Church of England, their involvement would be both inappropriate and irrelevant. The Sirdar, who had an especially soft spot for Father Robert Brindle, the Roman Catholic veteran of all the Sudan campaigns, would have none of it. Striking an early blow for ecumenicalism, he told Watson that he had the choice of conducting a joint service with all his fellow clergy or of catching the next steamer back to Cairo. The service, in common with everything else which happened in the Sudan for some time to come, was duly held in accordance with the Sirdar's wishes. In the event it was extremely moving and even Kitchener is said to have wept.

Before the religious ceremony the Union Jack and the Khedivial flag were run up on the shattered roof of the Palace to mark the successful outcome of the most important stage of the joint venture. Indeed, in business terms and setting aside humanitarian controversy, the campaign had been an object lesson in the maximum utilization of limited resources. Mahdist resistance had been ineffectual and, except at Kereri, half-hearted, but heat, disease and distance had proved to be mighty adversaries. They had been overcome and for the loss of about fifteen hundred Anglo-Egyptian lives, of which only about 15% were battle casualties, and at a cost of less than £2½ million pounds, of which nearly half was capital investment in railways, the whole of the northern half of the Sudan had been secured and the rest would follow. It was an achievement equal to the Mahdi's in the 1880s. Kitchener had earned his coronet and his cheque just as Mohamed Ahmed had deserved his lasting fame and brief fortune.

# 25 Settling the Dust

Soon the victors were scattered far and wide. The bulk of the British troops were borne away down river as fast as the steamers could carry them to the railhead at Atbara. Some were needed in Crete where the Turkish population was showing signs of rebellion against the consortium of the Powers by whom the island was temporarily governed. In any case, British soldiers left hanging about in the Sudan with nothing to do had a tendency to die at an alarming rate.

But the Sirdar and his staff had a new and quite different problem to contend with. The arrival of Commandant Marchand and his Senegalese troops at Fashoda on the White Nile, suspected for some time, was confirmed on 7 September when a Mahdist steamer, its crew unaware of the change of management, returned to Omdurman from a raiding sortie to the south. At Fashoda, the captain reported, his steamer, the *Tewfikiya* and another, the *Safiya*,[1] had fought a brisk action with black troops under white officers in which the *Safiya* had been damaged. Kitchener's instructions from Cromer were clear but at the same time vague: clear that the gallant Commandant was to be informed of his trespass upon Khedivial territory and invited to depart without delay, but vague as to how the Sirdar should enforce the invitation should it be declined.

Within hours the gunboats *Sultan, Fateh* and *Nasr*[2] and the steamer *Dal* had been warned for the 500-mile journey south and by dawn on 10 September the flotilla was chugging upstream. Although Marchand's force was known to be small and weak (about 150 men), Kitchener was taking no chances and the boats were packed with troops – two battalions of Soudanese, 11th (Jackson) and 13th

[1] Beresford's old gunboat. See Chapter 7.
[2] Later joined by the Abu Klea.

A Nile steamer in the 1960s, almost identical to those used by Kitchener in the 1890s.

(Smith-Dorrien), a company of Camerons (including Neville Cameron), an artillery battery and four Maxims (Peake).

Arriving at Fashoda on the 19th, Kitchener invited Marchand and his second-in-command Germain on board the *Dal* for discussions. Fortunately both Kitchener and Wingate spoke passable French and the meeting was held in a reasonably friendly, if somewhat tense, atmosphere. It was pointed out to the Frenchmen that they had encroached upon Egyptian territory and that the Upper Nile was not the No-Man's Land which the French Government purported to believe it to be. Theoretically the argument was sound; it had indeed been Egyptian territory in pre-Mahdist times and, to reinforce this point, the Sirdar, under some pressure from Wingate, flew only the Egyptian flag. Marchand, who described himself as "Commissioner for the French Government over the Upper Nile and the Bahr el Ghazal" held that he was under orders from that government to occupy this "vacant" territory and intended to do just that. Thus stalemate was reached at an early stage of the discussion. Short of the use of force, which would undoubtedly lead to a serious Anglo-French crisis and possibly war, Kitchener had no means of making Marchand leave Fashoda. For his part, Marchand must have been aware that his long-term position there was untenable without Anglo-Egyptian consent. Clearly the matter would have to be resolved between

A village near Fashoda in the 1960s.

Whitehall and the Quai d'Orsay and not on the deck of a steamer moored in a mosquito-infested swamp.

A few hours later, after a courtesy visit to Marchand's tidy and well-organized camp, a few toasts in excellent French wine, and the elaborate exchange of compliments, which, according to Newcombe of the *Abu Klea*, included a 21-gun salute using live ammunition, the Sirdar and part of his flotilla steamed on south to raise the Egyptian flag at the confluence of the White Nile and the Sobat. Colonel Herbert Jackson with his Soudanese battalion, several other British officers[3] and three of the gunboats were left at Fashoda to keep an eye on the Khedive's unwelcome and uninvited guests. By the 24th Kitchener was back in Omdurman and on 6 October he was reporting to Cromer in Cairo.

Happily for the peaceful outcome of the Fashoda incident both Jackson and

[3] Including Captain E. A. Stanton, Oxfordshire L. I. and 11th Soudanese, who designed the first Sudan postage stamp.

Marchand were men of tact and sensitivity, forming, within the limitations of the situation in which they found themselves, an immediate rapport. However, when Marchand travelled to Cairo for discussions with French officials, Jackson found the truculent Germain less easy to handle and considerable diplomatic skill was required to avoid conflict.

The full political story of the Fashoda affair is lengthy and rather tedious. Eventually, to the disgust of Marchand and his brave companions, French claims to the Upper Nile and Bahr el Ghazal were effectively abandoned and arrangements were made for the expedition to leave the Sudan via Abyssinia. No one was more relieved than Jackson, whose men, although themselves mostly Dinka and Shilluk from the region, had spent most of their lives in the dry climate of Upper Egypt and the northern Sudan. They suffered severely from malaria and, true to form, no wet weather equipment, not even ground sheets, had been provided. Worst of all, the local tribes, albeit their own kith and kin, refused to supply them with women. Parents were loth to part with their valuable daughters if, in due course, they were to disappear northwards with their dashing but impecunious bridegrooms – unpaid for.

By the end of the year, Fashoda (later renamed Kodok) had returned to dismal obscurity.

While the Sirdar had been thus occupied on the White Nile, General Hunter was busy on the Blue. The need to settle the agriculturally important Gezira area south of Khartoum was urgent and on 19 September Hunter set out for Wad Medani and Sennar in two gunboats, the *Tamai* and the *Sheikh*, with the steamer *Akasha*, the 10th Soudanese and two Maxims of the Royal Irish Fusilier detachment. Little resistance was encountered and a relative of Osman Digna and a number of his followers and other Mahdists surrendered. But the Standard of the Emir Ahmed Fadel, the main dervish force still intact, active and eager to join up with the Khalifa in Kordofan, was at large in the area between the Blue Nile and the Abyssinian frontier.

Colonel C. S. Parsons, RA, commandant of the Kassala garrison, upon learning of the victory at Kereri from the Italian Governor of Eritrea, marched on 7 September to occupy Ahmed Fadel's headquarters, Gedaref. In so doing he displayed more courage than prudence. His force was small – about 1,300 men – and weak – one battalion of Egyptian reservists (16th), one of Italian-trained "Arabs", originally recruited from the tribes in the Kassala area by the Italians and then handed over to the Anglo-Egyptians with the town, a small contingent of Slavery Department Camel Corps, known as Haggana, and a few hundred Friendlies. By contrast Ahmed Fadel was strong. Although half his Standard, under the Emir himself, had set out to fight at Kereri and was still on its way back from Rufaa where it had received word of the defeat, the Gedaref garrison numbered at least 3,000, half of it *jehadiya*.

Lt. the Hon. A. Hore-Ruthven, Highland Light Infantry, won the Victoria Cross at the Battle of Gedaref while attached to the Slavery Department Camel Corps.

It took Parsons over a week to cross the flooded Atbara in homemade boats and rafts and after a couple of brief skirmishes with Mahdist patrols arrived before Gedaref on 22 September. The action which followed took place a few miles to the north of the town. Parsons seized the advantage by occupying a saddle-backed ridge and forcing the Mahdists under Ahmed Fadel's lieutenant Saadallah to attack up hill. However, part of the enemy force worked round to the rear and launched a vigorous assault on the tempting baggage train guarded by 120 Friendlies and a few dozen Haggana. Despite the frantic efforts of the MO, Captain Fleming, who doubled as transport officer, and Sergeant Nicklin of the North Staffords, the Friendlies bolted, leaving the defence of the baggage to the Haggana. Under Captain Sandie Hore-Ruthven of the Highland Light Infantry Militia (later the Earl of Gowrie) the camelmen, all old Soudanese soldiers, fought with spirit, holding the enemy in check until a counterattack by the 16th Egyptians (Captain McKerrell, Cameron Highlanders) drove them off. During the fighting Hore-Ruthven rescued a wounded Egyptian officer, Mulazim Awal (Lieutenant)

Mahmud Moneib, under heavy fire and was awarded the last Victorian Cross of the Sudan campaigns.[4]

Saadallah's attempt to take the ridge was a costly failure which degenerated into a rout. Parsons occupied Gedaref but was trapped there by the rest of Ahmed Fadel's Standard returning from its abortive attempt to reach Omdurman in time for the battle of 2 September. On the morning of the 28th Ahmed assaulted the Anglo-Egyptian position from the north, south and west simultaneously but was repulsed with heavy losses. For the next few weeks Ahmed lingered around Gedaref hoping that Parsons would be foolhardy enough to emerge from his stronghold. However, the appearance of Colonel Collinson with reinforcements from Omdurman towards the end of October dashed Ahmed's hopes of settling with Parsons before making the long trek to Kordofan. Marching south-west he crossed the rivers Rahad and Dinder, finally clashing with a force under Colonel Lewis on the Blue Nile some 20 miles south of Rosaires on Boxing Day.

The Welshman's force was small and stricken with malaria but it consisted of the experienced 10th Soudanese under Lieutenant-Colonel Nason of the Cameronians, a small detachment of the 9th Soudanese under Captain Sir Henry Hill of the Royal Irish Fusiliers, two Maxims handled by Royal Marine sergeants and several hundred Friendlies under a former Mahdist, Sheikh Bakr Mustafa. On Christmas afternoon, Sheikh Bakr, patrolling the west bank, reported that Ahmed had attempted to cross the Blue Nile but had been forced back. Lewis, who marched down the east bank that same afternoon from Rosaires, found the Mahdist position the following morning at a point where the river divides into two fast-flowing streams around a large sandy island. Most of Ahmed's force was on this island but the wily emir himself had, contrary to Bakr's earlier report, reached the west bank with a group of riflemen, leaving Saadallah in command on the island. Sergeants Lambert and Trowbridge immediately opened up with their Maxims but the enemy were well protected from long-range fire by sandhills and it soon became apparent to Lewis that they could only be dislodged by an infantry attack.

With difficulty the 10th and Friendlies crossed the deep, fast torrent onto the island and with typically fearless Soudanese elan under a blizzard of fire drove the defenders from their positions into the river on the west side of the island where many, including Saadallah, were drowned. But Soudanese casualties too had

---

[4] The circumstances of the award of the Victoria Cross to Hore-Ruthven are probably unique in that the recipient was technically Absent Without Leave from his militia battalion in Scotland at the time that he won the medal! As he was in the process of applying for a regular commission this led to a protracted correspondence with officialdom, further complicated by the fact that, following his exertions in the Gedaref Campaign, he was below the required weight for his height. However, after the intervention of a certain Royal Personage, he was commissioned in the Cameron Highlanders and enjoyed a long and distinguished career.

Enclosure II.

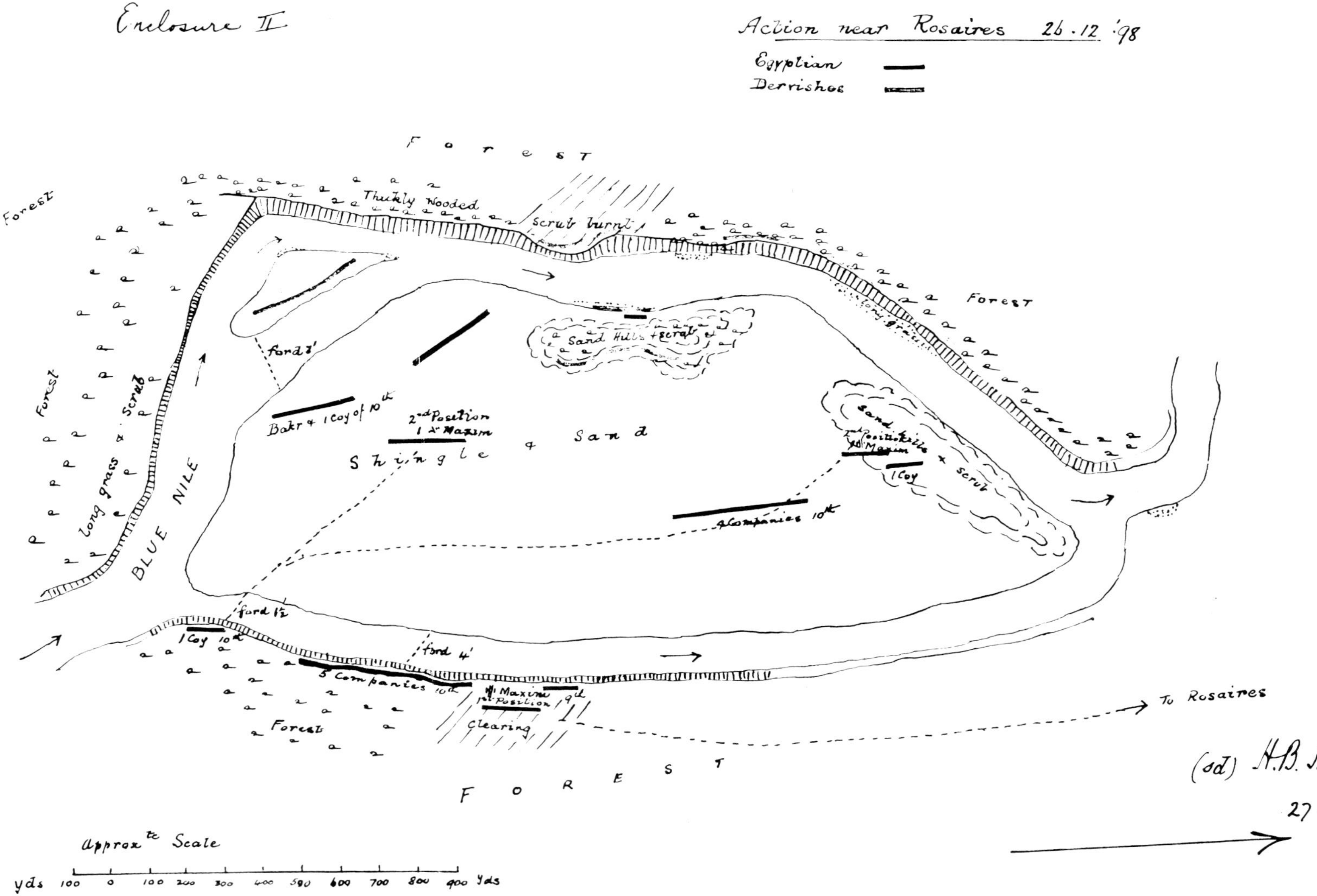

Action near Rosaires   26.12.'98

Egyptian ▬▬▬
Dervishes ▬▬▬

Forest

Thickly wooded

Scrub hurry.

Sand Hills forest

Sand

Shingle

Long grass & scrub

Forest

BLUE NILE

Ford 1'

Bakr + 1 Coy of 10th

Ford 2'

1 Coy 10th

Ford 3'

3 Companies 10th

Ford 4'

Maxims 1st Position

Clearing

F o r e s t

2nd Position 1st Maxim

10th

Rosaires 10th

Sand Hills Camboa's position

1 Coy

Sand + scrub

To Rosaires

Forest

(sd) H.B. Hill Rimt
27.12.98.

Approxte Scale

yds 100  0  100  200  300  400  500  600  700  800  900  yds been heavy in the fierce fighting around the sandhills and the 10th lost twenty-five men killed, one missing, presumably drowned, and 122 officers and men (including Major C. Fergusson, DSO, Grenadier Guards) wounded, nearly four times the battalion's casualties at the Battle of the Atbara. The Friendlies also lost a number of men killed and wounded. The two Marine sergeants who, aided by their escort of 9th Soudanese under Yuzbashi (Capt) Mohamed Abu Shaila, had managed to manhandle their machine-guns onto the island in support of the infantry and to engage Ahmed Fadel's riflemen on the west bank, were among those decorated, both receiving the DCM.

Ahmed Fadel, well placed for flight, escaped to join the Khalifa in Kordofan with a diminishing band of followers. In addition to Lewis's estimate of 500 Mahdist dead, about 1,700 had been captured.

The Sirdar was quick to capitalize on this success and within a few weeks an expedition had been organized under Walter Kitchener to follow Ahmed and the Khalifa into the depths of Kordofan (see map p. 15). After the fall of Omdurman Walter had been appointed Governor of the derelict city of Khartoum. He had done a fine job, using thousands of ansar PoWs to clear rubble and to begin the layout of the new city in its celebrated Union Jack pattern. Now he was to have his first independent command and a testing one at that, following the unenviable footsteps of Hicks into the thirsty wilderness. In view of Walter's relative inexperience in comparison with that of some of the long-serving officers of the Egyptian Army, the choice of leadership for this expedition must be open to criticism, although Churchill describes him as "the senior available officer". Perhaps his only qualification, other than the fact of being the Sirdar's brother, was the expertise he had acquired in camel transport management over the past three years. However, the veteran Tudway of the Camel Corps was appointed as his second-in-command and to his staff was added Major B. R. Mitford of the East Surreys, who spoke fluent Arabic, but was described by Walter as "a bumptious young boor".

The expedition, consisting of the 2nd Egyptians and 14th Soudanese, a troop of cavalry (mostly irregular), a company of Camel Corps, two Maxims and two small artillery pieces, left the White Nile near Aba Island on 23 January 1899 and marched west.

A fortnight later it was back and a depressed Walter sat down to write an account to his wife of his abortive attempt to kill or capture Abdullahi. Having covered 112 miles in six days through dense bush, Walter and his men had reached a place called Ageila to find, to their astonishment and consternation, a huge abandoned camp, capable of housing 6 to 10,000 men as opposed to the 2,500 which had been the Intelligence Department's estimate of the Khalifa's strength. For once that highly efficient body had made a serious and potentially fatal miscalculation.

Learning that his quarry was only ten or twelve miles further on, Walter was faced with the first of several agonising decisions. Should he advance or withdraw now? Almost certainly heavily outnumbered, with little water and encumbered by 1,500 camels and their drivers, he might be drawn into a Hickslike catastrophe. Common sense and Tudway told him to go no further. But to return to the river with his tail between his legs without even having seen the enemy would be to risk losing his brother's confidence and the chance of any further active command. So he pressed on, hacking a way through the bush for another five miles and then camped. The cavalry, which had been ranging ahead, brought in two women who confirmed that the Khalifa was indeed only a few miles away and expecting an attack in the morning. With only a day's water left and after "a terrible night weighing everything", at dawn Walter sent Mitford out to reconnoitre. Returning at 7 a.m. Mitford reported the movement of some 2,000 spearmen circling through the bush presumably either to attack the expedition's zariba or to cut off its retreat. Mitford may have been bumptious but he was also energetic and competent. Off he went again, this time returning at about 10 a.m. having located the Khalifa's position. From what he could see it appeared to be defended by about 2,000 riflemen and an indeterminate number of ansar armed with swords and spears. So, including the 2,000 Mitford had seen earlier in the morning, the enemy's strength could be estimated at a minimum of 5,000 men. If Walter attacked with his small force of 1,000 infantrymen, only half of them Soudanese including many ex-*jehadiya* and the attack failed it would be unlikely a single one of his men would survive a counterattack in the thick bush through which an organized fighting withdrawal would be almost impossible to achieve. On a rather smaller scale, history would repeat itself sixteen years after Sheikan with unforeseeable military and political consequences. A victory over the "Turk" might well revive Mahdism and bring thousands flocking back to the holy cause. Wisely, but with a heavy heart, Walter gave the order to withdraw while there was still time.

Next day two *jehadiya* deserters confirmed the partial accuracy of Mitford's reconnaissance and the wisdom of Walter's decision. In addition to the 2,000 ansar which Mitford had spotted circling the zariba and the 2,000 riflemen he had seen in defensive positions, the deserters revealed that there were a further 2,000 *jehadiya* and 1,200 ansar, a total of some 7–8,000 warriors.

Despite the rigours of the return march, Walter brought his force back to the river with the loss of only one man and seventy camels. There was some muted criticism of his handling of the expedition but his behaviour seems to have justified his brother's confidence. At any rate the Sirdar gave it as his opinion that it would have been "madness" to attack and a relieved Cromer, who had been on a visit to Omdurman, cabled, "Inform Col. Kitchener his action thoroughly approved".

It was now February and the short Sudan winter would soon begin to stoke up

An officer (left) and a soldier of the 13th Soudanese, c. 1898. Note the obsolete Martini-Henry rifle. This battalion took part in the final defeat of the Khalifa at Um Dibaykarat in November, 1899.

into summer (there is no spring). The Khalifa's considerable strength having been ascertained, it was clear that a more powerful force than Walter's would, in due course, have to be sent against him and this not until the fierce summer heat had partially abated. In late October the Sirdar assembled a force some 8,000 strong at Kaka on the White Nile some 380 miles south of Khartoum. A preliminary reconnaissance towards Jebel Gedir, where the Khalifa was reported to be, established that he had marched away to the north. On 13 November Ahmed Fadel appeared on the river near Aba Island and clashed briefly with his old adversary Colonel Taffy Lewis before withdrawing back into the wastes of Kordofan. On the 21st a follow-up force under Wingate left its base at Fachi Shoya taking roughly the same route as Walter Kitchener had (see map p. 15). His column consisted of an infantry brigade (Lewis) made up of two regular battalions, the 9th and 13th[5] Soudanese (Majors Doran, Royal Irish Regt and Maxse, Coldstream Guards), a company of the 2nd Egyptians, a battalion of ex-*jehadiya* (Major Gorringe, RE), a squadron of cavalry (Captain Bulkley-Johnson, Scots Greys), six companies of Camel Corps (Lieutenant-Colonel Henry, Northumberland Fusiliers), a Field Battery (12 pdrs) and six Maxims (Major Peake, RA).

Remarkably, in a long and illustrious career during which he reached the rank of full general, this was to be Wingate's only independent command in the field. The task, to hunt down and kill the Khalifa on his own ground, was a daunting one and the risks, similar to those faced by Hicks and Walter Kitchener, were formidable. But there is a symmetry, more usually found in fiction than in history, about this episode. At last the Mahdi's durable successor and his most implacable and tireless opponent were to come face to face within a few marches of Mahdism's great military triumph, Sheikan.

On the morning of the 22nd Ahmed Fadel was located by a patrol of irregular horse under Yuzbashi (Captain) Mahmud Hussein at a place called Abu Aadel. Receiving this report, Wingate immediately despatched one of his senior staff officers, the experienced Egyptian cavalryman Lieutenant-Colonel Bryan Mahon[6] of the 8th Hussars, with a strong force of Camel Corps and ex-*jehadiya*, four Maxims and two field guns to pin down Ahmed Fadel until Wingate himself could bring up the slower-moving regular infantry.

Mahon, seizing some high ground within 300 yards of Ahmed's position, opened fire. Ahmed's men counter-attacked bravely but were mown down by the Maxims, expertly handled by the inevitable Royal Marine NCOs, and by artillery and rifle fire. By now the regular infantry had arrived and the entire force swept down into Ahmed's position, shooting and bayonetting. Quantities of grain and large numbers of women, children and animals were captured. An estimated 400 Mahdists had been slain for the loss of one soldier killed and Yuzbashi Mustafa Shahin of the Camel Corps and three men wounded. Ahmed Fadel himself, almost rivalling Osman Digna in his ability to slip away from defeat, had escaped again.

That night the advance continued and on the following morning (23rd) a deserter reported that the Khalifa was encamped about seven miles to the

---

[5] This battalion, 1,000 strong, included 420 ex-jehadiya.
[6] General the Rt Hon Sir Bryan Mahon (1862–1930). Led the column which relieved Mafeking and commanded the British troops in the Salonika campaign 1915/16.

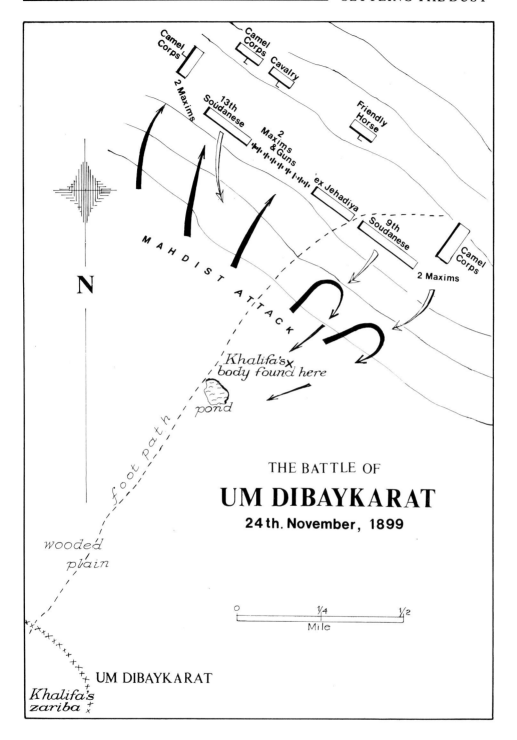

Camel Corps

Camel Corps

Cavalry

Friendly Horse

2 Maxims

13th Soudanese

2 Maxims & Guns

ex Jehadiya

9th Soudanese

Camel Corps

2 Maxims

N

MAHDIST ATTACK

Khalifa's body found here

pond

foot path

wooded plain

THE BATTLE OF

# UM DIBAYKARAT

### 24th. November, 1899

0      ¼      ½
Mile

UM DIBAYKARAT

Khalifa's zariba

south-east of the village of Gedid. The intrepid Yuzbashi Mahmud Hussein and his horsemen were again despatched to locate the exact position which they found at a spot known to history as Um Dibaykarat. To the south there was no water and to the north there was Wingate. Most of the Khalifa's supplies had been seized at Abu Aadel. Time was running out for Abdullahi and his loyal followers. Wingate resolved to attack at dawn next day.

At 12.20 a.m. on the 24th, with the cavalry leading and its flanks covered by the Camel Corps, the column started on its approach march and by 3 a.m. it was but three miles from its objective. With the cavalry and mule-drawn Maxims pushing on ahead, the infantry deployed for battle with the 9th Soudanese to the left of the 13th. From the direction of the Khalifa's zariba came the thump of noggaras (drums) and the braying of ombeyas (elephant tusk horns) indicating that the approaching "Turks" had been detected. Soon these sounds died away and Wingate halted his line in long grass atop a slight rise, drew in his cavalry and the Maxims, replacing them with infantry picquets to listen, watch and wait. At 5.10 a.m. the picquets started to trickle back to the line and in the first light of morning vague shapes could be seen moving behind them.

Apparently undeterred by previous bitter experience of overwhelming firepower, the Khalifa had again chosen to attack from the front in rapidly improving daylight. "Fire!" The Maxims opened up with their terrible staccato rattle, punctuated by artillery explosions and the crackle of the Martini-Henrys. But the responding musketry of the *jehadiya* and the *mulazimin* was heavy and for a time the left of the Soudanese line was under pressure. Wingate brought his right forward, pouring rifle and machine-gun fire into the Mahdist flank. The assault slackened and the Soudanese infantry started down the slope towards the zariba, bayonets fixed. The 9th had advanced only a few hundred yards when they came upon a huddle of bodies, separated and somehow apart from the rest of the fallen. This time the Khalifa had led from the front. "Seeing his followers retiring," reported Wingate, "he made an ineffectual attempt to rally them, but recognizing that the day was lost he had called on his Emirs to dismount from their horses and seating himself on his *furwa* or sheepskin – as is the custom of Arab chiefs who disdain surrender – he had placed Khalifa Ali Wad Helu on his right and Ahmed Fadel on his left, whilst the remaining Emirs seated themselves round him . . . and in this position they had unflinchingly met their death".

Wingate's report is an impressive document – clear, factual and free of any note of gloating triumph. Rather he prefers to give credit to his old adversary for the dignified manner of his departure from this world. In any case the sense of achievement which Wingate must have felt would have been tinged with regret. His friend Slatin was not there to share the moment (he was on leave in Austria) but, more importantly, both as an intelligence officer and as a student of all things

Sudanese, there must have been a thousand questions which Wingate would have wished to put to the Khalifa. On the other hand, Abdullahi's death was undoubtedly convenient. There need be no controversial trial, execution or long imprisonment and no living focus of future unrest in the Sudan.[7]

Osman Sheikh el Din was captured wounded (he died later in an Egyptian prison) and some 9,000 men, women and children surrendered. Wingate had lost three men killed and twenty-three wounded. A thousand more Mahdists had died. British and Khedivial decorations were lavishly distributed. The machine-gunners[8] Seabright, Seddon and Sears all received the DCM for their deadly and decisive work, but perhaps the most unusual award of this decoration went to Staff Sergeant McConnell of the Army Gymnastic Staff (fore-runner of the APTC) attached to the 9th Soudanese. "For his excellent instruction in fire discipline . . . and for his steadying effect on the men in the face of the enemy," reads Major Doran's recommendation. It will be recalled that the Khalifa's body had been found in the path of the 9th Soudanese and it is intriguing to speculate that the bullets which killed this medieval-style potentate may have been fired, or at least directed, by a man following such an emphatically twentieth-century profession as that of physical training instructor.

---

[7] Recently the suggestion has been made that Wingate kept the Khalifa's skull and used to drink a toast out of it on the anniversary of his death. It is hard to reconcile this story with Wingate's invariably tactful handling of any matter likely to ruffle the feathers of any section of the Sudanese people. Probably there is some confusion here with Kitchener's treatment of the Mahdi's skull recounted in Chapter 23.

[8] All Royal Marine NCOs. In the cases of Seabright and Sears the awards were bars to medals they had already won at the Battle of the Atbara. The fact that no less than ten awards of the DCM were made to Royal Marine machine-gunners serving with the Egyptian Army in 1898/99 emphasizes the immense importance placed upon the efficient handling of the Maxims. (See Appendix L).

# 26 Summing up

From these events have emerged three immortals. The Mahdi, a century after his death, is still a force to be reckoned with in the Sudan. His memory and philosophies are widely revered and to his followers, retaining the honoured name of ansar, Aba Island is a place of pilgrimage.

Gordon too lives on in the folk-memory of his race. Even at the time it was not entirely clear what standards and principles he stood for, but, whatever they may have been, he held to them firmly and to the death.

As for the third, perhaps it was not so much the Sudan which gave Kitchener his immortality but an advertisement. Alfred Leete's famous First World War recruiting poster is instantly recognizable as an item of pop-art, even to the victims of our current state educational system in which the likes of Kitchener have no place. Who he was and what he did may have been forgotten but the accusatory finger and luxuriant moustache are as timeless as the smile on the lips of the Mona Lisa.

The contemporaries and followers of this trio have been less fortunate. Today the Khalifa Abdullahi, although often confused with the Mahdi, and the emirs of the Mahdiya, are little more than names. Kitchener apart, the architects of their destruction have fared little better. Cromer? Was he not quite recently Governor of the Bank of England? Wingate? Ah! Yes, the eccentric hero of the Ethiopia and Burma campaigns of World War 2. Hunter? Who on earth was he? Well, he never became Sirdar, although Kitchener regarded him as his logical successor and made this plain in a letter to Sir Evelyn Wood, the Adjutant General. But Cromer preferred Wingate for the job and the decision was a wise one. Hunter's hand might have lain too heavily on a conquered people and he lacked Wingate's subtlety. But his career after the Sudan was distinguished. In South Africa he was counted one of the better generals and later he worked with his old chief Kitchener in the formation and training of the New Armies in the First World War. His term as Governor of Gibraltar from 1910–13 ended in resignation after a disagreement with the home government over defence preparations, but in 1918 he was elected Unionist MP for Lancaster, a seat which he held until 1922. Unfortunately for posterity, when he died in 1936 most of the memories and experiences of this oustanding front-line soldier died with him. He had committed them to paper but his orderly lit the fire with the manuscript!

In the early days of the Anglo-Egyptian re-occupation of the Sudan the country was governed by the military, thus the Sirdar automatically became Governor-General. The title Sirdar (held only by the British commanders of the Egyptian Army) was abolished after the assassination of General Sir Lee Stack by Egyptian terrorists in 1924. Thereafter the Governor-Generalship of the Sudan became a civilian appointment. At the same time the Soudanese battalions were separated from the Egyptian Army and reformed as the Sudan Defence Force.

Wingate succeeded Kitchener as Sirdar and Governor-General of the Sudan in January, 1900, and was at once faced with a crisis. Kitchener's obsession with economy had been undiminished by victory, following which he had arbitarily reduced the field allowances of the Egyptian officers serving in the Sudan. In December, 1899, the British Army in South Africa suffered a series of costly and humiliating reverses (Black Week) and a number of the aggrieved Egyptian officers in Omdurman spread the word among the Soudanese troops that they were to be sent to the war as reinforcements. Kitchener's terrifying presence was enough to prevent any immediate manifestation of discontent, but soon after his own departure for South Africa the pot boiled over.

Colonel Maxwell, now Governor of Omdurman, having received two anonymous letters threatening his life, ordered most of the ammunition withdrawn from the Soudanese battalions. Instead of obeying the order to hand in their ammunition some men of the 11th and 14th Soudanese, egged on by their junior Egyptian officers, hid it and defied their British commanders. Herbert Jackson, the wise former colonel of the veteran 11th, rushed to Omdurman from Berber where he was acting Governor. In conference with the wives of the battalion, Jackson persuaded these influential ladies that there was no intention of sending their menfolk to fight the dreaded Boer, nor, if the men handed in their ammunition forthwith, would they be punished. Negotiations conducted through the senior wife (el sheikha el harem) were successful and the mutineers of the 11th handed over their ammunition to three Soudanese officers commissioned from the ranks and personally loyal to Jackson.

The 14th, a more recently recruited battalion, lacking a father figure and including a large number of ex-*jehadiya*, was not quite so easily handled. However, Wingate, in a clever if not entirely honest ruse, invited any officer with

Colonel H. W. Jackson whose tact and diplomacy contributed much to peaceful settlements of the Fashoda incident and the mutiny of Soudanese troops in Omdurman.

a grievance to come forward and state it. A number did so, were immediately arrested and brought before a Court of Inquiry presided over by Jackson but including a majority of senior Egyptian officers. Of those who appeared before the Court, seven officers, three from the 11th, three from the 14th and one from the 8th (an Egyptian battalion) were deported to Egypt and dismissed the service. A corporal of the 14th was punished and discharged and several officers reprimanded or prematurely retired.

Eventually all the ammunition was recovered and no further action was taken against the men involved. Captain H. S. Sloman of the East Surreys, the commanding officer of the 14th Soudanese, was discreetly but rapidly packed off to South Africa.

Cromer believed that the plot, to spark off a general mutiny against the British throughout the Egyptian Army, had been inspired from within Khedivial circles. However, the findings of the Court of Inquiry indicate that it had been hatched by a group of junior Egyptian officers who were in the habit of meeting, boozing and grumbling in a Greek café (prop. Socrates Trapas) in Omdurman. Wingate, who handled a potentially explosive situation with great skill and tact, seems to have felt that the officers and men of the Egyptian Army in the Sudan did have some genuine grievances; that Maxwell's action had been hasty and that some of the British officers were not as closely in touch with their Egyptian juniors and the

Soudanese troops as they should have been. With only two companies of British troops (Seaforths) available to him in Omdurman, he consistently declined reinforcements from Egypt, believing, correctly, that his wits would be sharper than their bayonets.

As though the newly appointed Governor-General did not have enough on his hands, while the mutiny (if such it may be called) was in full swing, a new religious sect, known as the Milleniumists, appeared in Omdurman. The main item in its creed was that the demise of the Khalifa heralded the second coming of Issa (Jesus). Although only nine in number, these aspiring Apostles seemed to Wingate and his intelligence adviser, Milhem Shakoor, to constitute a threat to public order. They were arrested and whisked off to Wadi Halfa.

But we have diverged. Wingate remained in the Sudan until 1916, the longest serving of all the Governors-General, laying solid foundations for his successors. He had, incidentally, created the special appointment of Inspector-General of the Sudan for his friend and aide Slatin, one which the Austrian held until the outbreak of war in 1914. They remained life-long friends until Slatin's death in 1932. Transferred to Egypt in 1916 as High Commissioner, Wingate left the relative tranquillity of the Sudan for the turmoil of Egyptian politics and the problems of the war in the eastern Mediterranean. His success or failure in Egypt is outside the compass of this book but in 1919 disagreement with the British Government over the handling of Egyptian nationalism led to his dismissal and he never returned to public service. A successful business career followed and he died in 1953 in his ninety-second year.

The Earl of Cromer, the oldest and least enthusiastic of the Sudan's conquerers, remained on in Egypt until 1907 when, suddenly and almost without warning, he departed. Cold and aloof, he had not inspired affection and his carriage rumbled through empty streets as he drove for the last time to Cairo station. He had had difficulty in concealing his contempt for the Turko-Egyptian ruling class and little patience with the rising aspirations of the new intelligentsia. His sympathies lay with the fellahin and much of his work, including the abolition of forced labour, the dreaded corvée, was directed towards the alleviation of their miserable lot. The great public works of dam building and irrigation which were undertaken during his quarter century of unofficial rule are to this day the backbone of the Egyptian rural economy and stand as a memorial to the man who was perhaps the most effective and constructive ruler of Egypt in all her thousands of years of history.

When Cromer died in 1917, he had been preceded into the next world by his erstwhile protégé, Kitchener. The former Sirdar's contribution to the war effort in 1914–15 as Secretary of State for War was as important as his methods were controversial and his famous recruiting drive, upon which we have already touched, an unparalleled success. Nevertheless, by 1916 at the age of sixty-six he was tired, weary of political in-fighting, and his tendency to indecision had lost him the confidence of his Cabinet colleagues. An invitation from the Tsar to visit Russia and advise on the conduct of the war on the eastern front came to Kitchener as a temporary relief from drudgery and to the politicians as a welcome chance to be rid of him for a while. On the afternoon of 5 June, 1916, he sailed from Scapa Flow in the cruiser HMS *Hampshire*, which, within a few hours, struck a mine and sank. There were few survivors and Kitchener was not among them.

So the most soldierly of soldiers died a sailor's death. The politicians may not have been utterly dismayed by this turn of events but the British public was stunned and its refusal to accept the abrupt and unexpected demise of this great national figure gave rise to the wildest rumours. These ranged from the fantastic – that he lay in an enchanted sleep in some Orcadian cave awaiting a magic summons to his country's service once again – to the ridiculous, some years later – that he was Stalin. But many crises have come and gone without the intervention of Kitchener and, to the best of our knowledge, his feet were not webbed, as Stalin's were reputed to be!

South Africa from 1899 to 1902 was the graveyard, not only of many a good soldier, but of numerous reputations, including those of Butler, Buller and Gatacre. A lifetime spent in campaigning against brave but untrained and ill-armed tribesmen had done little to prepare such men for war against a well-equipped and relatively sophisticated foe. "True grit" (and sometimes even that was in short supply against the Boers) and Victorian parade-ground discipline was not enough. The day of the generation whose early training had been in the hands of Crimean veterans was passing. Buller's great record and popularity with the ordinary soldier saved him from total eclipse after dismissal. Gatacre was bowler-hatted and died of fever a few years later prospecting for rubber in Abyssinia. Butler, always the maverick, was sacked for pro-Boer sympathies.

The luck of many another Sudan survivor ran out in South Africa. Wauchope was killed leading his Highland Brigade in an attack in which he had no confidence. De Montmorency fell at the head of his troop of irregular horse, his batman at the time being none other than fellow Omdurman VC, Private Byrne, probably a unique relationship in the history of the highest award for valour. Byrne had to be physically restrained from charging off to recover De Montmorency's body from enemy-held territory. Somehow or other he managed to survive for another forty-four years and died at Canterbury aged seventy-eight, after over twenty years army service without quite making lance-corporal. The third VC of the 21st Lancers' celebrated charge, Kenna, was killed in the blood-bath of Gallipoli in 1915. To the best of our knowledge, all the other Sudan VCs died in their beds; Edwards, the English muleteer, who won his Cross at Tamai serving with a Highland regiment and attached to the Navy, lived the longest of all, dying aged ninety in 1953. He was survived only by Hore-Ruthven, who, as the Earl of Gowrie, was Governor-General of Australia and then Lieutenant-Governor of Windsor Castle until his death in 1955.

Wauchope's successor in command of the Highland Brigade, Hector MacDonald, survived the Boers but not the consequences of his own sexual inclinations. In 1903, as a major-general, he was appointed to command the troops in Ceylon. Vague rumours of his homosexual tendencies had followed him from South Africa and India but their origins were probably in the Egyptian Army where such activities would have been commonplace. In Ceylon rumour soon grew into accusation and, although the details are obscure, young schoolboys seem to have been involved. Faced with court-martial and disgrace, Fighting Mac took the only way out. Stopping in Paris on his return journey to Ceylon after a comfortless interview with the Commander-in-Chief, Roberts, at the War Office, he blew his brains out in his hotel room.

It is not easy to follow the fortunes of all those whose words and deeds have been recorded in these pages. Many played their little parts and passed beyond our ken. Of the diarists and letter writers, young talented Hale died of enteric (typhoid) within a few weeks of Omdurman, but the cheery Corporal Skinner survived to serve in Crete and South Africa before retiring as a Staff-Sergeant in 1910. Neville Cameron became a general and Colonel of his regiment and Frank Ferguson, the sabre-wielding cavalry trooper, leaping from one era to another, went into electrical goods distribution. Walter Kitchener, sound and reliable, achieved knighthood and a colonial governorship but died of peritonitis in 1912 at the early age of 54.

On the other side only a few of the leading figures survived the collapse of the Mahdiya. Of these the most notable was Osman Digna. Creeping from cave to cave in the hills of the Red Sea littoral, he was eventually outwitted by a man of his own race, a distinguished Soudanese officer, Mohamed Bey Ahmed, commandant of the Suakin police. Tradition has it that he was lured from his hiding place by the smell of roasting meat. Captured in 1900 and held for some years in Egyptian prisons, he was released in 1908 and allowed to live at Wadi Halfa. Unbending and unbowed, he made the pilgrimage to Mecca in 1924 and died two years later aged about 86.

Another famous slave-trader who returned to the Sudan in his declining years was Zubeir Pasha, living on his farm at Geili, north of Omdurman, until his death in 1913. In long discussions with Na'um Shuqair, he recounted his extraordinary life story which was later reproduced in book form by a Sudan official, H. C. Jackson (no relation to H. W.).

The third Khalifa, the Mahdi's son-in-law Mohamed Sherif, was executed with two of the Mahdi's sons in August, 1899, condemned, probably unjustly, for attempting to instigate a Mahdist revival.

And what of the Sudan itself? By the turn of the century it had retreated back into the obscurity whence it had burst so violently in the 1880s. Its fame, or perhaps more accurately, its notoriety was short-lived, and since then its story has been unspectacular.

After a year or so of rough justice under Kitchener and his military governors, the Sudan settled down to over half a century of enlightened rule and steady progress under the Anglo-Egyptian Condominium, a constitutional (or perhaps unconstitutional) device concocted by Cromer which enabled the British, maintaining the polite fiction of Egyptian partnership, to govern the Sudan without interference from the other Great Powers. On the whole, the Sudanese found their new rulers, mostly intelligent young Oxbridge athletes, congenial. They shared a remarkably similar sense of humour, freedom from pomposity and a dislike of unnecessary toil. That the Sudanese people benefitted greatly from this period of constructive paternalism is undeniable, although the anti-imperialist dogma of our day requires that it be repeatedly denied. Unfortunately, an independent Sudan has failed to live up to the expectations of its British friends or the aspirations of its own people. When the Condominium ended the irreconcilable differences between Moslem north and Christian south rapidly developed into civil war which has persisted, on and off, ever since. In Khartoum the soldiers soon lost patience with the squabbling and ineffectual politicians and took over, but the ruling group of generals grew fat and lazy, allowing themselves, in due course, to be overthrown by student mobs.

Various civilian leaders (including a descendant of the Mahdi) rose and fell, until a new military dictatorship was imposed. Demonstrating a remarkable capacity for survival if little else, Gen. Nimeiry remained in power for 16 years but eventually the Sudan's deteriorating economic and racial problems combined with the first famine for nearly a century to bring about his downfall in 1985. He had instituted fashionable Islamic puritanism and the ferocious punishments which go with it. Over 80 years on the Khalifa might have felt quite at home in Omdurman. At the time of writing little is known of the nature or intentions of the current regime.

And have the conquerors fared better? A Britain weakened by two World Wars, stripped of empire and demoralized by socialism, has replaced self-confidence with querulous self-doubt. Ashamed of a past which should be a source of pride, the pre-emptive cringe is today's substitute for the gunboat. When, with a strange instinctive jerk, the British lashed out at Argentina over the Falklands in 1982, incipient signs of patriotic revival so appalled the liberal establishment that churchmen, politicians and media verbalisers fell over each other to demand the surrender of a handful of sheep-farmers to a facist butcher. The spirit of the Great Britain which Gordon, Kitchener and the others served has disappeared almost without trace.

Of the three contestants in the Sudan conflict, perhaps the people of Egypt have undergone the least philosophical change. Impervious to the rise and fall of rulers, foreign or native, burdened with problems so intractable and permanent as to have become an accepted way of life, the Egyptian masses live as they have always lived, from day to day, hand to mouth, bending but not breaking, secure only in the knowledge that the life-giving Nile will flow for ever.

## *EPITAPH*

*On 20 January, 1977, there died at Weymouth at the age of 97 the last known British survivor of the Sudan campaigns. As a young Rifleman, former Regimental Sergeant-Major James Richard (Paddy) Miles had fought at Omdurman with the 2nd Battalion Rifle Brigade.*

*Towards the end of his life he was asked by an officer of his old regiment for his recollections of the battle. With the deference and brevity of a soldier of his generation addressing an officer, the old gentleman replied, "If you'll pardon the expression, sir, bloody hot!"*

# Appendices

---

*Europeans attached to Hicks's Army*

*Killed at or before the battle of Sheikan, 5 November, 1883*

Lieutenant-General W. Hicks (British)
Colonel A. Farquhar (British)
Colonel Baron von Seckendorf (German)
Major Warner (British)
Captain Massey (British)
Captain E. B. Evans (British)
Captain A. Herlth (Austrian)
Captain A. Mattiaga (Austrian)
Surgeon-General G. D. Douloglu (Greek)
Surgeon-Major Rosenberg (Nationality unknown)
ex-Sergeant-Major Brady (British)
Mr E. O'Donovan, journalist (British)
Mr A. Vizetelly, journalist (British)

*Invalided to Cairo before Kordofan expedition started*

Lieutenant-Colonel the Hon J. Colborne (British) died 1890
Major Martin (British) died Assouan 1886 of sunstroke
Captain F. H. Forestier-Walker (British) killed at first battle of El-Teb, February 1884
Second Lieutenant Morris (British) described by Hicks as "a mechanic for the Nordenfeldts". Nothing else is known about him but he seems to have gone sick on 6 September, 1883, with sunstroke.

*Invalided to Khartoum after Kordofan expedition started*

Mr F. Power, journalist and later acting British Consul at Khartoum, murdered with Colonel Stewart, September, 1884.

---

*At HQ Khartoum*

Colonel H. W. R. De Coetlogon (British) died 1908

There were also a number of European "other ranks", probably officers' servants, of whom Gustav Klootz was one, but their names have not been recorded. All except Klootz were killed at or before Sheikan.

# APPENDIX B *Victoria Cross Citations 1884/5*

## ROYAL NAVY

### Captain Arthur Knyvet Wilson

This Officer, on the staff of Rear-Admiral Sir William Hewett, at the battle of El-Teb, on the 29 February, attached himself during the advance to the right half battery, Naval Brigade, in the place of Lieutenant Royds, R.N., mortally wounded.

As the troops closed on the enemy's Krupp battery the Arabs charged out on the corner of the square and on the detachment who were dragging the Gardner gun. Captain Wilson then sprang to the front and engaged in single combat with some of the enemy, thus protecting his detachment till some men of the York and Lancaster Regiment came to his assistance with their bayonets. But for the action of this Officer Sir Redvers Buller thinks that one or more of his detachment must have been speared.

Captain Wilson was wounded but remained with the half battery during the day.

## 3rd BATTALION, KING'S ROYAL RIFLE CORPS, LATE MOUNTED INFANTRY.

### Lieutenant Percival Scrope Marling

For his conspicuous bravery at the battle of Tamai, on 13 March last, in risking his life to save that of Private Morley, Royal Sussex Regiment, who, having been shot, was lifted and placed in front of Lieutenant Marling on his horse. He fell off almost immediately, when Lieutenant Marling dismounted, and gave up his horse for the purpose of carrying off Private Morley, the enemy pressing close on to them until they succeeded in carrying him about 80 yards to a place of comparative safety.

## 19th HUSSARS

### Quartermaster-Sergeant William Marshall

For his conspicuous bravery during the Cavalry charge at El-Teb on 29 February last, in bringing Lieutenant-Colonel Barrow, 19 Hussars, out of action. That officer having been severely wounded, and his horse killed, was on the ground surrounded by the enemy, when Quartermaster-Sergeant Marshall, who stayed behind with him, seized his hand and dragged him through the enemy back to the regiment. Had Lieutenant-Colonel Barrow been left behind he must have been killed.

## 1st BATTALION, ROYAL HIGHLANDERS (Black Watch)

### Private Thomas Edwards

For the conspicuous bravery displayed by him in defence of one of the guns of the Naval Brigade, at the battle of Tamai on 13 March, 1884.

   This man (who was attached to the Naval Brigade as Mule Driver) was beside the gun with Lieutenant Almack, R.N., and a blue Jacket. Both the latter were killed, and Edwards, after bayonetting two Arabs, and himself receiving a wound with a spear, rejoined the ranks with his mules, and subsequently did good service in remaining by his gun throughout the action.

## ROYAL ARTILLERY

### Gunner Albert Smith

Date of Act of Bravery: 17 January 1885.

At the action of Abu Klea, on the 17 January 1885, when the enemy charged, the square fell back a short distance, leaving Lieutenant Guthrie, Royal Artillery, with his gun in a comparatively unprotected position. At this moment a native rushed at Lieutenant Guthrie with a spear, and would in all probability have killed that officer, who had no weapon in his hand at the time (being engaged in superintending the working of his gun), when Gunner Smith, with a handspike, warded off the thrust, thus giving Lieutenant Guthrie time to draw his sword, and with a blow bring the assailant to his knees, but as the latter fell he made a wild thrust at the officer with a long knife, which Gunner Smith again warded off, not, however, before the native had managed to inflict a wound in Lieutenant Guthrie's thigh. Before the Soudani could repeat the thrust, Gunner Smith killed him with the handspike, and thus for a time saved the life of his officer, though the latter unfortunately died some days afterwards of his wound.

## APPENDIX C  *Composition of Wolseley's Camel Regiments*

### Heavy Camel Regiment

| | |
|---|---|
| Commanding Officer | Lieutenant-Colonel Hon R. Talbot, Life Guards |
| Adjutant | Captain Lord St. Vincent, 16th Lancers |
| Medical Officer | Surgeon J. J. Falvey, Army Medical Dept |
| Quartermaster | Lieutenant G. Leigh, Life Guards |

No. 1 Company (1st & 2nd Life Guards)

Major Hon C. Byng
Captain Lord Cochrane
Lieutenant Lord Rodney
Lieutenant R. J. Beech
86 NCOs and men

No. 2 Company (Royal Horse Guards & Queen's Bays)

Major Lord A. Somerset (RHG)
Captain A. L. Gould (Bays)
Lieutenant Lord Binning (RHG)
Lieutenant R. F. Hibbert (Bays)
86 NCOs and men


No. 3 Company (4th & 5th Dragoon Guards)

Major W. H. Atherton (5DG)
Captain J. W. Darley (4DG)
Lieutenant C. W. Law (4DG)
Lieutenant St. J. Gore (5DG)
86 NCOs and men


No. 4 Company (Scots Greys & Royal Dragoons)

Major W. Gough (Royals)
Captain W. H. Hippisley (Greys)
Lieutenant J. F. Burn-Murdoch (Royals)
Lieutenant R. Wolfe (Greys)
86 NCOs and men


No. 5 Company (5th & 16th Lancers)

Major L. Carmichael (5L)
Major T. Davison (16L)
Lieutenant H. Costello (5L)
Lieutenant W. B. Browne (16L)
86 NCOs and men


Majors Atherton, Gough and Carmichael, Captains Lord St Vincent and Darley, Lieutenants Law, Wolfe and Costello, and 59 NCOs and men were killed in action or died of wounds. Lieutenant Browne and 28 NCOs and men died of disease and other causes.


*Light Camel Regiment*

| | |
|---|---|
| Commanding Officer | Colonel Stanley Clarke |
| Adjutant & Quartermaster | Captain H. Paget, 7th Hussars |
| Medical Officer | Surgeon P. B. Connolly, Army Medical Dept. |

| Regimental Contingents | |
|---|---|
| 3rd Hussars | Major C. E. Beckett |
| | Lieutenant J. S. Scott |
| 4th Hussars | Captain C. W. Peters |
| | Lieutenant R. Kincaid-Smith |
| 7th Hussars | Lieutenant-Colonel H. McCalmont |
| | Lieutenant Hon R. Lawley |

| | |
|---|---|
| 10th Hussars | Lieutenant-Colonel J. P. Brabazon |
| | Lieutenant Hon G. Bryan |
| 11th Hussars | Major C. E. Swaine |
| | Lieutenant W. Harrison |
| 15th Hussars | Captain A. G. Holland |
| | Lieutenant P. K. Coke |
| 18th Hussars | Major C. O. Gould |
| | Lieutenant E. G. Knox |
| 20th Hussars | Captain E. R. Courteney |
| | Lieutenant R. M Richardson |
| 21st Hussars | Major W. G. Crole Wyndham |
| | Lieutenant J. Fowle |

43 NCOs and men from each regiment
The Light Camel Regiment suffered no battle casualties but Major Gould and several NCOs and men died of disease and other causes.

*Guards Camel Regiment*

| | |
|---|---|
| Commanding Officer | Lieutenant Colonel Hon E. E. Boscawen, Coldstream Guards |
| Adjutant | Lieutenant C. Crutchley, Scots Guards |
| Quartermaster | Captain E. M Crabbe, Grenadier Guards |
| Medical Officer | Surgeon Major J. Magill, Coldstream Guards |
| Signals Officer | Lieutenant Colonel H. Bonham, Grenadier Guards |

Regimental Contingents

| | |
|---|---|
| 1st Bn Grenadier Guards | Lieutenant Colonel. C. R. Rowley |
| | Lieutenant Count A. E. Gleichen |
| 2nd Bn Grenadier Guards | Lieutenant Colonel I. C. Herbert |
| | Lieutenant L. D'Aguilar |
| 3rd Bn Grenadier Guards | Captain E. M. Crabbe |
| | Lieutenant R. Wolridge-Gordon |
| 1st Bn Coldstream Guards | Lieutenant V. J. Dawson |
| | Lieutenant Hon H. Amherst |
| 2nd Bn Coldstream Guards | Lieutenant-Colonel F. Graves Sawle |
| | Lieutenant D. Dawson |
| 1st Bn Scots Guards | Lieutenant-Colonel Sir W. Gordon-Cumming |
| | Lieutenant F. Romilly |
| 2nd Bn Scots Guards | Lieutenant-Colonel M. Wilson |
| | Lieutenant A. Drummond |
| Royal Marines | Major W. H. Poe |
| | Captain A. C. Pearson |
| | Lieutenant C. V. Townshend |
| | Lieutenant H. N. White |

Each Guards battalion contributed 43 NCOs and men and the Royal Marines 102 NCOs and men. 26 NCOs and men were killed in action or died of wounds and 23 died of disease and other causes.

*Mounted Infantry Camel Regiment*

| | |
|---|---|
| Commanding Officer | Major Hon G. H. Gough, 14th Hussars |
| Adjutant | Captain J. H. Sewell, Norfolk Regt |
| Quartermaster | Lieutenant R. A. Grant, Gordon Highlanders |
| Staff Officers | Major C. T. Barrow, Cameronians |
| | Captain T. H. Phipps, 7th Hussars |

A Company

| | |
|---|---|
| Company Commander | Captain C. H. Payne, Gordon Highlanders |
| South Staffordshire Regt | Lieutenant C. O. Hore |
| Black Watch | Lieutenant C. P. Livingstone |
| Gordon Highlanders | Lieutenant H. K. Stewart |
| KRRC (60th Rifles) | Lieutenant P. S. Marling, VC |
| | Lieutenant R. I. Bower |

30 NCOs and men from each regiment.

B Company

| | |
|---|---|
| Company Commander | Captain H. A. Walsh, Somersest L I |
| West Kent Regt | Captain A. T. Morse |
| Sussex Regt | Lieutenant F. G. Todd Thornton |
| Essex Regt | Lieutenant R. J. Tudway |
| Duke of Cornwall's L I | Lieutenant C. G. Martyr |

30 NCOs and men from each regiment

C Company

| | |
|---|---|
| Company Commander | Captain R. S. Fetherstonhaugh, 60th Rifles |
| KRRC (60th Rifles) | Lieutenant A. E. Miles |
| | Lieutenant W. P. Campbell |
| Rifle Brigade | Lieutenant Hon H. C. Hardinge |
| | Lieutenant W. M Sherston |

60 NCOs and men from each regiment

D Company

| | |
|---|---|
| Company Commander | Captain C. B. Pigott, 21st Hussars |
| Somerset L I | Lieutenant T. Snow |
| West Kent Regt | Lieutenant E. A. Alderson |
| Connaught Rangers | Lieutenant C. J. Carden |
| Royal Scots Fusiliers | Lieutenant H. S. Stanuell |

30 NCOs and men from each regiment
11 NCOs and men were killed in action or died of wounds. Captain Phipps and several NCOs and men died of disease and other causes.

The total number of wounded in all the Camel Regiments amounted to eleven officers and 136 NCOs and men.

# APPENDIX D *Men of the Royal Sussex Regiment on the Steamers*

*Members of C Company 1st Battalion The Royal Sussex Regiment on board the steamers Talahawiya and Bordein.*
(By courtesy of the West Sussex Record Office and the Trustees of the Royal Sussex Regiment Museum).

*Talahawiya*

| | |
|---|---|
| Captain L. J. Trafford | (commanding) |
| Corporal Smith | |
| Drummer W. Gilbert | |
| Private C. Cowstick | (awarded the Distinguished Conduct Medal) |
| Private C. Paine | (awarded the Distinguished Conduct Medal) |
| Private Mitchell | |
| Private H. Nealan | |
| Private J. Canning | |
| Private M. Poole | |
| Private G. Woods | |

*Bordein*

| | |
|---|---|
| Colour-Sergeant E. Wellstead | |
| Lance-Corporal N. Othen | (awarded the Distinguished Conduct Medal) |
| Private G. Benford | |
| Private E. Dale | (awarded the Distinguished Conduct Medal) |
| Private J. Jones | |
| Private H. Temple | |
| Private J. Gausden | |
| Private Patching | |
| Private W. Leggett | |
| Private H. Ings | |

*N.B.*
In his journal Captain Trafford lists a Private Ings on both steamers but there seems to have been only one Ings in the battalion; therefore there may have been another man whom Trafford mistakenly listed as Ings.

## APPENDIX E  *A letter to the widow of Captain Dalison*

Letter from Sam Heron to the widow of Captain M. D. D. Dalison, Scots Guards, killed in action at Hashin 20 March, 1885.
(By kind permission of the Kent Archives Office and the late Lieutenant Colonel W. D. Keown-Boyd).

Suakin 21st

Madam,

It is with the deepest regret that I write a few lines to you on this sad occasion. Dr Cummings told me that word had been sent you of the unexpected death of my master.

I will try and give as near account of it as I can. We went out yesterday morning to take some wells of the enemy and were very successful until we were going back to camp. We had one man slightly wounded in the morning. Then we had a private [killed/wounded?]. Then my dear master got the fatal shot. He was about fifty yards from me when it happened but it was instantaneous he never spoke a single word. He got struck a little above the left breast and went downwards. I got everything he had with the exception of his clothes in which he was buried today. I have everything packed in his big box. The little bag that you told me to look after is also in it. They have kept some of his things that they thought would be of no use to send back. Colonel Paget has been very attentive and took to looking after everything. He also told me that he would give all the details as soon as possible. I need scarcely add the death of Mr Dalison was very deeply felt by the whole camp. I cannot tell you when to expect his things but I saw everything sealed up this morning before the burial. I went and saw him laid in his last resting place in an island out of Suakin.

I hope you will excuse this short letter as my heart is too full to write any more as I have lost a good master and my best friend.

I will conclude praying that God will bless you and the poor orphans at this sad time.

I will write again when the things are sent away.

I ever remain yours
sorrowful

Sam Heron


## APPENDIX F  *Ranks in the Egyptian Army (Khedivial period)*

| | |
|---|---|
| Commander-in-Chief (British only) | Sirdar |
| Lieutenant-General | Farik |
| Major-General | Lewa |
| Colonel | Miralai |
| Lieutenant-Colonel | Kaimakam |
| Major | Bimbashi |
| Adjutant-Major | Saghkolaghasi |

| | |
|---|---|
| Captain | Yuzbashi |
| Lieutenant | Mulazim awal |
| Second Lieutenant | Mulazim tani |
| Quartermaster | Solkolaghasi |
| British NCO | Mulahiz |
| Sergeant-Major | Bash Shawish |
| Quartermaster Sergeant | Buluk Amin |
| Sergeant | Shawish |
| Corporal | Ombashi |
| Private | Nafar |

*N.B.*

No British officer held a rank lower than Bimbashi. The British NCOs retained their British Army ranks, usually Colour Sergeant or Sergeant, and were directly responsible to the British officers.

## APPENDIX G  *Wad-el-Nejumi*

Head Quarters, Egyptian Army,
War Office,
Cairo.

Abdurahman Wad-el-Nejumi, Commander-in-Chief of the Dervish Force which recently invaded Egypt, was by birth an Arab of the JAALIN tribe, a powerful and warlike race of arabs, who inhabit the desert on the East Bank of the Nile, and holding large tracts of country west and south of Khartoum.

In 1882 Nejumi is reported to have been exercising the calling of Fikeh, or religious mendicant in Khartoum. In that year he was probably about 35 years of age, and was notorious for the severity with which he adhered to the religious rites imposed by the Mohammedan religion on Fikehs, and many stories are told of the wonderful asceticism of his life.

When the rebellion of the Mahdi Mohammed-Ahmed was first kindled in the Sudan, Nejumi was at once singled out as a man likely to embrace with fervour a movement of so truly a religious character, and he is reported to have gone to Kordofan, where he speedily became one of the most powerful and astute of the Mahdi's followers.

In the early conflicts of Mahdism against the authority of the Egyptian Government, Nejumi soon distinguished himself as a fearless as well as popular leader of men, and this quality, added to his intense fanaticism, rendered him speedily the most trusted of Mohammed-Ahmed's Emirs; thus we find that when the late Hicks Pasha started on his ill-fated expedition towards Obeid, he was opposed by overwhelming numbers of fanatical dervishes under the direct leadership of Nejumi – for the late Mahdi, Mohammed-Ahmed, though the nominal leader, was never permitted sufficiently near the scene of action to make it possible for him to personally direct the movements of his followers. Thus the brunt of the fighting fell to the share of Nejumi, and the success of the strategy which enabled him to practically annihilate an army of 10,000 men soon caused him to be recognised as the best and most powerful of the Dervish leaders and the righthand man of the Mahdi.

The Dervish successes which followed up the defeat of Hicks Pasha, and the subsequent advance of the enormous force against General Gordon in Khartoum, were all planned and carried out by Nejumi – and he is credited throughout the Sudan, as being the conqueror of Khartoum and of Gordon, and on the fall of that city and its occupation by the Mahdi, Nejumi was appointed the Governor of Omdurman and Commander-in-Chief of the Khartoum armies.

During the lifetime of the Mahdi, Nejumi enjoyed the highest favours, but even in the height of his success, he is reported never to have abandoned the role of Fikeh; he still lived an abstemious life, and even his garb was but that of an ordinary dervish soldier, except on state occasions, when he wore a very distinguishing suit of chain armour.

From all accounts he appears to have been above all others a man of extreme religious fervour, and his influence over his followers on this account was very great. He was widely known as a severe though just Commander and a man of his word, both rare qualities in an Eastern ruler, and these characteristics doubtless gained for him his ascendancy over his subordinate Emirs.

On the death of the late Mahdi, Mohammed-Ahmed, his Vakeel, or Vizier, Abdullah Taashi, was appointed ruler and Nejumi does not appear to have been held in the same favour by him. Abdullah Taashi no doubt tacitly regarded Nejumi as a dangerous rival, and he would probably have suffered the usual fate of Eastern rivals, but his influence with the dervish soldiers was too great to be tampered with and the allegiance of the Jaalin tribe was so necessary to the welfare of the dervish cause, that Nejumi was with great pomp and show inducted as Emir of the Dongola Province, and thus removed to a safe distance from the immediate seat of the dervish Government.

The appointment of Nejumi to the Province of Dongola, though partially for the above reasons, was also in a large measure occasioned by the desire of the Khalifa to carry out the long talked of invasion of Egypt, and he well knew that Nejumi was the only one of his Emirs to whom he could entrust such an undertaking, with, as he thought, a certainty of success. Nejumi was for two years the Governor of the Dongola Province and during that time he quite sustained his reputation as a fighting emir. He placed his most warlike and trusted emirs, Abdul Halim and Osman Azrak, at the advanced post of SARRAS within 30 miles of the Egyptian frontier station of Wadi Halfa, and by continuous raids succeeded in keeping the Egyptian garrison on the frontier alert.

All this activity was to prepare the way for ultimate invasion and many expeditions on a large scale were planned, but owing to dervish troubles in other parts of the country, their troops were repeatedly recalled – elated, however, by his recent successes against the Abyssinians, the Khalifa Abdullah at length ordered a general advance north from Dongola, for the purpose of subduing Egypt, then Turkey, and eventually the whole world, which was to be brought to acknowledge the faith of the Mahdi!

This expedition consisting chiefly of the Baggara and Jaalin tribes, the most warlike in the Sudan, left Dongola in June last under the direct leadership of Nejumi, who was supported by all the most prominent fighting emirs. Marching by short stages and driving along with them the population of the countries through which they passed, this large mass of men, women and children, numbering over 15,000 with numerous horses, camels and donkeys, at length crossed over the frontier into Egyptian territory, and began that almost unparalleled march through waterless tracts of desert, which occasioned the most harrowing sufferings from famine and thirst, and yet this extraordinary leader succeeded in keeping together this enormous mass of human beings, and inspiring them with a religious fanatacism which even the most acute sufferings failed to diminish.

It would seem almost incredible that any one individual should have such power over his fellow creatures, but this strange attachment to their leader was evinced in the most striking manner, only a few days before the final struggle at Toski – when, in reply to a summons to surrender, the warriors drew their swords and waving them in the air, shouted that they would stand by their Chief and would never yield.

It is needless to repeat the details of the action before Toski on 3rd August, when the brave but misguided Nejumi died, fighting bravely to the last. One of his faithful followers and relations who stood by his leader till all was over, thus briefly describes the part taken by Nejumi on that fatal day: he says, "Early in the fight Abdurahman-el-Nejumi was wounded by a bullet in the chest and suffering from loss of blood he dismounted from his horse and rested on a high rock watching the battle. Presently one of his emirs came running towards him crying out that the day was lost, and that almost all his leaders had been slain. Nejumi called for his horse and rapidly tightening the bandage round his wound leaped up crying, 'I cannot leave my people to die alone' and galloped into the midst of the fight. He was seen galloping up and down, amongst his retreating followers endeavouring to rally them, but the British and Egyptian cavalry charging down dispersed them and Nejumi, wounded a second time, was borne away by some of his faithful mulazimen or bodyguard. By them he was carried off the field, and placed in a dying condition on a camel, still escorted by his faithful bodyguard of 20 men. They attempted to make good their retreat, but were pursued by a troop of cavalry, who, ignorant of who the wounded man might be, engaged the bodyguard who fought around their Chief, until all were killed in the skirmish and Nejumi received his last fatal wound – a bullet through the heart."

Thus died the bravest of the Dervish fighting leaders, and one whose loss to the Dervish cause is irreparable. Fanatical to a degree he inspired his followers with the same fearless spirit and yet he was esteemed – even beloved – by the men on whom his reckless fanaticism had brought such terrible sufferings. His body when brought into the camp at Toski was identified by numbers of prisoners of his own tribe and as they were marshalled round for a farewell look at their dead chief, there were few dry eyes amongst them, there was but one interpretation of the universal wail. "Our good and brave Chief is dead" and the desolate expression of their faces, told how much this "savage hero" had been respected and beloved.

(F. R. Wingate)

This memorandum is held in the Sudan Archive, University of Durham, and is reproduced here by kind permission of the University.

## APPENDIX H  *The Last Cavalry Charge*

Mr George O'Farrell, who served with F Troop 390th (Surrey Yeomanry) Battery R.A. and later with the Sudan Defence Force, has provided the author with the following account of an action which took place during the Eritrean campaign in 1941.

"The last cavalry charge faced by British troops took place at Keru gorge on the approach to Agordat 7 a.m. on 21 January, 1941. About 60 Eritrean cavalry firing from the saddle and hurling hand grenades led by an Italian officer on a grey horse made a surprise charge on the 25 pdr. guns of 390th (Surrey Yeomanry) Battery RA. The guns were quickly swung round and engaged the cavalry over open sights at point blank range. Some shells hit the horses and others ricocheted off the ground without exploding. Officers and command post staff joined in the defence with all available automatic and small arms and when the gallant survivors turned and galloped back they left behind 25 dead and 16 wounded on the position. The climax of the charge was when the artificer of F Troop shot off the head of one of the Italian officers with a round from the ill-famed Boyes anti-tank rifle. There were no casualties on the British side.

The mounted (lorried) infantry of the Sudan Defence Force debussed at the gun position, moved forward with their .5 Vickers machine guns, enfiladed the cavalry in a khor to which they had retreated from us and virtually wiped them out."

Mr O'Farrell goes on to say ". . . the SDF (Sudan Defence Force) were mostly, if not all, descendants of the Sudanese troops who fought at Omduran in the Egyptian Army. There were lots of Nuba and southerners in the SDF I knew."

## APPENDIX I *The Sirdar's letter to the Khalifa*

The Sirdar's letter to the Khalifa of 30 August, 1898.

I write to warn you that your evil conduct in the Sudan, and the number of Moslems you have caused to be killed unjustly and without cause, whose blood calls for vengeance, has necessitated the advance of my army to put an end to your unjust and unlawful rule, but as in such cases innocent people, old men and women and children, and those that detest the way you have been treating and reigning in the Sudan, may fall victim if exposed to our bullets, you should remove all such to a place of safety and you with your adherents alone stand to meet the army and the fate God has prepared for you. Should you and your emirs desire to surrender to avoid the effusion of blood, any messenger will be well-received and you may rest assured of my just treatment. Should you not do so the responsibility for such innocent blood-shed will be on your head.

## APPENDIX J *Victoria Cross Citations, 1898*

*21st LANCERS*

*Captain Paul Aloysius Kenna*

At the Battle of Khartoum on the 2 September, 1898, Captain P.A. Kenna assisted Major Crole Wyndham, of the same Regiment, by taking him on his horse, behind the saddle (Major Wyndham's horse having been killed in the charge), thus enabling him to reach a place of safety; and, after the charge of the 21st Lancers, Captain Kenna returned to assist Lieutenant de Montmorency, who was endeavouring to recover the body of Second Lieutenant R. G. Grenfell.

*Lieutenant the Hon Raymond Harvey Lodge Joseph de Montmorency*

At the Battle of Khartoum on the 2 September, 1898, Lieutenant de Montmorency, after the charge of the 21st Lancers, returned to assist Second Lieutenant R. G. Grenfell, who was lying surrounded by a large body of dervishes. Lieutenant de Montmorency drove the dervishes off, and, finding Lieutenant Grenfell dead, put the body on his horse which then broke away. Captain Kenna and Corporal Swarbrick then came to his assistance, and enabled him to rejoin the Regiment, which had begun to open a heavy fire on the enemy.

*Private Thomas Byrne*

At the Battle of Khartoum on the 2 September, 1898, Private Byrne turned back in the middle of the charge of the 21st Lancers and went to the assistance of Lieutenant the Honourable R. F. Molyneux, Royal Horse Guards, who was wounded, dismounted, disarmed, and being attacked by several dervishes. Private Byrne, already severely wounded, attacked these dervishes, received a second severe wound, and, by his gallant conduct, enabled Lieutenant Molyneux to escape.

*2nd DRAGOON GUARDS*

*Captain Neville Maskelyne Smyth*

At the Battle of Khartoum on the 2 September, 1898, Captain Smyth galloped forward and attacked an Arab who had run amok among some Camp Followers. Captain Smyth received the Arab's charge, and killed him, being wounded with a spear in the arm in so doing. He thus saved the life of one at least of the Camp Followers.

*3rd (MILITIA) BTN. HIGHLAND LIGHT INFANTRY*

*Captain the Hon Alexander Gore Arkwright Hore-Ruthven*

On 22 September, 1898, during the action at Gedaref, Captain Hore-Ruthven seeing an Egyptian officer lying wounded within 50 yards of the advancing dervishes, who were firing and charging, picked him up and carried him towards the 16th Egyptian Battalion. He dropped the wounded officer two or three times and fired upon the dervishes who were following to check their advance. Had this officer been left where he first dropped he must have been killed.

## APPENDIX K *The Anglo-Egyptian Army and Fleet of Gunboats at Omdurman*

The Anglo-Egyptian Army and Fleet of Gunboats at Omdurman, 2 September, 1898. (British officers of the Egyptian Army are given their Egyptian Army ranks and their British Army parent regiments are given in brackets.)

| | |
|---|---|
| Commander | El Sirdar Sir Herbert Kitchener (R.E.) |
| Chief-of-Staff | El Lewa H. M. L. Rundle (R.A.) |
| Director of Intelligence | El Miralai F. R. Wingate (R.A.) |
| Principal Medical Officer | Surgeon-General W. Taylor, R.A.M.C. |
| Director of Transport | Brevet Lieutenant-Colonel F. W. Kitchener, W. Yorkshire Regt |

## BRITISH DIVISION
(1st & 2nd British Brigades)

| | |
|---|---|
| Divisional Commander | Major-General W. F. Gatacre, 77th (Middlesex) Regt |
| Commanding 1st British Brigade | Brigadier-General A. G. Wauchope, Black Watch |
| Brigade Major | Major T. d'O. Snow, Royal Inniskillin Fusiliers |
| 1st Bn Royal Warwickshire Regt | Lieutenant-Colonel W. E. G. Forbes |
| 1st Bn Lincolnshire Regt | Lieutenant-Colonel F. R. Lowth |
| 1st Bn Seaforth Highlanders | Brevet Colonel R. H. Murray |
| 1st Bn Cameron Highlanders | Brevet Colonel G. L. C. Money |
| Commanding 2nd British Brigade | Brigadier-General the Hon. N. G. Lyttelton, Rifle Brigade |
| Brigade Major | Major C. a'Court, Rifle Brigade |
| 1st Bn Grenadier Guards | Colonel V. Hatton |
| 1st Bn Northumberland Fusiliers | Lieutenant-Colonel C. G. C. Money |
| 2nd Bn Lancashire Fusiliers | Lieutenant-Colonel C. G. Collingwood |
| 2nd Bn Rifle Brigade | Brevet Colonel F. Howard |
| Maxim Det. 1st Bn Royal Irish Fusiliers | Captain D. W. Churcher |
| 32nd Field Bty Royal Artillery | Major H. W. Williams |
| 37th Field Bty Royal Artillery | Major F. B. Elmslie |
| Royal Artillery Maxim Bty (attached 1st Brigade) | Captain C. O. Smeaton |
| 21st Lancers | Brevet Colonel R. H. Martin |
| 2nd Fortress Company Royal Engineers | Major L. B. Friend |
| Divisional Principal Medical Officer | Surgeon Lieutenant-Colonel W. H. McNamara, R.A.M.C |
| Army Service Corps | Lieutenant-Colonel L. A. Hope |

## EGYPTIAN DIVISION

| | |
|---|---|
| Divisional Commander | El Lewa A. Hunter (King's Own) |
| Commanding 1st Brigade | El Miralai H. A. MacDonald (Royal Fusiliers) |
| Brigade Major | El Kaimakam C. E. Keith-Falconer (Northumberland Fusiliers) |
| 2nd Egyptian Battalion | El Kaimakam F. J. Pink (Queen's W. Surrey Regt) |
| 9th Soudanese Battalion | El Kaimakam W. F. Walter (Lancs Fusiliers) |

| | |
|---|---|
| 10th Soudanese Battalion | El Kaimakam F. J. Nason (Cameronians) |
| 11th Soudanese Battalion | El Kaimakam H. W. Jackson (Gordon Highlanders) |
| | |
| Commanding 2nd Brigade | El Miralai J. G. Maxwell (Black Watch) |
| Brigade Major | El Bimbashi F. I. Maxse (Coldstream Guards)[1] |
| 8th Egyptian Battalion | El Bimbashi F. I. Maxse (Coldstream Guards) |
| 12th Soudanese Battalion | El Kaimakam C. V. F. Townshend (Indian Staff Corps) |
| 13th Soudanese Battalion | El Kaimakam H. L. Smith Dorrien (Sherwood Foresters) |
| 14th Soudanese Battalion | El Kaimakam H. P. Shekleton (S. Lancs Regt) |
| | |
| Commanding 3rd Brigade | El Miralai D. F. Lewis (Cheshire Regt) |
| Brigade Major | El Bimbashi J. J. Asser (Dorset Regt) |
| 3rd Egyptian Battalion | El Kaimakam J. Sillem (Welsh Regt) |
| 4th Egyptian Battalion | El Kaimakam W. S. Sparkes (Welsh Regt) |
| 7th Egyptian Battalion | El Kaimakam Ibrahim Fathi |
| 15th Egyptian Battalion | El Kaimakam T. E. Hickman (Worcs. Regt) |
| | |
| Commanding 4th Brigade | El Miralai J. Collinson (Northants Regt) |
| Brigade Major | El Bimbashi O. H. Pedley (Connaught Rangers) |
| 1st Egyptian Battalion | El Kaimakam R. H. G. Heygate (Border Regt) |
| 5th Egyptian Battalion (Half) | El Kaimakam Abdel Gawad Borham |
| 17th Egyptian Battalion | El Kaimakam V. T. Bunbury (Leics. Regt) |
| 18th Egyptian Battalion | El Bimbashi H. G. Matchett (Connaught Rangers) |
| | |
| Commanding Artillery | El Miralai C. J. Long (R.A.) |
| Horse Battery | El Bimbashi N. E. Young (R.A.) |
| Maxim Battery | El Bimbashi C. E. Lawrie (R.A.) |
| Field Batteries (four) | El Bimbashi M. Peake (R.A.) |
| | |
| Commanding Cavalry (nine Squadrons) | El Miralai L. G. Broadwood (12th Lancers) |
| Commanding Camel Corps (eight cos.) | El Kaimakam R. J. Tudway (Essex Regt) |
| Principal Medical Officer | El Miralai T. J. Gallwey (R.A.M.C.) |

*Gunboats*

| | |
|---|---|
| Flotilla Commander | Commander C. Keppel, R.N. |
| | |
| *Sultan* | Lieutenant W. H. Cowan, R.N. |
| *Melik* | El Kaimakam W. S. Gordon (R.E.) |
| *Sheikh* | Lieutenant J. B. Sparks, R.N. |

[1] This officer was in temporary command of 8th Battalion during the battle.

| | |
|---|---|
| *Fateh* | Lieutenant D. Beatty, R.N. |
| *Nasr* | Lieutenant the Hon A. Hood, R.N. |
| *Tamai* | Lieutenant H. F. Talbot, R.N. |
| *El Teb* (renamed Hafir) | Lieutenant C. M. Stavely, R.N. |
| *Abu Klea* | El Bimbashi E. O. Newcombe (R.E.) |
| *Metemma* | El Bimbashi A. G. Stevenson (R.E.) |

*Tribal Irregulars ("Friendlies")*

| | |
|---|---|
| In command | Major the Hon E. J. Montagu-Stuart-Wortley, 60th Rifles |
| Second-in-command | Lieutenant C. Wood, Northumberland Fusiliers |

# APPENDIX L *British NCOs of the Egyptian Army Commissioned and/or Decorated, 1885–99*

*Commissioned*

Staff Sergeant W. E. Bailey,[2] East Yorkshire Regt
Sergeant S. K. Flint, Royal Irish Rifles
Sergeant T. H. Healey, DCM & 2 bars, Cameron Highlanders
Sergeant C. McKey, Middlesex Regt
Sergeant A. Nicklin, DCM, Oxfordshire Light Infantry
Sergeant J. Scott-Barbour,[3] DCM, Highland Light Infantry

*Distinguished Conduct Medal*

Squadron Sergeant-Major W. D. Blake, 17th Lancers
Sergeant E. A. T. Handley, KOYLI
Sergeant T. H. Healey,[4] (and 2 bars), Cameron Highlanders
Sergeant G. Hilton, Scots Guards
Colour Sergeant F. Jenvey, Royal Marine Artillery
Colour Sergeant A. R. L. Kelham, Buffs

---

[2] Bailey was the Sirdar's Chief Clerk during the campaign of reconquest and one of the most trusted members of his staff.

[3] Scott-Barbour was ambushed and killed by Dinka tribesmen in the Bahr el Ghazal region in 1902. His death led to the Shambe Expedition of that year commanded by Lee Stack, a future Sirdar.

[4] The author can find no record of any other holder of the DCM *with two bars* prior to the Great War 1914–18. Healey won all three decorations while serving with the 9th Soudanese.

Sergeant J. C. Lambert, Royal Marine Artillery
Staff Sergeant S. W. McConnell, Army Gymnastic Staff
Sergeant S. T. Mathieson, Royal Marine Artillery
Sergeant A. Nicklin, North Staffs (commissioned in Oxfordshire L I )
Sergeant A. Russel, Scots Guards
Colour Sergeant W. Russell, Royal Marine Artillery
Colour Sergeant F. E. Seddon, Royal Marine Artillery
Colour Sergeant G. E. Seabright, (and bar), Royal Marine Artillery
Sergeant F. T. Sears, (and bar), Royal Marine Artillery
Sergeant J. Scott-Barbour, Gordon Highlanders (commissioned in H.L.I.)
Colour Sergeant H. Sheppard, West Kents
Sergeant R. A. Trowbridge, Royal Marine Artillery

*N.B.*
One British private soldier was awarded the DCM while attached to the Egyptian Army. This was Private J. Warburton, Durham Light Infantry, attached to the 1st Egyptian Battalion as orderly-room clerk and decorated after the Battle of Ginnis in 1885.

Egyptian and Soudanese soldiers were not normally awarded British decorations but one Private Ali Omry of the Egyptian Cavalry is listed as having received the DCM after an action at Handub on 1 February, 1885. It is not known what he did or why an exception was made in his case.

# Bibliography

## Some published sources

Alford, H. & Sword, W., *The Egyptian Soudan, Its Loss & Recovery*, 1898
Anglesey, Marquess of, *History of the British Cavalry*, Vol. 3, 1982
Arthur, Sir G., *The Letters of Lord & Lady Wolseley*, 1922
Brook-Shepherd, G., *Between Two Flags*, 1972
Churchill, W. S., *The River War*, Vols 1 & 2, 1900
Cromer, Earl of, *Modern Egypt*, Vols 1 & 2, 1908
Farwell, B., *Prisoners of the Mahdi*, 1967
Haggard, Lieutenant-Colonel A., *Under Crescent & Star*, 1895
Hake, A. E., *The Journals of Major-General Gordon at Khartoum*, 1895
Hill, R., *Biographical Dictionary of the Sudan*, 1951
Magnus, P., *Kitchener, Portrait of an Imperialist*, 1958
Preston, A., *In Relief of Gordon*, 1967
Sandes, Lieutenant-Colonel E., *The Royal Engineers in Egypt & the Sudan*, 1937
Shibeika, M., *British Policy in the Sudan 1882–1902*, 1952
Slatin, R., *Fire and Sword in the Sudan*, 1896
Symons, J., *England's Pride*, 1965
Theobald, A. B., *The Mahdiya*, 1951
Wilson, Colonel C. W., *From Korti to Khartoum*, 1886
Wingate, Major F. R., *Mahdiism and the Egyptian Soudan*, 1891
Zulfo, I., *Karari*, 1980

*Manuscript and unpublished sources*

The Wingate and other Sudan papers, Oriental Section, Durham University Library
Documents relating to the Sudan campaigns at the National Army Museum
Egyptian Army Intelligence Reports, Ministry of Defence Library

War Office and Foreign Office Reports, Public Record Office
Records of the Royal Sussex Regiment, West Sussex Record Office
The Maxse papers, West Sussex Record Office
The Dalison papers, Kent Archives Office
Lord Edward Cecil's diary (1896), Hatfield House Library
Manuscript of "The Sirdar's Camel Corps" by Colonel H. C. B. Hopkinson
The letters of Lieutenant-General Sir Walter Kitchener
The letters and journal of the Earl of Gowrie, VC
The letters of Lieutenant William Lonsdale Hale
Documents from numerous Regimental Headquarters, Museums and Archives

# Index